Fodor's 96
San Diego

"When it comes to information on regional history, what to see and do, and shopping, these guides are exhaustive."

—*USAir Magazine*

"Usable, sophisticated restaurant coverage, with an emphasis on good value."

—Andy Birsh, *Gourmet Magazine* columnist

"Valuable because of their comprehensiveness."

—*Minneapolis Star-Tribune*

"Fodor's always delivers high quality...thoughtfully presented...thorough."

—*Houston Post*

"An excellent choice for those who want everything under one cover."

—*Washington Post*

Fodor's Travel Publications, Inc.
New York • Toronto • London • Sydney • Auckland

Fodor's San Diego

Editor: Christopher Billy

Editorial Contributors: Steven K. Amsterdam, Rob Andrews, Lori Chamberlain, Albert M. Columbo, Edie Jarolim, Maribeth Mellin, Tracy Patruno, Kathryn Shevelow, M.T. Schwartzman, Dinah Spritzer

Creative Director: Fabrizio La Rocca

Cartographer: David Lindroth

Cover Photograph: Peter Guttman

Text Design: Between the Covers

Copyright

Special Sales

Fodor's Travel Publications are available at special discounts for bulk purchases for sales promotions or premiums. Special editions, including personalized covers, excerpts of existing guides, and corporate imprints, can be created in large quantities for special needs. For more information, contact your local bookseller or write to Special Markets, Fodor's Travel Publications, 201 East 50th Street, New York, NY 10022. Inquiries from Canada should be directed to your local Canadian bookseller or sent to Random House of Canada, Ltd., Marketing Department, 1265 Aerowood Drive, Mississauga, Ontario L4W 1B9. Inquiries from the United Kingdom should be sent to Fodor's Travel Publications, 20 Vauxhall Bridge Road, London SW1V 2SA.

MANUFACTURED IN THE UNITED STATES OF AMERICA

10 9 8 7 6 5 4 3 2 1

CONTENTS

Maps

ON THE ROAD WITH FODOR'S

A GOOD TRAVEL GUIDE is like a wonderful traveling companion. It's charming, it's brimming with sound recommendations and solid ideas, it pulls no punches in describing lodging and dining establishments, and it's consistently full of fascinating facts that make you view what you've traveled to see in a rich new light. In the creation of *San Diego 96*, we at Fodor's have gone to great lengths to provide you with the very best of all possible traveling companions— and to make your trip the best of all possible vacations.

About Our Writers

The information in these pages is the result of a collaboration of a number of extraordinary writers.

Freelance writer **Edie Jarolim** was a senior editor at Fodor's before moving to Tucson—which is within easy driving distance of San Diego. She first fell in love with the city while doing dissertation research at UCSD's spaceship-shaped Central Library and now returns yearly for a fix of sand and surf.

A longtime resident of San Diego, travel writer and photographer **Maribeth Mellin** is a former senior editor at *San Diego Magazine,* the author of *Fodor's Baja,* and a contributor to several magazines and newspapers.

Attorney **Lori Chamberlain** wrote the chapter on traveling in San Diego with kids. Her own two small children, Sophie and Ryder, were her research assistants.

When she's not busy tracking down interesting new restaurants, **Katheryn Shevelow** teaches in the Literature Department of the University of California at San Diego.

After a four-year stint in the U.S. Navy— which included duty in Desert Shield and Desert Storm and service as a journalist for the Admiral of the Atlantic Surface Fleet— freelance writer and part-time fund-raiser **Albert Columbo** returned to his hometown to pursue a journalism degree at San Diego State University. He is now a staff writer for SDSU's *The Daily Aztec* and a proud member of the Alpha Delta chapter of the national gay fraternity Delta Lambda Phi. At press-time he had been elected to be the chapter's president and was looking forward to planning and producing fraternity fund-raisers and events in San Diego's gay community. Albert's other interests include art, drawing, nightclubbing, music (especially retro, old school, deep house, and tribal), comedy, and keeping up lively correspondences with friends.

What's New

A New Design

If this is not the first Fodor's guide you've purchased, you'll immediately notice our new look. More readable and easier to use than ever? We think so—and we hope you do, too.

New Takes on Nightlife

Albert Columbo has completely revised the Arts and Nightlife chapter, adding a few new categories and providing a thorough, up-to-date listing of the hippest and hottest nightspots.

Let Us Do Your Booking

Our writers have scoured San Diego to come up with an extensive and well-balanced list of the best B&Bs, inns, and hotels, both small and large, new and old. But you don't have to beat the bushes to come up with a reservation. Now we've teamed up with an established hotel-booking service to make it easy for you to secure a room at the property of your choice. It's fast, it's free, and confirmation is guaranteed. If your first choice is booked, the operators can line up your second right away. Just call 1–800/FODORS–1 or 1–800/363–6771 (0800–89–1030 when in Great Britain; 0014–800–12–8271 when in Australia; 1–800/55–9101 when in Ireland).

Travel Updates

In addition, just before your trip, you may want to order a Fodor's Worldview Travel Update. From local publications all over San Diego, the lively, cosmopolitan editors at Worldview gather information on concerts, plays, opera, dance performances, gallery and museum shows, sports competitions, and other special events that coincide with your visit. See the order blank at the back of this book, call 800/799–9609, or fax 800/799–9619.

And in San Diego

The event that's sure to change the quality of life in San Diego in 1996 (at least for a month) is the **Republican National Convention.** The GOP will gather from August 10 to 17 (the actual meeting dates are Aug. 12–15), and hordes of people (19,400 of them delegates to the convention) are expected to descend on the city, and, it's hoped, spend at least part of their time (over)crowding the city's attractions and nightspots. The official noise-making and platform-building will take place in the San Diego Convention Center, which overlooks the bay.

The downtown San Diego skyline continues to change in subtle and startling ways. Although hotel and office-tower construction seems to have peaked in this newly developed area, growth and refinement of already existing sites are continuing apace. At press-time, downtown's **Horton Plaza** was undergoing a $16-million renovation, most of the work concentrated on converting the former Robinson-May building into a 120,000-square-foot dining/entertainment/fashion complex. A new **Planet Hollywood** restaurant littered with movie and television memorabilia recently opened as part of the expansion. Other additions to Horton Plaza will include a 14-screen movie theater complex and music and clothing stores.

In 1995 the 150-acre **Arco Training Center** for Olympic athletes had its grand opening. Overlooking Lower Otay Lake, 10 miles east of San Diego Bay, the facility is a warm-weather counterpart to the U.S. Olympic centers in Lake Placid, NY, and Colorado Springs, CO. Guests can survey the complex and watch athletes training for events, including archery, track, cycling, tennis, and various water-related sports; guided tours begin at the visitor center, which houses gift shops, interactive exhibits, and an observation deck.

There's always something new at the **San Diego Zoo.** At the zoo's newest habitat, **Hippo Canyon**—a 2-acre African rain forest opened at the base of Tiger River in 1995—you can watch the huge but surprisingly graceful beasts frolicking underwater. These newcomers, however, are likely to be overshadowed for a while by two glamorous visitors who arrived in the spring: **Shi Shi and Bay Yun,** a pair of giant pandas on 12-year loan from the People's Republic of China.

One of San Diego's most delightful museums was scheduled to move to new quarters in late 1995. The **Mingei International Museum of World Folk Art,** one of only five facilities in the world devoted to this subject, is planning to move from the University Towne Center into Balboa Park's House of Charm. You should be able to get up-to-date information on the new facility by calling the museum's current number (☎ 619/453–5300).

How to Use This Book

Organization

Up front is the **Gold Guide,** comprising two sections on gold paper that are chock-full of information about traveling within your destination and traveling in general. Both are in alphabetical order by topic. **Important Contacts A to Z** gives addresses and telephone numbers of organizations and companies that offer destination-related services and detailed information or publications. Here's where you'll find information about how to get to San Diego from wherever you are. **Smart Travel Tips A to Z,** the Gold Guide's second section, gives specific tips on how to get the most out of your travels, as well as information on how to accomplish what you need to in San Diego.

At the end of the book you'll find Portraits, a wonderful essay about San Diego, followed by suggestions for pretrip reading, both fiction and nonfiction.

Stars

Stars in the margin are used to denote highly recommended sights, attractions, hotels, and restaurants.

Credit Cards

The following abbreviations are used: **AE,** American Express; **D,** Discover; **DC,** Diners Club; **MC,** MasterCard; and **V,** Visa.

Please Write to Us

Everyone who has contributed to Fodor's *San Diego '96* has worked hard to make the text accurate. All prices and opening times are based on information supplied to us at press time, and the publisher cannot accept responsibility for any errors that may have occurred. The passage of time will bring changes, so it's always a good idea to call ahead and confirm information when it matters—particularly if you're making a detour to visit specific sights or attractions. When making reservations at a hotel or inn, be sure to mention if you have a disability or are traveling with children, if you prefer a private bath or a certain type of bed, or if you have specific dietary needs or any other concerns.

Were the restaurants we recommended as described? Did our hotel picks exceed your expectations? Did you find a museum we recommended a waste of time? We would love your feedback, positive and negative. If you have complaints, we'll look into them and revise our entries when the facts warrant it. If you've happened upon a special place that we haven't included, we'll pass the information along to the writers so they can check it out. So please send us a letter or postcard (we're at 201 East 50th Street, New York, New York 10022). We'll look forward to hearing from you. And in the meantime, have a wonderful trip!

Karen Cure

Editorial Director

N

Torrey Pines
State Beach

S21

Mira Mesa Blvd.

Genesee Ave.

805

Miramar Rd.

MIRAMAR

University of California
San Diego (UCSD)

MIRAMAR
NAVAL AIR
STATION

Gilman Dr.

Torrey Pines Rd.

Ardath Rd.

52

LA JOLLA

Clairemont Mesa Blvd.

5

163

Clairmont Dr.

Balboa Ave.

Genesee Ave.

Aero Dr.

La Jolla Blvd.

PACIFIC
BEACH

Grand Ave.

Ingraham St.

LINDA
VISTA

Vista Rd.

Cabrillo Fwy.

805

Mission Blvd.

MISSION
BEACH

Mission Bay

Linda Vista Rd.

Friars Rd.

Adams Ave.

Mission Bay Dr.

Sea World

8

163

OCEAN
BEACH

Sunset Cliffs Blvd.

Nimitz Blvd.

Rosecrans Blvd.

OLD
TOWN

University

Catalina Blvd.

209

Harbor Dr.

Pacific Hwy.

Balboa Park

POINT
LOMA

Cabrillo Memorial Dr.

North Island
U.S. NAVAL
AIR STATION

Broadway
Market St.
DOWNTOWN

94

Imperial

Harbor Dr.

Av

Natio

Cabrillo
National
Monument

Coronado
Beach

75

San Diego-
Coronado Bay
Bridge

San Diego Bay

NA

Strand Blvd.

PACIFIC OCEAN

Silver Strand
State Beach

Chula
Wild
Rese

Southern California

World Time Zones

Numbers below vertical bands relate each zone to Greenwich Mean Time (0 hrs.).
Local times frequently differ from these general indications,
as indicated by light-face numbers on map.

Algiers, **29**
Anchorage, **3**
Athens, **41**
Auckland, **1**
Baghdad, **46**
Bangkok, **50**
Beijing, **54**

Berlin, **34**
Bogotá, **19**
Budapest, **37**
Buenos Aires, **24**
Caracas, **22**
Chicago, **9**
Copenhagen, **33**
Dallas, **10**

Delhi, **48**
Denver, **8**
Djakarta, **53**
Dublin, **26**
Edmonton, **7**
Hong Kong, **56**
Honolulu, **2**

Istanbul, **40**
Jerusalem, **42**
Johannesburg, **44**
Lima, **20**
Lisbon, **28**
London
(Greenwich), **27**
Los Angeles, **6**
Madrid, **38**
Manila, **57**

Prime Meridian

Prime Meridian

-1   0   +1   +2   +3   +4   +5   +6   +7   +8   +9   +10
Greenwich
Mean Time

IMPORTANT CONTACTS A TO Z

*An Alphabetical Listing of Publications,
Organizations, and Companies That Will Help You
Before, During, and After Your Trip*

No single travel resource can give you every detail about every topic that might interest or concern you at the various stages of your journey—when you're planning your trip, while you're on the road, and after you get back home. The following organizations, books, and brochures will supplement the information in Fodor's *San Diego '96.* For related information, including both basic tips on visiting San Diego and background information on many of the topics below, study Smart Travel Tips A to Z, the section that follows Important Contacts A to Z.

A

AIR TRAVEL

San Diego is served by **Lindbergh Field** (☎ 619/231–2100). Flying time is 5 hours from New York, 3½ hours from Chicago, and ¾ hour from Los Angeles. The airport is a five-minute drive from downtown.

CARRIERS

Carriers serving San Diego include **Aeromexico** (☎ 800/237–6639), **Alaska Airlines** (☎ 800/426–0333), **America West** (☎ 800/235–9292), **American** (☎ 800/433–7300), **Continental** (☎ 800/525–

0280), **Delta** (☎ 800/221–1212), **Mark Air** (☎ 800/627–5247), **Midwest Express** (☎ 800/452–2022), **Northwest** (☎ 800/225–2525), **Sky West** (☎ 800/453–9417), **Southwest** (☎ 800/435–9792), **TWA** (☎ 800/221–2000), **United** (☎ 800/241–6522), and **USAir** (☎ 800/428–4322).

LOW-COST CARRIERS

For inexpensive, no-frills flights, contact **Midwest Express** (☎ 800/452–2022) and **Reno Air** (☎ 800/736–6247).

COMPLAINTS

To register complaints about charter and scheduled airlines, contact the U.S. Department of Transportation's **Office of Consumer Affairs** (400 7th St. NW, Washington, DC 20590, ☎ 202/366–2220 or 800/322–7873).

PUBLICATIONS

For general information about charter carriers, ask for the Office of Consumer Affairs' brochure **"Plane Talk: Public Charter Flights."** The Department of Transportation also publishes a 58-page booklet, **"Fly Rights"** ($1.75; Consumer Information Center, Dept. 133-B, Pueblo, CO 81009).

For other tips and hints, consult the Consumers Union's monthly **"Consumer Reports Travel Letter"** ($39 a year; Box 53629, Boulder CO 80322, ☎ 800/234–1970) and the newsletter **"Travel Smart"** ($37 a year; 40 Beechdale Rd., Dobbs Ferry, NY 10522, ☎ 800/327–3633); *The Official Frequent Flyer Guidebook,* by Randy Petersen (\$14.99 plus $3 shipping; 4715-C Town Center Dr., Colorado Springs, CO 80916, ☎ 719/597–8899 or 800/487–8893); *Airfare Secrets Exposed,* by Sharon Tyler and Matthew Wonder (Universal Information Publishing; $16.95 plus $3.75 shipping from Sandcastle Publishing, Box 3070-A, South Pasadena, CA 91031, ☎ 213/255–3616 or 800/655–0053); and *202 Tips Even the Best Business Travelers May Not Know,* by Christopher McGinnis ($10 plus $3.00 shipping; Irwin Professional Publishing, 1333 Burr Ridge Pkwy. Burr Ridge, IL 60521, ☎ 708/789–4000 or 800/634–3966).

AIRPORT TRANSFERS

BY BUS

San Diego Transit (☎ 619/233–3004) Route 2 buses leave every 10 to 15 minutes Monday through Friday and every 15 to 20 minutes Saturday and Sunday from about 5:30 AM–1 AM. Buses depart from the front of East Terminal's USAir section and travel along Broadway, downtown. The fare is $1.50 per person, 75¢ for senior citizens.

Cloud 9 Shuttle (☎ 619/278–8877 or 800/974–8885 in San Diego) and **Public Shuttle** (☎ 619/990–8770) offer van shuttles that take you directly to your destination, often for less than a cab would cost.

BY CAR

If you have rented a car at the airport, you can take Harbor Drive, at the perimeter of the airport, to downtown, only about 3 miles away.

BY TAXI

Taxi fare is $6–$8 plus tip to most center-city hotels.

B

BETTER BUSINESS BUREAU

San Diego Better Business Bureau (3111 Camino del Rio N., Suite 600, San Diego, CA 92108, ☎ 619/521–5898). For other local contacts, consult the **Council of Better Business Bureaus** (4200 Wilson Blvd., Arlington, VA 22203, ☎ 703/276–0100).

BUS TRAVEL

Greyhound (☎ 619/239–8082 or 800/231–2222) operates more than 20 buses a day between the downtown terminal at 120 West

Broadway and Los Angeles, connecting with buses to all major U.S. cities. Many buses are express or nonstop; others make stops at coastal towns en route.

WITHIN SAN DIEGO

The **San Diego Transit Information Line** (☎ 619/233–3004, TTY/TDD 619/234–5005; open daily 5:30 AM–8:30 PM) can provide details on getting to and from any location.

Regional bus companies that service areas outside the city include **ATC Van Co.** (☎ 619/427–5660), for Coronado, the Silver Strand, and Imperial Beach; **Chula Vista Transit** (☎ 619/233–3004), for Bonita and Chula Vista; **National City Transit** (☎ 619/474–7505), for National City; **North County Transit District** (☎ 619/722–6283), for the area bound by the ocean, east to Escondido, north to Camp Pendleton, and south to Del Mar; and **Northeast Rural Bus System** (☎ 619/765–0145) or **Southeast Rural Bus System** (☎ 619/478–5875), for access to rural county towns.

DISCOUNT PASSES

The **Day Tripper Transit Pass** is good for unlimited trips on the same day on San Diego Transit buses and on the trolley and the ferry for $5; there's also a four-day pass for $15. Passes are available at the **Transit Store** (449 Broadway, ☎ 619/234–1060) as well as at the ferry landing and the

downtown Amtrak station.

C

CAR RENTAL

Major car-rental companies represented in San Diego include **Alamo** (☎ 800/327–9633, 0800/272–2000 in the U.K.), **Avis** (☎ 800/331–1212, 800/879–2847 in Canada), **Budget** (☎ 800/527–0700, 0800/181–181 in the U.K.), **Dollar** (known as Eurodollar outside North America, ☎ 800/800–4000 in the U.S. and Canada, 0181/952–6565 in the U.K.), **Hertz** (☎ 800/654–3131, 800/263–0600 in Canada, 0181/679–1799 in the U.K.), and **National** (☎ 800/227–7368, 0181/950–5050 in the U.K., where it is known as Europcar). **Rent-A-Wreck** (☎ 800/535–1391) can offer less expensive rentals. Rates in San Diego begin at $25 a day and $179 a week for an economy car with unlimited mileage.

CHILDREN AND TRAVEL

FLYING

Look into **"Flying with Baby"** ($5.95 plus $1 shipping; Third Street Press, Box 261250, Littleton, CO 80126, ☎ 303/595–5959), cowritten by a flight attendant. **"Kids and Teens in Flight,"** free from the U.S. Department of Transportation's Office of Consumer Affairs, offers tips for children flying alone. Every two years the February issue of *Family Travel Times* (*see* Know-How, *below*)

details children's services on three dozen airlines.

KNOW-HOW

Family Travel Times, published 10 times a year by Travel with Your Children (TWYCH, 45 W. 18th St., New York, NY 10011, ☎ 212/206–0688; annual subscription $55), covers destinations, types of vacations, and modes of travel.

The *Family Travel Guides* catalogue ($1 postage; ☎ 510/527–5849) lists about 200 books and articles on family travel. Also check *Take Your Baby and Go! A Guide for Traveling with Babies, Toddlers and Young Children,* by Sheri Andrews, Judy Bordeaux, and Vivian Vasquez ($5.95 plus $1.50 shipping; Bear Creek Publications, 2507 Minor Ave., Seattle, WA 98102, ☎ 206/322–7604 or 800/326–6566). *The 100 Best Family Resorts in North America,* by Jane Wilford with Janet Tice ($12.95), and the two-volume *50 Great Family Vacations in North America* ($18.95 per volume), both from Globe Pequot Press (plus $3 shipping; Box 833, 6 Business Park Rd., Old Saybrook, CT 06475, ☎ 203/395–0440 or 800/243–0495, 800/962–0973 in CT) help plan your trip with children, from toddlers to teens.

LOCAL INFORMATION

San Diego Family Press, a monthly magazine for parents, is filled with listings of events and resources; it is available by mail (Box 23960, San Diego 92193, ☎ 619/685–6970) for $2.50, which covers postage and handling, or free in San Diego at Longs drugstores, Boney's grocery stores, and local libraries.

Also consult the lively by-parents, for-parents *Where Should We Take the Kids? California* ($17.00; Fodor's Travel Publications, ☎ 800/533–6478 and in bookstores).

Places to Go with Children in Southern California, by Stephanie Kegan ($9.95; Chronicle Books, 275 5th St., San Francisco, CA 94103, ☎ 415/777–7240), gives you suggestions for traveling with kids in this area.

TOUR OPERATORS

Contact **Grandtravel** (6900 Wisconsin Ave., Suite 706, Chevy Chase, MD 20815, ☎ 301/986–0790 or 800/247–7651), which has tours for people traveling with grandchildren ages 7 to 17.

CANADIANS

Contact **Revenue Canada** (2265 St. Laurent Blvd. S, Ottawa, Ontario, K1G 4K3, ☎ 613/993–0534) for a copy of the free brochure **"I Declare/Je Déclare"** and for details on duties that exceed the standard duty-free limit.

U.K. CITIZENS

HM Customs and Excise (Dorset House, Stamford St., London SE1 9NG, ☎ 0171/202–4227) can answer questions about U.K. customs regulations and publishes **"A Guide for Travellers,"** detailing standard procedures and import rules.

D

FOR TRAVELERS WITH DISABILITIES

COMPLAINTS

To register complaints under the provisions of the Americans with Disabilities Act, contact the U.S. Department of Justice's **Public Access Section** (Box 66738, Washington, DC 20035, ☎ 202/514–0301, TDD 202/514–0383, FAX 202/307–1198).

LOCAL INFORMATION

The Access Center of San Diego (Information and Referrals, 1295 University Ave., Suite 10, San Diego 92103, ☎ 619/293–3500, TDD 619/293–7757) publishes lists of hotels, motels, and restaurants with access for the disabled. **Accessible San Diego** (2466 Bartell St., San Diego 92123, ☎ 619/279–0704) has a visitor information center and telephone hot line, makes hotel referrals, and provides guides to San Diego's attractions for visitors with mobility problems.

ORGANIZATIONS

For Travelers with Hearing Impairments➤ Contact the **American Academy of Otolaryngology** (1 Prince St., Alexandria, VA 22314, ☎ 703/836–4444, FAX

703/683–5100, TTY 703/519–1585).

FOR TRAVELERS WITH MOBILITY PROBLEMS➤ Contact the **Information Center for Individuals with Disabilities** (Fort Point Pl., 27–43 Wormwood St., Boston, MA 02210, ☎ 617/727–5540, 800/462–5015 in MA, TTY 617/345–9743); **Mobility International USA** (Box 10767, Eugene, OR 97440, ☎ and TTY 503/343–1284; FAX 503/343–6812), the U.S. branch of an international organization based in Belgium (*see below*) that has affiliates in 30 countries; **MossRehab Hospital Travel Information Service** (1200 W. Tabor Rd., Philadelphia, PA 19141, ☎ 215/456–9603, TTY 215/456–9602); the **Society for the Advancement of Travel for the Handicapped** (347 5th Ave., Suite 610, New York, NY 10016, ☎ 212/447–7284, FAX 212/725–8253); the **Travel Industry and Disabled Exchange** (TIDE, 5435 Donna Ave., Tarzana, CA 91356, ☎ 818/344–3640, FAX 818/344–0078); and **Travelin' Talk** (Box 3534, Clarksville, TN 37043, ☎ 615/552–6670, FAX 615/552–1182).

FOR TRAVELERS WITH VISION IMPAIRMENTS➤ Contact the **American Council of the Blind** (1155 15th St. NW, Suite 720, Washington, DC 20005, ☎ 202/467–5081, FAX 202/467–5085) or the **American Foundation for the Blind** (15 W. 16th St., New York,

NY 10011, ☎ 212/620–2000, TTY 212/620–2158).

IN THE U.K.

Contact the **Royal Association for Disability and Rehabilitation** (RADAR, 12 City Forum, 250 City Rd., London EC1V 8AF, ☎ 0171/250–3222) or **Mobility International** (Rue de Manchester 25, B1070 Brussels, Belgium, ☎ 00–322–410–6297), an international clearinghouse of travel information for people with disabilities.

PUBLICATIONS

Several free publications are available from the U.S. Information Center (Box 100, Pueblo, CO 81009, ☎ 719/948–3334): *"New Horizons for the Air Traveler with a Disability"* (address to Dept. 355A), describing legally mandated changes; the pocket-size *"Fly Smart"* (Dept. 575B), good on flight safety; and the Airport Operators Council's worldwide *"Access Travel: Airports"* (Dept. 575A).

Fodor's *Great American Vacations for Travelers with Disabilities* ($18; available in bookstores, or call 800/533–6478) details accessible attractions, restaurants, and hotels in U.S. destinations. The 500-page *Travelin' Talk Directory* ($35; Box 3534, Clarksville, TN 37043, ☎ 615/552–6670) lists people and organizations who help travelers with disabilities. For specialist travel agents worldwide, consult the *Directory of Travel*

Agencies for the Disabled ($19.95 plus $2 shipping; Twin Peaks Press, Box 129, Vancouver, WA 98666, ☎ 206/694–2462 or 800/637–2256). The Sierra Club publishes *Easy Access to National Parks* ($16 plus $3 shipping; 730 Polk St., San Francisco, CA 94109, ☎ 415/776–2211 or 800/935–1056).

PUBLIC TRANSPORTATION

About one-third of the bus lines are served by buses with elevator ramps; call the **San Diego Transit Information Line** (*see* Bus Travel, *above*) for detailed information. The **San Diego Trolley** (☎ 619/233–3004), which goes as far as the Mexican border, has wheelchair lifts. Round-the-clock wheelchair transportation throughout San Diego is available through **Self-Reliance Shuttle** (Box 90458, San Diego 92169, ☎ 619/272–4117).

TRAVEL AGENCIES, TOUR OPERATORS

The Americans with Disabilities Act requires that travel firms serve the needs of all travelers. However, some agencies and operators specialize in making group and individual arrangements for travelers with disabilities, among them **Access Adventures** (206 Chestnut Ridge Rd., Rochester, NY 14624, ☎ 716/889–9096), run by a former physical-rehab counselor; and **Tailored Tours** (Box 797687, Dallas, TX

75379, ☎ 214/612–1168 or 800/628–8542). In addition, many general-interest operators and agencies (*see* Tours Operators, *below*) can also arrange vacations for travelers with disabilities.

FOR TRAVELERS WITH HEARING IMPAIRMENTS➤ One agency is **International Express** (7319-B Baltimore Ave., College Park, MD 20740, ☎ TDD 301/699–8836, FAX 301/699–8836), which arranges group and independent trips.

FOR TRAVELERS WITH MOBILITY IMPAIRMENTS➤ A number of operators specialize in working with travelers with mobility impairments, including **Hinsdale Travel Service** (201 E. Ogden Ave., Suite 100, Hinsdale, IL 60521, ☎ 708/325–1335 or 800/303–5521), a travel agency that will give you access to the services of wheelchair traveler Janice Perkins; and **Wheelchair Journeys** (16979 Redmond Way, Redmond, WA 98052, ☎ 206/885–2210), which can handle arrangements worldwide.

FOR TRAVELERS WITH DEVELOPMENTAL DISABILITIES➤ Contact the nonprofit **New Directions** (5276 Hollister Ave., Suite 207, Santa Barbara, CA 93111, ☎ 805/967–2841), for travelers with developmental disabilities and their families, as well as the general-interest operations *above*.

DISCOUNTS

Options include **Entertainment Travel Editions** (fee $28–$53, depending on destination; Box 1068, Trumbull, CT 06611, ☎ 800/445–4137), **Great American Traveler** ($49.95 annually; Box 27965, Salt Lake City, UT 84127, ☎ 800/548–2812), **Moment's Notice Discount Travel Club** ($25 annually, single or family; 163 Amsterdam Ave., Suite 137, New York, NY 10023, ☎ 212/486–0500), **Privilege Card** ($74.95 annually; 3391 Peachtree Rd. NE, Suite 110, Atlanta GA 30326, ☎ 404/262–0222 or 800/236–9732), **Travelers Advantage** ($49 annually, single or family; CUC Travel Service, 49 Music Sq. W, Nashville, TN 37203, ☎ 800/548–1116 or 800/648–4037), and **Worldwide Discount Travel Club** ($50 annually for family, $40 single; 1674 Meridian Ave., Miami Beach, FL 33139, ☎ 305/534–2082).

E
EMERGENCIES

Dial 911 for **police, ambulance,** and **fire** departments in an emergency.

DOCTORS

Hospital emergency rooms, with physicians on duty, are open 24 hours. Major hospitals are **Mercy Hospital and Medical Center** (4077 5th Ave., ☎ 619/294–8111), **Scripps Memorial Hospital** (9888 Genesee Ave., La Jolla, ☎ 619/457–4123), **Veterans**

Administration Hospital (3350 La Jolla Village Dr., La Jolla, ☎ 619/552–8585), and **UCSD Medical Center** (200 W. Arbor Dr., Hillcrest, ☎ 619/543–6222).

Doctors on Call (☎ 619/275–2663) offers 24-hour medical service to guests at San Diego hotels.

DENTIST

The **San Diego County Dental Society** (☎ 619/275–0244) can provide referrals Monday through Friday to those with dental emergencies. Doctors on Call (*see above*) provides 24-hour dental emergency referrals.

F
FERRY TRAVEL

The **San Diego-Coronado Ferry** (☎ 619/234–4111) leaves from the Broadway Pier daily, every hour on the hour, 9 AM–9:30 PM Sunday–Thursday, until 10:30 PM Friday and Saturday. The fare is $2 each way.

G
GAY AND LESBIAN TRAVEL

ORGANIZATION

The **International Gay Travel Association** (Box 4974, Key West, FL 33041, ☎ 800/448–8550), a consortium of 800 businesses, can supply names of travel agents and tour operators.

PUBLICATIONS

The premiere international travel magazine for gays and lesbians is **Our World** ($35 for 10 issues; 1104 N. Nova Rd., Suite 251, Daytona Beach, FL 32117, ☎ 904/441–5367). The 16-page monthly "Out & About" ($49 for 10 issues; ☎ 212/645–6922 or 800/929–2268), covers gay-friendly resorts, hotels, cruise lines, and airlines.

TOUR OPERATORS

Vacations are handled by **R.S.V.P. Travel Productions** (2800 University Ave. SE, Minneapolis, MN 55414, ☎ 800/328–RSVP); **Toto Tours** (1326 W. Albion Suite 3W, Chicago, IL 60626, ☎ 312/274–8686 or 800/565–1241) have group tours worldwide.

TRAVEL AGENCIES

The largest agencies serving gay travelers are **Advance Travel** (10700 Northwest Freeway, Suite 160, Houston, TX 77092, ☎ 713/682–2002 or 800/695–0880), **Islanders/Kennedy Travel** (183 W. 10th St., New York, NY 10014, ☎ 212/242–3222 or 800/988–1181), **Now Voyager** (4406 18th St., San Francisco, CA 94114, ☎ 415/626–1169 or 800/255–6951), and **Yellowbrick Road** (1500 W. Balmoral Ave., Chicago, IL 60640, ☎ 312/561–1800 or 800/642–2488). **Skylink Women's Travel** (746 Ashland Ave., Santa Monica, CA 90405, ☎ 310/452–0506 or 800/225-5759) works with lesbians.

I

INSURANCE

Travel insurance covering baggage, health, and trip cancellation or interruptions is available from **Access America** (Box 90315, Richmond, VA 23286, ☎ 804/285–3300 or 800/284–8300), **Carefree Travel Insurance** (Box 9366, 100 Garden City Plaza, Garden City, NY 11530, ☎ 516/294–0220 or 800/323–3149), **Near** (Box 1339, Calumet City, IL 60409, ☎ 708/868–6700 or 800/654–6700), **Tele-Trip** (Mutual of Omaha Plaza, Box 31716, Omaha, NE 68131, ☎ 800/228–9792), **Travel Insured International** (Box 280568, East Hartford, CT 06128-0568, ☎ 203/528–7663 or 800/243–3174), **Travel Guard International** (1145 Clark St., Stevens Point, WI 54481, ☎ 715/345–0505 or 800/826–1300), and **Wallach & Company** (107 W. Federal St., Box 480, Middleburg, VA 22117, ☎ 703/687–3166 or 800/237–6615).

IN THE U.K.

The **Association of British Insurers** (51 Gresham St., London EC2V 7HQ, ☎ 0171/600–3333; 30 Gordon St., Glasgow G1 3PU, ☎ 0141/226–3905; Scottish Provident Bldg., Donegall Sq. W., Belfast BT1 6JE, ☎ 01232/249176; call for other locations) gives advice by phone and publishes the free **"Holiday Insurance,"** which

sets out typical policy provisions and costs.

L

LIMOUSINES

Limousine companies offer airport shuttles and customized tours. Rates vary and are per hour, per mile, or both, with some minimums established. Companies that offer a range of services include **Advantage Limousine Service** (☎ 619/563–1651), **La Jolla Limousines** (☎ 619/459–5891), **Limousines by Linda** (☎ 619/234–9145), and **Olde English Livery** (☎ 619/232–6533).

LODGING

APARTMENT AND VILLA RENTALS

Among the companies to contact are **Vacation Home Rentals Worldwide** (235 Kensington Ave., Norwood, NJ 07648, ☎ 201/767–9393 or 800/633–3284). Members of the travel club **Hideaways International** ($99 annually; 767 Islington St., Portsmouth, NH 03801, ☎ 603/430–4433 or 800/843–4433) receive two annual guides plus quarterly newsletters, and arrange rentals among themselves.

HOME EXCHANGE

Principal clearinghouses include **Intervac International** ($65 annually; Box 590504, San Francisco, CA 94159, ☎ 415/435–3497), which has three annual directories; and **Loan-a-Home** ($35–$45 annually; 2 Park La., Apt. 6E, Mount Vernon, NY 10552-3443, ☎ 914/664–7640), which specializes in long-term exchanges.

M
MONEY MATTERS

ATMS

For specific **Cirrus** locations in the United States and Canada, call 800/424–7787. For U.S. **Plus** locations, call 800/843–7587 and enter the area code and first three digits of the number you're calling from (or of the calling area where you want an ATM).

WIRING FUNDS

Funds can be wired via **American Express MoneyGram℠** (☎ 800/926–9400 from the U.S. and Canada for locations and information) or **Western Union** (☎ 800/325–6000 for agent locations or to send using MasterCard or Visa, 800/321–2923 in Canada).

P
PASSPORTS AND VISAS

U.K. CITIZENS

For fees, documentation requirements, and to get an emergency passport, call the **London Passport Office** (☎ 0171/271–3000). For visa information, call the **U.S. Embassy Visa Information Line** (☎ 0891/200–290; calls cost 49p per minute or 39p per minute cheap rate) or write the **U.S. Embassy Visa Branch** (5 Upper Grosvenor St., London W1A 2JB). If you live in Northern Ireland, write the **U.S. Consulate General** (Queen's House, Queen St., Belfast BTI 6EQ). In

Scotland, apply to the consulate at 3 Regent Terrace, Edinburgh EH7 5BW.

PHOTO HELP

The **Kodak Information Center** (☎ 800/242–2424) answers consumer questions about film and photography.

R
RAIL TRAVEL

Amtrak trains (☎ 800/872–7245) from Los Angeles arrive at Santa Fe Depot (1050 Kettner Blvd., corner of Broadway, near the heart of downtown, ☎ 619/239–9021). There are additional stations in Del Mar (☎ 619/481–0114) and Oceanside (☎ 619/722–4622), both in north San Diego County. Eight trains operate daily in either direction.

TROLLEYS

The **San Diego Trolley** (☎ 619/233–3004) travels from downtown to within 100 feet of the U.S.–Mexican border, stopping at 21 suburban stations en route. The basic fare is $1.75 one way. The trolley also travels from downtown to Encanto, Lemon Grove, La Mesa, and El Cajon in East County. Tickets must be purchased before boarding. Ticket-vending machines, located at each station, require exact change. Trolleys operate daily, approximately every 15 minutes, 5 AM–9 PM, then every 30 minutes until 1 AM. The Bayside line serves the Convention Center and Seaport Village; lines to Old Town, Mission Valley,

and North County are under construction.

S
SENIOR CITIZENS

EDUCATIONAL TRAVEL

The nonprofit **Elderhostel** (75 Federal St., 3rd Floor, Boston, MA 02110, ☎ 617/426–7788), for people 60 and older, has offered inexpensive study programs since 1975. The nearly 2,000 courses cover everything from marine science to Greek myths and cowboy poetry. Fees for programs in the United States and Canada, which usually last one week, run about $300, not including transportation.

ORGANIZATIONS

Contact the **American Association of Retired Persons** (AARP, 601 E St. NW, Washington, DC 20049, ☎ 202/434–2277; $8 per person or couple annually). Its Purchase Privilege Program gets members discounts on lodging, car rentals, and sightseeing, and the AARP Motoring Plan furnishes domestic trip-routing information and emergency road-service aid for an annual fee of $39.95 per person or couple ($59.95 for a premium version).

For other discounts on lodgings, car rentals, and other travel products, along with magazines and newsletters, contact the **National Council of Senior Citizens** (membership $12 annually; 1331 F St. NW, Washington, DC

20004, ☎ 202/347–8800) and **Mature Outlook** (subscription $9.95 annually; 6001 N. Clark St., Chicago, IL 60660, ☎ 312/465–6466 or 800/336–6330).

PUBLICATIONS

The 50+ Traveler's Guidebook: Where to Go, Where to Stay, What to Do, by Anita Williams and Merrimac Dillon ($12.95; St. Martin's Press, 175 5th Ave., New York, NY 10010, ☎ 212/674–5151 or 800/288–2131), offers many useful tips. **"The Mature Traveler"** ($29.95; Box 50400, Reno, NV 89513, ☎ 702/786–7419), a monthly newsletter, covers travel deals.

SIGHTSEEING

BALLOON TOURS

Six-passenger hot-air balloons lift off from San Diego's North Country. Most flights are at sunrise or sunset and are followed by a traditional champagne celebration. Companies that offer daily service, weather permitting, are **Air Affaire** (☎ 619/560–6373 or 800/331–1979), **Pacific Horizon** (☎ 619/756–1790 or 800/244–1790), and **Skysurfer** (☎ 619/481–6800 or 800/660–6809 in CA). Balloon flights average $145 per person.

BUS TOURS

Gray Line Tours (☎ 619/491–0011 or 800/331–5077) and **San Diego Mini Tours** (☎ 619/477–8687) offer two daily sightseeing excursions for about $25.

Old Town Trolley (☎ 619/298–8687) travels to almost every attraction and shopping area on open-air trackless trolleys. Drivers double as tour guides. You can take the full two-hour, narrated city tour or get on and off as you please at any of the nine stops. An all-day pass costs $16 for adults, $7 for children 6–12. The trolley, which leaves every 30 minutes, operates daily 9–5 in summer, 9–4 in winter.

Free two-hour trolley tours of the downtown redevelopment area, including the Gaslamp Quarter, are hosted by **Centre City Development Corporation's Downtown Information Center** (☎ 619/235–2222). Groups of 35 passengers leave from 255 G Street, downtown, the first and third Saturday of each month at 10 AM. Reservations are necessary. The tour may be canceled if there aren't enough passengers.

CRUISES

San Diego Harbor Excursion (☎ 619/234–4111) and **Hornblower Invader Cruises** (☎ 619/234–8687) sail on narrated cruises of San Diego Harbor, departing from Broadway Pier. Both companies offer one-hour cruises ($10), departing several times daily, and a two-hour tour ($15) each day at 2 PM (additional tours in summer). No reservations are necessary, and both vessels have snack bars on board. **Classic Sailing Adventures** (☎ 619/224–0800) has morning and afternoon

tours of the harbor and San Diego Bay and nighttime summer cruises for $45 per person.

HELICOPTER TOURS

Civic Helicopters (☎ 619/438–8424 or 800/438–4354) has helicopter tours starting at $69 per person per half hour.

WALKING TOURS

The Gaslamp Quarter Association (410 Island Ave., ☎ 619/233–5227) leads 1½-hour architectural tours of the restored downtown historic district on Saturday at 11 AM ($5 adults, $3 senior citizens and students). Self-guided tour brochures are available at the office, weekdays 10–4:30.

On weekends, the State Park Department (☎ 619/220–5422) gives free walking tours of **Old Town.** Groups leave from 4002 Wallace Street at 2 PM daily, weather permitting.

Walkabout (☎ 619/231–7463) offers several different free walking tours throughout the city each week.

WHALE-WATCHING

Gray whales migrate south to Mexico and back north from mid-December to mid-March. As many as 200 whales pass the San Diego coast each day, coming within yards of tour boats. During whale-watching season, *The Apollo* (☎ 619/221–8500), a luxury motor yacht, offers narrated tours twice a day. **Classic Sailing Adventures** (☎ 619/

224–0800) tailors whale-watching expeditions for up to six people. **H&M Landing** (☎ 619/222–1144) and **Seaforth Sportfishing** (☎ 619/224–3383) have daily whale-watching trips in large party boats.

STUDENTS

GROUPS

Major tour operators include **Contiki Holidays** (300 Plaza Alicante, Suite 900, Garden Grove, CA 92640, ☎ 714/740–0808 or 800/466–0610).

HOSTELING

Contact **Hostelling International–American Youth Hostels** (733 15th St. NW, Suite 840, Washington, DC 20005, ☎ 202/783–6161) in the United States, **Hostelling International–Canada** (205 Catherine St., Suite 400, Ottawa, Ontario K2P 1C3, ☎ 613/237–7884) in Canada, and the **Youth Hostel Association of England and Wales** (Trevelyan House, 8 St. Stephen's Hill, St. Albans, Hertfordshire AL1 2DY, ☎ 01727/855215 and 01727/845047) in the United Kingdom. Membership ($25 in the U.S., C$26.75 in Canada, and £9 in the U.K.) gets you access to 5,000 hostels worldwide that charge $7–$20 nightly per person.

I.D. CARDS

To be eligible for discounts on transportation and admissions, get the **International Student Identity Card** (ISIC) if you're a bona fide student or the **International Youth Card** (IYC) if you're under 26. In the United States, the ISIC and IYC cards cost $16 each and include basic travel-accident and illness coverage, plus a toll-free travel hot line. Apply through the Council on International Educational Exchange (*see* Organizations, *below*). Cards are available for $15 each in Canada from **Travel Cuts** (187 College St., Toronto, Ontario M5T 1P7, ☎ 416/979–2406 or 800/667–2887) and in the United Kingdom for £5 each at student unions and student travel companies.

ORGANIZATIONS

A major contact is the **Council on International Educational Exchange** (CIEE, 205 E. 42nd St., 16th Floor, New York, NY 10017, ☎ 212/661–1450) with locations in Boston (729 Boylston St., Boston, MA 02116, ☎ 617/266–1926), Miami (9100 S. Dadeland Blvd., Miami, FL 33156, ☎ 305/670–9261), Los Angeles (1093 Broxton Ave., Los Angeles, CA 90024, ☎ 310/208–3551), 43 college towns nationwide, and the United Kingdom (28A Poland St., London W1V 3DB, ☎ 0171/437–7767). Twice a year, it publishes *Student Travels* magazine. The CIEE's Council Travel Service offers domestic air passes for bargain travel within the United States and is the exclusive U.S. agent for several student-discount cards.

Campus Connections (325 Chestnut St., Suite 1101, Philadelphia, PA 19106, ☎ 215/625–8585 or 800/428–3235) specializes in discounted accommodations and airfares for students. The **Educational Travel Centre** (438 N. Frances St., Madison, WI 53703, ☎ 608/256–5551) offers rail passes and low-cost airline tickets, mostly for flights departing from Chicago.

In Canada, also contact **Travel Cuts** (*see above*).

PUBLICATIONS

See the *Berkeley Guide to California* ($17.50; Fodor's Travel Publications, 800/533–6478 or from bookstores).

T

TAXIS

Cab companies that serve most areas of the city are **Coast Shuttle** (☎ 619/477–3333), **Co-op Silver Cabs** (☎ 619/280–5555), **Coronado Cab** (☎ 619/435–6211), **La Jolla Cab** (☎ 619/453–4222), **Orange Cab** (☎ 619/291–3333), and **Yellow Cab** (☎ 619/234–6161).

TOUR OPERATORS

Among the companies selling tours and packages to San Diego, the following have a proven reputation, are nationally known, and have plenty of options to choose from.

GROUP TOURS

For deluxe escorted tours to San Diego, contact **Maupintour** (Box 807, Lawrence KS 66044, ☎ 800/255–4266 or 913/843–

1211) and **Tauck Tours** (11 Wilton Rd., Westport, CT 06880, ☎ 800/468–2825 or 203/226–6911). Another operator falling between deluxe and first-class is **Globus** (5301 South Federal Circle, Littleton, CO 80123-2980, ☎ 800/221–0090 or 303/797–2800). In the first-class and tourist range, try **Collette Tours** (162 Middle St., Pawtucket, RI 02860, ☎ 800/832–4656 or 401/728–3805), **Domenico Tours** (750 Broadway, Bayonne, NJ 07002, ☎ 800/554–8687 or 201/823–8687) and **Mayflower Tours** (1225 Warren Ave., Downers Grove, IL 60515, ☎ 708/960–3430 or 800/323–7604). For budget and tourist class programs, try **Cosmos** (*see* Globus, *above*).

PACKAGES

Independent vacation packages are available from major tour operators and airlines. Contact **American Airlines Fly AAway Vacations** (☎ 800/321–2121), **SuperCities** (139 Main St., Cambridge, MA 02142, ☎ 800/333–1234 or 617/621–0099), **Continental Airlines' Grand Destinations** (☎ 800/634–5555), **Delta Dream Vacations** (☎ 800/872–7786), **Certified Vacations** (Box 1525, Ft. Lauderdale, FL 33302, ☎ 305/522–1414 or 800/233–7260), **United Vacations** (☎ 800/328–6877), **Kingdom Tours** (300 Market St., Kingston, PA 18704, ☎ 717/283–4241 or 800/872–8857), and

USAir Vacations (☎ 800/455–0123). **Funjet Vacations**, based in Milwaukee, Wisconsin, and **Gogo Tours**, based in Ramsey, New Jersey, sell packages to San Diego only through travel agents.

FROM THE U.K.➤ Tour operators offering packages to San Diego include **British Airways Holidays** (Astral Towers, Betts Way, London Rd., Crawley, West Sussex RH10 2XA, ☎ 01293/518–022), **Jetsave** (Sussex House, London Rd., East Grinstead, West Sussex RH19 1LD, ☎ 01342/312033), **Key to America** (1–3 Station Rd., Ashford, Middlesex TW15 2UW, ☎ 01784/248777), **Kuoni Travel Ltd.** (Kuoni House, Dorking, Surrey RH5 4AZ, ☎ 01306/742–222), **Premier Holidays** (Premier Travel Center, Westbrook, Milton Rd., Cambridge CB4, 1YG, ☎ 01223/516–688), and **Trailfinders** (42–50 Earl's Court Rd., London W8 6FT, ☎ 0171/937–5400; 58 Deansgate, Manchester, M3 2FF, ☎ 0161/839–6969).

Some travel agencies that offer cheap fares to San Diego include Trailfinders (*see above*); **Travel Cuts** (295a Regent St., London W1R 7YA, ☎ 0171/637–3161), the Canadian Students' travel service; and **Flightfile** (49 Tottenham Court Rd., London W1P 9RE, ☎ 0171/700-2722).

THEME TRIPS

BICYCLING➤ Bike tours are available from

Backroads (1516 5th St., Suite L101, Berkeley, CA 94710, ☎ 510/527–1555 or 800/462–2848), **Imagine Tours** (917 3rd St., Davis, CA 95616, ☎ 800/228–7041), and **Native Cycles** (70–053 Hwy. 111, Rancho Mirage, CA 92262, ☎ 800/952–5068).

ECOTOURS➤ **Oceanic Society Expeditions** (Fort Mason Center, Bldg. E, San Francisco, CA 94124, ☎ 415/441–1106 or 800/326–7491) goes to Baja for snokeling with sea lions, desert nature walks, and whale-watching boat trips. **Eco Tour!** (San Diego North County Convention & Visitors Bureau, 720 N. Broadway, Escondido, CA 92025, ☎ 619/745–4796 or 800/848–3336) combines familiar vacation elements with hands-on environmental activities.

GOLF➤ **Best Golf Tours** (332 Forest Ave., Laguna Beach, CA 92651, ☎ 714/752–8881 or 800/227–0212) and **Golf America, Inc.** (7514 Girard Ave., No. 243, La Jolla, CA 92037, ☎ 800/435–5775 or 619/454–2026) have design-your-own golf packages in Palm Springs. Also contact **Golf Amtrak/Great American Vacations** (1220 Kensington, Oakbrook, IL 60521, ☎ 800/872–7245 or 800/321–8684 in southern California).

HORSEBACK RIDING➤ For a riding vacation at a ranch once owned by John Wayne, contact **FITS Equestrian** (685

Important Contacts A to Z

THE GOLD GUIDE / IMPORTANT CONTACTS

Lateen Rd., Solvang, CA 93463, ☎ 805/688–9494 or 800/666–3487.)

NATIVE CULTURE➤ **Agua Caliente Band of Cahuilla Indians Reservation** (110 N. Indian Canyon Dr., Palm Springs, CA 92262, ☎ 619/325–5673) has day-long excursions to three spectacular Indian canyons and trading posts.

WHALE WATCHING➤ Whale-watching trips in search of the gray whale are available from **Biological Journeys** (1696 Ocean Dr., McKinleyville, CA 95521, ☎ 800/548–7555) **Oceanic Society Expeditions** (see Ecotours, *above*) and **Pacific Sea-Fari Tours.**

WINE TOURS➤ **Burbury Wine Tour** (2554 Lincoln Blvd., No. 525, Marina del Rey, CA 90291, ☎ 310/208–0980) offers picnic wine tours to wineries in Temecula Valley.

ORGANIZATIONS

The **National Tour Association** (546 E. Main St., Lexington, KY 40508, ☎ 606/226–4444 or 800/682–8886) and **United States Tour Operators Association** (USTOA, 211 E. 51st St., Suite 12B, New York, NY 10022, ☎ 212/750–7371) can provide lists of member operators and information on booking tours.

PUBLICATIONS

Consult the brochure on tour and ask for a current list of member operators from the National Tour Association (*see above*). Also

get a copy of the **"Worldwide Tour & Vacation Package Finder"** from the USTOA (*see above*) and the Better Business Bureau's **"Tips on Travel Packages"** (publication No. 24-195, $2; 4200 Wilson Blvd., Arlington, VA 22203).

For names of reputable agencies in your area, contact the **American Society of Travel Agents** (1101 King St., Suite 200, Alexandria, VA 22314, ☎ 703/739–2782).

V

VISITOR INFORMATION

For information before your trip, contact the **San Diego Convention & Visitors Bureau** (401 B St., Suite 1400, San Diego 92101, ☎ 619/232–3101) for *The San Diego Official Visitors Guide.* The **Visitor Information Center** (2688 E. Mission Bay Dr., San Diego 92109, ☎ 619/276–8200) can make your lodging reservations and publishes a newspaper, *Pathfinder* (enclose a SASE when requesting a copy). You can get information about other communities within San Diego County from the visitors bureaus or chambers of commerce, including those in **Borrego Springs** (622 Palm Canyon Dr., Box 66, 92004, ☎ 619/767–5555), **Carlsbad** (Box 1246, 92018, ☎ 619/434–6093), **Coronado** (1111 Orange Ave., Suite A, 92118, ☎ 619/437–8788 or 800/622–8300), **Del Mar** (1104

Camino del Mar, 92014, ☎ 619/755–4844), **San Diego North County Convention & Visitors Bureau** (720 N. Broadway, Escondido, 92025, ☎ 619/745–4741 or 800/848–3336), **Julian** (2123 Main St., Box 413, 92036, ☎ 619/765–1857), **La Jolla** (1055 Wall St., Box 1101, 92038, ☎ 619/454–1444), and **Oceanside** (928 N. Hill St., 92054, ☎ 619/722–1534 or 800/350–7873). The **California Office of Tourism** (801 K St., Suite 1600, Sacramento, CA 95814, ☎ 916/322–2881) can answer many questions about travel in the state. You can also order a visitors guide, which includes an informative section on San Diego (free; ☎ 800/862–2543).

In the U.K., also contact the **United States Travel and Tourism Administration** (Box 1EN, London W1A 1EN, ☎ 0171/495–4466). For a free USA pack, write the USTTA at Box 170, Ashford, Kent TN24 0ZX. Enclose stamps worth £1.50.

When you're in San Diego, stop in at the **International Visitor Information Center** (11 Horton Plaza, at 1st Ave. and F St., ☎ 619/236–1212; open Mon.–Sat., 8:30–5 year-round, Sun. 11–5 June–Aug.) at the **Balboa Park Visitors Center** (1549 El Prado, in Balboa Park, ☎ 619/239–0512; open daily 9–4), or at the **Mission Bay Visitor Information Center** (2688 E. Mission Bay Dr., off I–5 at the

Mission Bay Dr. exit, ☎ 619/276–8200; open Mon.–Sat. 9–5, Sun. 9:30–4:30 in winter, open later in summer).

W
WEATHER

Call the **San Diego City Beach and Weather**

Conditions Information Line (☎ 619/221–8884). For current conditions and forecasts, plus the local time and helpful travel tips,

call the **Weather Channel Connection** (☎ 900/932–8437; 95¢ per minute) from a touch-tone phone.

SMART TRAVEL TIPS A TO Z

Basic Information on Traveling in San Diego and Savvy Tips to Make Your Trip a Breeze

The more you travel, the more you know about how to make trips run like clockwork. To help make your travels hassle-free, Fodor's editors have rounded up dozens of tips from our contributors and travel experts all over the world, as well as basic information on visiting San Diego. For names of organizations to contact and publications that can give you more information, *see* Important Contacts A to Z, *above.*

A
AIR TRAVEL

If time is an issue, **always look for nonstop flights,** which require no change of plane and make no stops. If possible, **avoid connecting flights,** which stop at least once and can involve a change of plane, although the flight number remains the same; if the first leg is late, the second waits.

CUTTING COSTS

The Sunday travel section of most newspapers is a good source of deals.

MAJOR AIRLINES➤ The least-expensive airfares from the major airlines are priced for round-trip travel and are subject to restrictions. You must usually **book in advance and buy the ticket within 24 hours** to get cheaper fares, and

you may have to **stay over a Saturday night.** The lowest fare is subject to availability, and only a small percentage of the plane's total seats are sold at that price. It's good to **call a number of airlines—and when you are quoted a good price, book it on the spot**—the same fare on the same flight may not be available the next day. Airlines generally allow you to change your return date for a $25 to $50 fee, but most low-fare tickets are nonrefundable. However, if you don't use it, you can apply the cost toward the purchase price of a new ticket, again for a small charge.

CONSOLIDATORS➤ Consolidators, who buy tickets at reduced rates from scheduled airlines, sell them at prices below the lowest available from the airlines directly—usually without advance restrictions. Sometimes you can even get your money back if you need to return the ticket. Carefully read the fine print detailing penalties for changes and cancellations. If you doubt the reliability of a consolidator, **confirm your reservation with the airline.**

ALOFT

AIRLINE FOOD➤ If you hate airline food, **ask for special meals when**

booking. These can be vegetarian, low-cholesterol, or kosher, for example; commonly prepared to order in smaller quantities than standard catered fare, they can be tastier.

JET LAG➤ To avoid this syndrome, which occurs when travel disrupts your body's natural cycles, try to maintain a normal routine. At night, **get some sleep.** By day, move about the cabin to **stretch your legs, eat light meals, and drink water—not alcohol.**

SMOKING➤ Smoking is banned on all flights within the U.S. of less than six hours' duration and on all Canadian flights; the ban also applies to domestic segments of international flights aboard U.S. and foreign carriers. Delta has banned smoking system-wide.

C
CAMERAS, CAMCORDERS, AND COMPUTERS

LAPTOPS

Before you depart, **check your portable computer's battery,** because you may be asked at security to turn on the computer to prove that it is what it appears to be. At the airport, you may prefer to **request a manual inspection,** although security X-rays do not harm hard-disk or floppy-disk storage.

PHOTOGRAPHY

If your camera is new or if you haven't used it for a while, **shoot and develop a few rolls of film** before you leave. Always **store film in a cool, dry place**—never in the car's glove compartment or on the shelf under the rear window.

Every pass of film through an X-ray machine increases the chance of clouding. To protect it, carry it in a clear plastic bag and **ask for hand inspection at security.** Such requests are virtually always honored at U.S. airports. Don't depend on a lead-lined bag to protect film in checked luggage—the airline may increase the radiation to see what's inside.

VIDEO

Before your trip, **test your camcorder, invest in a skylight filter to protect the lens, and charge the batteries.** (Airport security personnel may ask you to turn on the camcorder to prove that it's what it appears to be).

Videotape is not damaged by X-rays, but it may be harmed by the magnetic field of a walk-through metal detector, so **ask that videotapes be hand-checked.**

CHILDREN AND TRAVEL

BABY-SITTING

For recommended local sitters, **check with your hotel desk.**

DRIVING

If you are renting a car, **arrange for a car seat when you reserve.** Sometimes they're free.

FLYING

On domestic flights, children under 2 not occupying a seat travel free, and older children currently travel on the "lowest applicable" adult fare.

BAGGAGE➤ In general, the adult baggage allowance applies for children paying half or more of the adult fare.

SAFETY SEATS➤ According to the FAA, it's a good idea to **use safety seats aloft.** Airline policy varies. U.S. carriers allow FAA-approved models, but airlines usually require that you buy a ticket, even if your child would otherwise ride free, because the seats must be strapped into regular passenger seats.

FACILITIES➤ When making your reservation, **ask for children's meals or a freestanding bassinets** if you need them; the latter are available only to those with seats at the bulkhead, where there's enough legroom. If you don't need the bassinet, **think twice before requesting bulkhead seats**—the only storage for in-flight necessities is in the inconveniently distant overhead bins.

LODGING

Most hotels allow children under a certain age to stay in their parents' room at no extra charge, while others charge them as extra adults; be sure to

ask about the cut-off age.

CUSTOMS AND DUTIES

IN SAN DIEGO

U.K. CITIZENS➤ British visitors age 21 or over may import the following into the United States: 200 cigarettes or 50 cigars or 2 kilograms of tobacco; one U.S. liter of alcohol; gifts to the value of $100. Restricted items include meat products, seeds, plants, and fruits. Never carry illegal drugs.

BACK HOME

IN CANADA➤ Once per calendar year, when you've been out of Canada for at least seven days, you may bring in C$300 worth of goods duty-free. If you've been away less than seven days but more than 48 hours, the duty-free exemption drops to C$100 but can be claimed any number of times (as can a C$20 duty-free exemption for absences of 24 hours or more). You cannot combine the yearly and 48-hour exemptions, use the C$300 exemption only partially (to save the balance for a later trip), or pool exemptions with family members. Goods claimed under the C$300 exemption may follow you by mail; those claimed under the lesser exemptions must accompany you.

Alcohol and tobacco products may be included in the yearly and 48-hour exemptions but not in the 24-hour exemption. If you meet the age requirements of the province through which you reenter Canada, you may bring in, duty-free, 1.14 liters (40 imperial ounces) of wine or liquor *or* 24 12-ounce cans or bottles of beer or ale. If you are 16 or older, you may bring in, duty-free, 200 cigarettes, 50 cigars or cigarillos, and 400 tobacco sticks or 400 grams of manufactured tobacco. Alcohol and tobacco must accompany you on your return.

An unlimited number of gifts valued up to C$60 each may be mailed to Canada duty-free. These do not count as part of your exemption. Label the package "Unsolicited Gift— Value Under $60." Alcohol and tobacco are excluded.

In the U.K.➤ From countries outside the EU, including the United States, you may import duty-free 200 cigarettes, 100 cigarillos, 50 cigars or 250 grams of tobacco; 1 liter of spirits or 2 liters of fortified or sparkling wine; 2 liters of still table wine; 60 milliliters of perfume; 250 milliliters of toilet water; plus £136 worth of other goods, including gifts and souvenirs.

D

FOR TRAVELERS WITH DISABILITIES

Most of San Diego is easily accessible to visitors using wheelchairs. Most public buses and trolleys are equipped with lifts. Although the Old Town district has some moderately uneven streets, curb cuts and smooth sidewalks are decidedly the rule rather than the exception for the city as a whole. The extensive network of walkways in Balboa Park affords views that are both lovely and accessible.

When discussing accessibility with an operator or reservationist, **ask hard questions.** Are there any stairs, inside *or* out? Are there grab bars next to the toilet *and* in the shower/tub? How wide is the doorway to the room? To the bathroom? For the most extensive facilities, meeting the latest legal specifications, **opt for newer facilities,** which more often have been designed with access in mind. Older properties or ships must usually be retrofitted and may offer more limited facilities as a result. Be sure to **discuss your needs before booking.**

DISCOUNT CLUBS

Travel clubs offer members unsold space on airplanes, cruise ships, and package tours at as much as 50% below regular prices. Membership may include a regular bulletin or access to a toll-free hot line giving details of available trips departing from three or four days to several months in the future. Most also offer 50% discounts off hotel rack rates. Before booking with a club, **make sure the hotel or other supplier isn't offering a better deal.**

DIVERS' ALERT

Scuba divers take note: **Do not fly within 24 hours of scuba diving.**

DRIVING

Interstate 5 stretches from Canada to the Mexican border and bisects San Diego. Interstate 8 provides access from Yuma, Arizona, and points east. Drivers coming from Nevada and the mountain regions beyond can reach San Diego on I–15. To avoid traffic, **steer clear of rush-hour periods.**

I

INSURANCE

Travel insurance can protect your investment, replace your luggage and its contents, or provide for medical coverage should you fall ill during your trip. Most tour operators, travel agents, and insurance agents sell specialized health-and-accident, flight, trip-cancellation, and luggage insurance as well as comprehensive policies with some or all of these features. Before you make any purchase, **review your existing health and homeowner's policies** to find out whether they cover expenses incurred while traveling.

BAGGAGE

Airline liability for your baggage is limited to $1,250 per person on domestic flights. On international flights, the airlines' liability is $9.07 per pound or $20 per kilogram for checked baggage (roughly $640 per 70-

pound bag) and $400 per passenger for unchecked baggage. However, this excludes valuable items such as jewelry and cameras that are listed in your ticket's fine print. You can buy additional insurance from the airline at check-in, but first **see if your home-owner's policy covers lost luggage.**

FLIGHT

You should **think twice before buying flight insurance.** Often purchased as a last-minute impulse at the airport, it pays a lump sum when a plane crashes, either to a beneficiary if the insured dies or some-times to a surviving passenger who loses eyesight or a limb. Supplementing the airlines' coverage de-scribed in the limits-of-liability paragraphs on your ticket, it's expen-sive and basically unnecessary. Charging an airline ticket to a major credit card often automatically entitles you to coverage and may also embrace travel by bus, train, and ship.

HEALTH

FOR U.K. TRAVELERS➤ According to the Asso-ciation of British Insur-ers, a trade association representing 450 insur-ance companies, it's wise to **buy extra medical coverage when you visit the United States.** You can buy an annual travel-insurance policy valid for most vacations during the year in which it's pur-chased. If you go this route, make sure it covers you if you have a preexisting medical condition or are preg-nant.

TRIP

Without insurance, you will lose all or most of your money if you must cancel your trip due to illness or any other reason. Especially if your airline ticket, cruise, or package tour is nonrefundable and cannot be changed, it's essential that you **buy trip-cancellation-and-interruption insurance.** When considering how much coverage you need, look for a policy that will cover the cost of your trip plus the nondiscounted price of a one-way airline ticket should you need to return home early. Read the fine print carefully, especially sections defining "family mem-ber" and "preexisting medical conditions." Also **consider default or bankruptcy insurance,** which protects you against a supplier's failure to deliver. How-ever, such policies often do not cover default by a travel agency, tour operator, airline, or cruise line if you bought your tour and the coverage directly from the firm in question.

L
LODGING

APARTMENT AND VILLA RENTALS

If you want a home base that's roomy enough for a family and comes with cooking facilities, **consider a furnished rental.** It's generally cost-wise, too, although not always—some rentals are luxury properties (economical only when your party is large). Home-exchange directories do list rentals—often second homes owned by prospective house swappers—and some services search for a house or apartment for you (even a castle if that's your fancy) and handle the paperwork. Some send an illustrated catalogue and others send photographs of specific properties, sometimes at a charge; up-front registration fees may apply.

HOME EXCHANGE

If you would like to find a house, an apart-ment, or other vacation property to exchange for your own while on vacation, **become a member of a home-exchange organization,** which will send you its annual directories listing available ex-changes and will in-clude your own listing in at least one of them. Arrangements for the actual exchange are made by the two parties to it, not by the organi-zation.

M
MONEY AND EXPENSES

ATMS

Chances are that you can **use your bank card at ATMs** to withdraw money from an account and get cash advances on a credit-card account if your card has been programmed with a personal identification number, or PIN. Before leaving home, **check in on frequency limits** for withdrawals and cash advances.

SMART TRAVEL TIPS / THE GOLD GUIDE

On cash advances you are charged interest from the day you receive the money, whether from an ATM or a teller. Transaction fees for ATM withdrawals outside your home turf may be higher than for withdrawals at home.

TRAVELER'S CHECKS

Whether or not to buy traveler's checks depends on where you are headed; **take cash to rural areas and small towns, traveler's checks to cities.** The most widely recognized are American Express, Citicorp, Thomas Cook, and Visa, which are sold by major commercial banks for 1% to 3% of the checks' face value—it pays to **shop around.** Both American Express and Thomas Cook issue checks that can be counter-signed and used by you or your traveling companion.

WIRING MONEY

You don't have to be a cardholder to send or receive funds through MoneyGram^{SM} from American Express. Just go to a MoneyGram agent, located in retail and convenience stores and in American Express Travel Offices. Pay up to $1,000 with cash or a credit card, anything over that in cash. The money can be picked up within 10 minutes in cash or check at the nearest MoneyGram agent. The cost, which includes a free long-distance phone call, runs from 3% to 10%, depending on the amount sent, the

destination, and how you pay.

You can also send money using Western Union. Money sent from the United States or Canada will be available for pickup at agent locations in 100 countries within 15 minutes. Once the money is in the system, it can be picked up at any one of 25,000 locations. Fees range from 4% to 10%, depending on the amount you send.

P

PACKAGES AND TOURS

A package or tour to San Diego can make your vacation less expensive and more convenient. Firms that sell tours and packages purchase airline seats, hotel rooms, and rental cars in bulk and pass some of the savings on to you. In addition, the best operators have local representatives to help you out at your destination.

A GOOD DEAL?

The more your package or tour includes, the better you can predict the ultimate cost of your vacation. Make sure you know exactly what is included, and **beware of hidden costs.** Are taxes, tips, and service charges included? Transfers and baggage handling? Entertainment and excursions? These can add up.

Most packages and tours are rated deluxe, first-class superior, first class, tourist, or budget. The key difference is

usually accommodations.

BUYER BEWARE

Each year consumers are stranded or lose their money when operators go out of business—even very large ones with excellent reputations. If you can't afford a loss, take the time to **check out the operator**—find out how long the company has been in business, and ask several agents about its reputation. Next, **don't book unless the firm has a consumer-protection program.** Members of the United States Tour Operators Association and the National Tour Association are required to set aside funds exclusively to cover your payments and travel arrangements in case of default. Nonmember operators may instead carry insurance; look for the details in the operator's brochure—and the name of an underwriter with a solid reputation. Note: When it comes to tour operators, **don't trust escrow accounts.** Although there are laws governing those of charter-flight operators, no governmental body prevents tour operators from raiding the till.

Next, **contact your local Better Business Bureau and the attorney general's office** in both your own state and the operator's; have any complaints been filed? Last, **pay with a major credit card.** Then you can cancel payment, provided that you can document your complaint. Always **consider** trip-cancellation insurance (*see* Insurance, *above*).

BIG VS. SMALL➤ An operator that handles several hundred thousand travelers annually can use its purchasing power to give you a good price. Its high volume may also indicate financial stability. But some small companies provide more personalized service; because they tend to specialize, they may also be experts on an area.

USING AN AGENT

Travel agents are an excellent resource. In fact, large operators accept bookings only through travel agents. But it's good to **collect brochures from several agencies,** because some agents' suggestions may be skewed by promotional relationships with tour and package firms that reward them for volume sales. If you have a special interest, **find an agent with expertise in that area;** the American Society of Travel Agents can give you leads in the United States. (Don't rely solely on your agent, though; agents may be unaware of small-niche operators, and some special-interest travel companies only sell direct).

SINGLE TRAVELERS

Prices are usually quoted per person, based on two sharing a room. If traveling solo, you may be required to pay the full double occupancy rate. Some operators eliminate this surcharge if you agree to be matched up with a roommate of the same sex, even if one is not found by departure time.

PACKING FOR SAN DIEGO

San Diego's casual lifestyle and year-round mild climate set the parameters for what you'll want to pack. You can **leave formal clothes and cold-weather gear behind.**

Plan on warm weather at any time of the year. Cottons, walking shorts, jeans, and T-shirts are the norm at tourist attractions. **Pack bathing suits and shorts regardless of the season.** Casual attire is generally acceptable; only a few restaurants require a jacket and tie for men. Women may want to bring something a little dressier than their sightseeing garb.

Evenings are cool, even in summer, so be sure to **bring a sweater or a light jacket.** Rainfall in San Diego is not usually heavy; you won't need a raincoat except during the winter months, and even then, an umbrella may be sufficient protection. Be sure you **take proved, comfortable walking shoes** with you. Even if you don't walk much at home, you'll find yourself covering miles while sightseeing on your vacation.

Sunglasses are a must in San Diego. Binoculars can also come in handy, especially if you're in town during whale-watching season.

Bring an extra pair of eyeglasses or contact lenses in your carry-on luggage, and if you have a health problem, **pack enough medication** to last the trip. In case your bags go astray, **don't put prescription drugs or valuables in luggage to be checked.**

LUGGAGE

Free airline baggage allowances depend on the airline, the route, and the class of your ticket; ask in advance. In general, on domestic flights you are entitled to check two bags—neither exceeding 62 inches, or 158 centimeters (length + width + height), or weighing more than 70 pounds (32 kilograms). A third piece may be brought aboard; its total dimensions are generally limited to less than 45 inches (114 centimeters), so it will fit easily under the seat in front of you or in the overhead compartment. In the United States, the Federal Aviation Administration gives airlines broad latitude to limit carry-on allowances and tailor them to different aircraft and operational conditions. Charges for excess, oversize, or overweight pieces vary.

SAFEGUARDING YOUR LUGGAGE➤ Before leaving home, **itemize your bags' contents and** their worth, and label them with your name, address, and phone number. (If you use your home address, cover it so that potential thieves can't see it.) Inside your bag, **pack a copy of your itinerary.**

THE GOLD GUIDE / SMART TRAVEL TIPS

At check-in, **make sure that your bag is correctly tagged** with the airport's three-letter destination code. If your bags arrive damaged or not at all, file a written report with the airline before leaving the airport.

PASSPORTS AND VISAS

CANADIANS

No passport is necessary to enter the United States.

U.K. CITIZENS

British citizens need a valid passport. If you are staying fewer than 90 days and traveling on a vacation, with a return or onward ticket, you will probably not need a visa. However, you will need to fill out the Visa Waiver Form, 1-94W, supplied by the airline.

While traveling, **keep one photocopy of the data page** separate from your wallet and leave another copy with someone at home. If you lose your passport, promptly call the nearest embassy or consulate, and the local police; and having the data page can speed replacement.

R
RENTING A CAR

A car is essential for San Diego's sprawling freeway system and comes in handy for touring Baja California, although it's not necessary in Tijuana.

CUTTING COSTS

To get the best deal, **book through a travel agent and shop around.**

When pricing cars, **ask where the rental lot is located.** Some off-airport locations offer lower rates—even though their lots are only minutes away from the terminal via complimentary shuttle. You may also want to **price local car-rental companies,** whose rates may be lower still, although service and maintenance standards may not be up to those of a national firm. Also **ask your travel agent about a company's customer-service record.** How has it responded to late plane arrivals and vehicle mishaps? Are there often lines at the rental counter, and, if you're traveling during a holiday period, does a confirmed reservation guarantee you a car?

INSURANCE

When you drive a rented car, you are generally responsible for any damage or personal injury that you cause as well as damage to the vehicle. Before you rent, **see what coverage you already have** under the terms of your personal auto-insurance policy and credit cards. For about $14 a day, rental companies sell insurance, known as a collision damage waiver (CDW), that eliminates your liability for damage to the car; it's always optional and should never be automatically added to your bill. California, New York, and Illinois have outlawed the sale of CDW altogether.

SURCHARGES

Before picking up the car in one city and leaving it in another, **ask about drop-off charges or one-way service fees,** which can be substantial. Note, too, that some rental agencies charge extra if you return the car before the time specified on your contract. To avoid a hefty refueling fee, **fill the tank just before you turn in the car.**

FOR U.K. CITIZENS

In the United States you must be 21 to rent a car; rates may be higher for those under 25. Extra costs cover child seats, compulsory for children under 5 (about $3 per day), and additional drivers (about $1.50 per day). To pick up your reserved car you will need the reservation voucher, a passport, a U.K. driver's license, and a travel policy covering each driver.

S
SENIOR-CITIZEN DISCOUNTS

Many discounts are available to older travelers: Meals, lodging, entry to various attractions, car rentals, tickets for buses and trains, and campsites are among the prime examples. Some discounts are given solely on the basis of age, without membership requirement; others require membership in an organization. In California, the state park system, which includes more than 200 locations, provides a $2 discount on campsites for anyone 62 or over and others in the same private vehicle; ask for this discount when you make reservations.

If you are 50 or older, ask about senior discounts even if there is no posted notice. A 10% cut on a bus ticket and $2 off a pizza may not seem like major savings, but they add up, and you can cut the cost of a trip appreciably if you remember to take advantage of these options.

To qualify for age-related discounts, **mention your senior-citizen status up front** when booking hotel reservations, not when checking out, and before you're seated in restaurants, not when paying your bill. Note that discounts may be limited to certain menus, days, or hours. When renting a car, **ask about promotional car-rental discounts**—they can net lower costs than your senior-citizen discount.

STUDENTS ON THE ROAD

To save money, **look into deals available** through student-oriented travel agencies. To qualify, you'll need to have a bona fide student I.D. card. Members of international student groups are also eligible. *See* Students *in* Important Contacts A to Z, *above.*

T
TAXIS

Taxi fares are regulated at the airport—all companies charge the same rate (generally $2 for the first mile, $1.40 for each additional mile). Fares vary among companies on other routes, however, including the ride back to the airport.

TELEPHONES

LONG-DISTANCE

The long-distance services of AT&T, MCI, and Sprint make calling home relatively convenient and let you avoid hotel surcharges; typically, you dial an 800 number.

W
WHEN TO GO

For the most part, **any time of the year is the right time** for a trip to San Diego. The climate is generally close to perfect. Typical days are sunny and mild, with low humidity—ideal for sightseeing and for almost any sport that does not require snow and ice. From mid-December through mid-March, gray whales can be seen migrating along the coast. And in early spring, wildflowers transform the desert into a rainbow of colors.

CLIMATE

The annual high temperature averages 70°F with a low of 55°F, and the annual rainfall is usually less than 10 inches. Most of the rain occurs in January and February, but precipitation usually lasts for only part of the day or for a day or two at most. The rainfall during the winters of 1992 and 1993, which dampened the spirits of visitors but ended a five-year drought, was uncharacteristic.

The following are average maximum and minimum temperatures for San Diego.

Climate in San Diego

Jan.	62F	17C	May	66F	19C	Sept.	73F	23C
	46	8		55	13		62	17
Feb.	62F	17C	June	69F	21C	Oct.	71F	22C
	48	9		59	15		57	14
Mar.	64F	18C	July	73F	23C	Nov.	69F	21C
	50	10		62	17		51	11
Apr.	66F	19C	Aug.	73F	23C	Dec.	64F	18C
	53	12		64	18		48	9

1 Destination: San Diego

WARM AND WELCOMING

EACH YEAR, San Diego absorbs thousands of visitors who are drawn by the climate: sunny, dry, and warm nearly year-round. They swim, surf, and sunbathe on long beaches facing the turquoise Pacific, where whales, seals, and dolphins swim offshore. They tour oases of tropical palms, sheltered bays fringed by golden pampas grass, and far-ranging parklands blossoming with brilliant bougainvillea, jasmine, ice plant, and birds of paradise.

They run and bike and walk down wide streets and paths planned for the recreation of the natives, who thrive on San Diego's varied health, fitness, and sports scenes. They drive by Mission Bay, a 4,600-acre aquatic park, where dozens of colorful, intricate kites fly above hundreds of picnickers lounging in the sun. They wander through the streets of downtown, where the fanciful Horton Plaza shopping center serves as a vibrant city center, with theaters, restaurants, and shops drawing crowds from nearby steel-and-glass office towers.

San Diego County is the nation's sixth largest— larger than nearly a dozen U.S. states— with a population of more than 2.5 million. It sprawls east from the Pacific Ocean through dense urban neighborhoods to outlying suburban communities that seem to sprout on canyons and cliffs overnight. Its eastern boundaries are the Cleveland National Forest, where the pines and manzanita are covered with snow in the winter, and the Anza-Borrego Desert, where delicate pink and yellow cactus blooms herald the coming of spring. San Diegans visit these vast wildernesses for their annual doses of seasonal splendors, then return to the city, where flowers bloom year-round and the streets are dry and clean. One of the busiest international borders in the United States marks the county's southern line, where approximately 60 million people a year legally cross between Mexico's Baja California peninsula and San Diego. To the north, the marines at Camp Pendleton practice land, sea, and air maneuvers in southern California's largest coastal greenbelt, marking the demarcation zone between the congestion of Orange and Los Angeles counties and the more relaxed expansiveness of San Diego.

The city of San Diego is the state's second largest, after Los Angeles. It serves as a base for the U.S. Navy's 11th Naval District and a port for ships from many nations. A considerable number of its residents were stationed here in the service and decided to stay put. Others either passed through on vacation or saw the city in movies and TV shows and became enamored of the city and its reputation as a prosperous Sunbelt playground. From its founding San Diego has attracted a steady stream of prospectors, drawn to the nation's farthest southwest frontier. Nearly 10,000 new residents arrive in San Diego each year.

Tourism is San Diego's third-largest industry, after manufacturing and the military. In the past few years, the San Diego Convention and Visitors Bureau and other local boosters have courted and won internationally important events that have brought uncalculated tourism benefits to the city. Worldwide media events, such as the America's Cup race, keep San Diego very visible as a vacation option.

The waterfront has assumed a completely new look and ambience since the 1990 opening of the 760,000-square-foot San Diego Convention Center at the foot of 5th Avenue, its sail-like rooftop thrust before downtown's skyline. The convention center's completion spurred development of the area at an unprecedented rate, and the thousands of conventioneers who visit San Diego annually are boosting the downtown business climate and image as never before. Hotel development seems to have peaked after a spate of building on what seemed every patch of available land, but San Diego's politicians, business leaders, and developers have set the city's course toward a steadily increasing influx of visitors—which gives residents pleasant attractions as well as not-so-enjoyable distractions. With growth comes congestion, even in San Diego's vast expanse.

Fortunately, there are many reminders of the city's more peaceful times. In Old Town, San Diego's original city center, the courthouse, newspaper offices, and haciendas are historical adobe buildings covered with ancient twisted vines. The village of La Jolla, often compared with Monte Carlo, has retained its gentle charm despite continual development. And Balboa Park, the city's centerpiece, is a permanent testimonial to the Spanish architecture and natural ecology that give San Diego its unique character and charisma.

If San Diego sounds just a bit too laid-back and serene, consider its proximity to Mexico. Tijuana, a typically colorful and frenetic border town and an intrinsically foreign land, is only 30 minutes away. San Diegans think of Tijuana and all the Baja peninsula as their backyard playground.

During Prohibition, Americans drove down dusty, rutted roads to the spectacular gambling halls of Tijuana, Rosarito Beach, and Ensenada, where unbridled hedonism was not only tolerated but encouraged. Hollywood stars settled in for the duration, waiting out the dry days north of the border in lavish grandeur and investing their dollars in Mexican real estate. Some of Baja's grandest hotels were built during this era, when U.S. financiers recognized the value of the peninsula's rugged coastal wilderness.

THOSE PLEASURE PALACES of the past have since crumbled, but Baja is undergoing a new surge of development now that the Mexican government has targeted the area as a premier tourist destination. The coastline from Tijuana through Rosarito Beach to Ensenada is rapidly being transformed from an isolated hideaway with a few resorts and vacation-home communities into a major holiday destination. Every month brings another elegant condominium and time-share development. New, full-scale RV parks have more amenities than most hotels, and there are enough restaurants, artisans' markets, and bars to keep the onslaught of weekend travelers content. Tijuana's main Avenida Revolución continues to attract shoppers and those looking for the border city's wild side, but such cultural attractions as Mexitlan, the out-

door museum–entertainment center, are gaining in popularity as well.

Visiting Baja is easier than ever, thanks to the San Diego–Tijuana trolley, which runs from the Santa Fe Depot in downtown San Diego to the international border in San Ysidro. The trolley travels south through the suburbs of National City and Chula Vista, where giant shipyards and fish canneries have been replaced by fancy marinas. Near San Ysidro, the trackside billboards display Spanish ads for Tijuana's shopping centers, highlighting bargains in brand-name clothing from Ralph Lauren and Guess?. Still, for all its familiarity, Tijuana could never be mistaken for an American town. Therein lies its appeal.

If you prefer more organized attractions, San Diego has its share of theme parks and specialized museums. Sea World, on the shores of Mission Bay, highlights San Diego's proximity to the sea with spectacular aquariums, whale shows, shark exhibits, and penguin habitats. The San Diego Zoo, often called the country's finest zoological-botanical park, is a must-see attraction. The Wild Animal Park, 30 minutes east of downtown, preserves the natural wonders of San Diego's chaparral country while protecting endangered wildlife from around the world. Balboa Park, site of the 1915 Panama-California Exposition, houses not only the zoo but the city's finest museums in historical Spanish-Moorish palaces set amid lush lawns and rocky canyons.

San Diego has always been recognized as an environmental paradise. As the city grows, its cultural base expands to meet more sophisticated demands. Today San Diego retains its sense of a western frontier as it develops into a major cosmopolitan centerpiece for the nation. No wonder visitors from all over the world come for vacations and decide to stay for life.

— *Maribeth Mellin*
A longtime resident of San Diego, travel writer and photographer Maribeth Mellin is a former senior editor at San Diego Magazine, *the author of* Fodor's Baja, *and a contributor to several magazines and newspapers.*

WHAT'S WHERE

which extend in a long arc to the south from the body of the island.

Downtown and the Embarcadero

Downtown San Diego's main arteries are Harbor Drive, which runs along the waterfront; Broadway, which cuts through the center of downtown; and 6th Avenue as far as Balboa Park. Numbered streets run roughly north–south; the lettered and named streets (Broadway, Market, Island, and Ash) run east–west. In one of the few successful California examples of urban revitalization, San Diego's downtown and waterfront came back to life in the mid-'80s as a bustling, colorful jumble of hotels, restaurants, shopping centers, floating gift shops, and sea-going vessels of every size and shape. The centerpiece of the area is Horton Plaza, a shopping, dining, and entertainment mall that fronts Broadway and G Street from 1st to 4th avenues and covers more than six city blocks. Surrounding Horton Plaza is the Gaslamp Quarter, an area that features art galleries, antiques, and specialty shops housed in Victorian buildings and renovated warehouses. Another of downtown's main attractions is the Embarcadero, the section of waterfront that follows Harbor Drive along the curve of San Diego Bay. This is the best spot to linger for views of the bay and its docked boats, ranging from huge cruise ships to old sailing vessels. South of the Embarcadero on Harbor Drive is Seaport Village, 14 acres of shopping plazas designed to reflect the architectural styles of early California.

Coronado

Across the water from the Embarcadero, Coronado Island is a combination of wealthy suburban enclave and naval air base. Visible from downtown and Point Loma and accessible from the San Diego–Coronado Bridge, Coronado is an island of wide, graceful streets, neighborhood parks, and grand Victorian homes. The community grew up around the ornate Hotel Del Coronado, a celebrity hangout from the late 19th century and now a National Historic Site. Those who aren't interested in Victorian architecture come to Coronado to catch some rays and splash in the surf at Silver Strand Beach State Park and Imperial Beach,

Point Loma

Acting as a buffer against the temperamental Pacific, Point Loma curves along San Diego Bay and extends south into the sea. Beyond its main streets—which are cluttered with fast-food restaurants and motels—Point Loma is made up of well-to-do neighborhoods and bayside estates (it's a favorite retirement spot for naval officers). From the bay side you can enjoy a terrific view of downtown San Diego, and for an incomparable view of the Pacific, head to Sunset Cliffs, between Point Loma and Mission Beach, among the most dramatic places in San Diego to watch the sunset.

Balboa Park

Straddling two mesas that overlook downtown, Balboa Park offers visitors a respite from urban San Diego. Its 1,400 landscaped acres boast a world-famous zoo, a complex of 13 museums, and lots of open space in which to play. The park is the city's cultural center as well as a recreational paradise for animal lovers and picnickers. Most of the museums are grouped around El Prado, the park's central pedestrian mall; they're housed in big Spanish-Moorish buildings that were built for the Panama-California International Exposition of 1915. Most of the downtown thoroughfares lead north to the park (it's hard to miss). From the west side of downtown, take any east–west street until you hit Park Boulevard, and drive north into the park. From Old Town, take I–8 east to Route 163 south into the park. From I–5, take any of the well-marked exit signs.

Old Town

A few miles north of downtown off I–5, Old Town is essentially a collection of remnants from the original San Diego, the first European settlement in California (the first Spanish mission, which preceded the town, was established by Father Junipero Serra on a hill north of Old Town now known as Presidio Park). The former pueblo of San Diego is now preserved as a state historic park and contains several original and reconstructed buildings. The historic sites are clustered around Old Town Plaza, which is bounded by Wallace Street, Calhoun Street, Mason

Street, and San Diego Avenue. If you're not too distracted by Old Town's commercial aspects, it can be a fascinating afternoon trip into California's past.

Mission Bay and Sea World

Situated northwest of Old Town, the Mission Bay area is San Diego's monument to sports and fitness. This is where locals and visitors interested in boating, running, sunning, or jet skiing spend their days. Some parts of the amorphous 4,600-acre aquatic park, with numerous coves and inlets and about 27 miles of bayfront beach, are specifically designated for swimming, waterskiing, and sailing. Terrestrial types can jog, play basketball, toss a frisbee, or fly a kite on the bay's peninsulas and two main islands, Vacation Island and Fiesta Island. Easily the most popular attraction in Mission Bay (and for some, in all of San Diego), Sea World displays fish and captive marine mammals, including sea otters, dolphins, seals, and the trademark killer whales.

La Jolla

Spanish for "the jewel," La Jolla lives up to its name in both beauty and expense, offering dramatic beachfront, spectacular views, and huge, expensive homes. Boutiques and restaurants cater to the affluent local gentry, but the largely unspoiled scenery of its coast, coves, and verdant hillsides is still free. North of Mission Bay, La Jolla can be approached by the meandering coastal road (Mission Blvd. and La Jolla Blvd.) or via the speedier I–5.

The North Coast

The seaside towns of the northern coastal extension of San Diego developed separately from San Diego, and from each other; all offer the visitor a glimpse into a part of southern California's past. Del Mar, which actually lies within the limits of the city of San Diego, is a seaside preserve for aspiring urban professionals, with inordinately expensive lodging and exclusive boutiques. Solana Beach is a small, very beach-oriented town with a mellow ambience and acres of sand. Encinitas is justly famous for its fabulous fields of flowers and gardens, which extend inland from excellent surfing waters. Carlsbad flaunts its history as a spa town to visitors lured annually by package tours, and Oceanside shows off its harbor and Mis-

sion San Luis Rey (the oldest of the California missions), as well as Camp Pendleton, the country's largest marine base. The coastal portion of North County is best accessed via I–5, but traveling along Route S21 (old Highway 101) once you reach the general area will give you a better feel for the differences of each settlement.

Tijuana, Rosarito Beach, and Ensenada

If you've ventured this far south in California, you ought to at least consider a daytrip across the border to Baja California. Just 23 miles south of San Diego, Tijuana has grown over the last 20 years from a border town of 700,000 to a city of nearly 2 million inhabitants; it continues to attract hordes of "yanquis" with its souvenir shops, sports events, and great Mexican dining. Eighteen miles further south, laidback Playas de Rosarito (Rosarito Beach) has become something of a weekend hangout for southern Californians. And another 40 miles down the coast is the charming port city of Ensenada.

PLEASURES & PASTIMES

Beaches

The 70 miles of coastline in and around San Diego are dotted with some of the best beaches on the West Coast. Some are wide and sandy, others narrow and rocky; some are almost always crowded with athletes and sun-worshippers, others seem created for solitary beachcombers and romantic pairs. Among the stand-outs are Imperial Beach in South Beach, a classic southern California beach favored by surfers, swimmers, and Frisbee maniacs; Silver Strand State Beach, a relatively calm, family-friendly beach on the isthmus of Coronado; Ocean Beach, a.k.a. Dog Beach because of the number of canines found romping next to volleyball players and sunbathers; Mission Beach, which has a boardwalk popular with strollers, roller skaters, and bicyclists; La Jolla Cove, where tidal pools and cliff coves provide exciting diversions for explorers; and Torrey Pines State Beach in Del Mar, one of the easeist and most comfortable beaches to visit in the area. (*See* Chapter 5, Beaches, for details.)

Outdoor Activities

At least one stereotype of San Diego is true—it is an active, outdoors-oriented community. People recreate here more than they spectate, and as a visitor, it's hard not to join in, with such a wide variety of choices available. As you would expect, the emphasis is on fun in the sun and surf—beaches, sailing, swimming, surfing, diving, and fishing head the list. Here is a sampling of favorite activities and best place to enjoy them: scuba diving off La Jolla Cove, surfing at almost any of the beaches, golfing at Torrey Pines, roller skating at Mission Bay, jogging along the Embarcadero, playing volleyball on Ocean Beach, windsurfing on Mission Bay, and jet-skiing at the Snug Harbor Marina. (*See* Chapter 7, Sports and the Outdoors, for details.)

Shopping

San Diego's many shopping districts are a mélange of self-contained megamalls, historic districts, quaint villages, funky neighborhoods, and chic suburbs. Horton Plaza, in the heart of center city, is the place to go for department stores and one-of-a-kind shops; the adjoining Gaslamp Quarter is chock full of art galleries, antiques shops, and specialty stores. The Paladion, also adjoining Horton Plaza, is a posh grouping of upscale boutiques. Seaport Village on the waterfront is thick with theme shops and arts-and-crafts galleries. Coronado Island has a few blocks of fancy boutiques and galleries as well as Old Ferry Landing, a waterfront shopping center. The historic Old Town district has what resembles a colorful Mexican marketplace, where you can browse in shops selling international goods, toys, souvenirs, and arts and crafts. Kensington, north and east of downtown, is the city's unofficial Antiques Row and nearby Hillcrest is the place to go for vintage clothing, furnishings, and accessories. (*See* Chapter 4, Shopping, for details.)

FODOR'S CHOICE

Special Moments

★ **Driving across the San Diego–Coronado Bridge.** The view of the harbor, downtown, and Coronado Island from this landmark is breathtaking, day or night.

★ **An evening stroll about La Jolla Cove.** Palm-tree-lined Ellen Browning Scripps Park on the cliffs overlooking the cove is one of the prettiest spots in the world. The ocean is stunningly clear, serene in brilliant tones of blue and green until it smashes into a white foam against the rocky shoreline below.

★ **Spotting a gray whale spouting during the winter migration.** As many as 200 whales pass the San Diego coast each day on their way south to Mexico (starting in mid-December) or back north (until mid-March); many pass within yards of tour boats out on whale-watching trips.

★ **Hiking at Cabrillo National Monument on Point Loma.** Perched at the end of the peninsula, this 144-acre preserve of rugged cliffs and shores and outstanding overlooks was set aside as a National Park Service site to commemorate Portuguese explorer Juan Rodríguez Cabrillo.

★ **A Sunday picnic in Balboa Park.** Forget about the park's museums (for one day, anyway) and settle down to your own custom-made meal on a grassy spot near one of the park's many beautifully landscaped gardens.

Restaurants

★ **Dobson's.** Local movers and shakers come to this clubby eatery to see and be seen. That aside, Dobson's has one of the most innovative and consistent kitchens in the city. $$$

★ **George's at the Cove.** It's hard to say what's better here: the stunning view overlooking La Jolla Cove or the superb cooking. $$$

★ **Rainwater's.** If you're dying for a steak, this is the place. Homey, satisfying side dishes also consistently get high marks. $$$

★ **California Cuisine.** Innovative nouvelle-American cuisine in a minimalist dining room is what you'll encounter at this outstanding Uptown restaurant. The grilled items are especially tasty. $$

★ **Trattoria La Strada.** This downtown Italian spot has taken the cuisine of Tuscany to new heights. None of the pastas fails to please. $$–$$$

★ **Bayou Bar and Grill.** Cajun and Creole specialties are faithfully re-created in a dining room that looks (almost) as if it was imported from New Orleans. If you're dieting, skip the main course so that you can justify ordering one of the dreamy desserts (they're not to be missed). $–$$

★ **Palenque.** Come to this family-run Pacific Beach restaurant for an introduction to the various delights of regional Mexican cooking. $–$$

★ **Panda Inn.** The best Chinese restaurant in San Diego, this Horton Plaza stand-out serves both Mandarin and Szechuan specialties in an elegant setting. $–$$

★ **Thai Chada.** It won't win any awards for design or ambience, but this is one of the best Thai restaurants in the city. $–$$

Lodging

★ **Hyatt Regency San Diego.** Opened in 1992, this Hyatt has received high marks from business and leisure travelers alike. Right next to Seaport Village, it offers an unbeatable location. $$$$

★ **Le Meridien.** Lushly landscaped grounds and flamingos set the scene for the deluxe accommodations you'll find indoors. The top-of-the-line spa facilities are an added draw. $$$$

★ **La Valencia.** An Art-Deco landmark near the shops and restaurants of La Jolla Village, the venerable La Valencia is still in great shape and continues to attract repeat visitors enchanted by its lovely setting. $$$–$$$$

★ **U.S. Grant Hotel.** Just across the street from Horton Plaza, this historic hotel recently underwent a meticulous renovation. $$$

★ **Hanalei Hotel.** This Hawaii-theme complex on the so-called Hotel Circle (between Mission Valley and Old Town) offers great value for the money. The adjacent golf course is an added draw. $$

★ **Torrey Pines Inn.** It may be a bit off the beaten path—on a bluff between La Jolla and Del Mar—but it's not every hotel that can offer proximity to scenic beaches, pristine coastline, a nature reserve, and one of the best golf courses in the country. $$

★ **Gaslamp Plaza Suites.** San Diego's first skyscraper, this hotel in the Gaslamp district offers comfortable European-style accommodations and complimentary Continental breakfast on the rooftop terrace. $–$$

★ **La Pensione.** If you're planning an extended stay, this downtown budget hotel with kitchenettes is an outstanding option. $

FESTIVALS AND SEASONAL EVENTS

WINTER

FEB.➤ **The Buick Invitational Golf Tournament** attracts more than 100,000 people, including local and national celebrities, to the Torrey Pines Golf Course (☎ 800/888–2842).

SPRING

MAR.➤ **The Ocean Beach Kite Festival** is an annual kite-decorating and -flying contest for all ages at Ocean Beach (☎ 619/531–1527).

APR.➤ **The San Diego Crew Classic** brings together more than 2,000 athletes on college teams from across the United States for a rowing competition at Crown Point in Mission Bay (☎ 619/488–0700). **The Downtown ArtWalk,** an annual open house for downtown's art galleries, has become a weekend-long festival in the G Street neighborhood (☎ 619/232–4395).

MAY➤ **The Cinco de Mayo Festival** (☎ 619/299–6055) brings lively entertainment and booths to town for this yearly Mexican celebration in Old Town State Park and the Bazaar del Mundo (☎ 619/299–6055). **The Del Mar National Horse Show,** at the Del Mar Fairgrounds, presents thousands of show horses in competition (☎ 619/792–4288). **The Pacific Beach Block Party** is an annual street fair with live music, food stands, and games (☎ 619/272–7282).

SUMMER

JUNE➤ **The Indian Fair** attracts Native Americans from throughout the southwest for arts, crafts, ethnic foods, and dances at the Museum of Man in Balboa Park (☎ 619/239–2001). **The San Diego County Fair at Del Mar** (☎ 619/755–1161) is a classic county fair, with live entertainment, flower and garden shows, displays, a carnival, and livestock shows (☎ 619/755–1161).

JULY➤ **The Old Globe Festival,** which runs from July until September, features works of Shakespeare in repertory with other classic and contemporary plays at the Old Globe Theatre in Balboa Park (☎ 619/239–2255). **The Over-the-Line Tournament** is a rowdy party that takes place over two weekends, with more than 1,000 three-person teams competing in a sport that's a cross between softball and stickball, on Fiesta Island in Mission Bay (☎ 619/688–0817). **Sand Castle Days,** at Imperial Beach Pier, brings sand sculptors of all ages together for one of the largest sand-castle events in the United States (☎ 619/424–6663).

AUG.➤ **America's Finest City Week** gives San Diegans a chance to proclaim their pride with a half-marathon, parades, and concerts (☎ 619/437–0369).**During the Annual Hillcrest Cityfest Street Fair** 5th Avenue is blocked off for a fun day of local arts and crafts, displays, live entertainment, a beer garden, and food (☎ 619/299–3330). **Las Californias/Tijuana Fair,** a south-of-the-border festival, features Mexican arts and crafts, food booths, and lively music and dancing (☎ 619/298–4105 or 66/84–05–37 in Tijuana).

AUTUMN

SEPT.➤ **Street Scene** transforms the historic Gaslamp Quarter into a rollicking two-day music festival, with 10 stages showcasing more than 60 bands from around the world (☎ 619/557–8490). The **Texaco Star Mart Cup** unlimited hydroplane races draw thunderboat enthusiasts to Mission Bay (☎ 619/268–1250).

OCT.➤ **Zoo Founders Day** means that everyone has free admission to the world-famous San Diego Zoo (☎ 619/231–1515).

NOV.➤ **The Dixieland Jazz Festival** presents a weekend filled with performances by well-known bands at the Town & Country Hotel (☎ 619/297–5277). El Cajon's **Mother Goose Parade** is a two-hour, nationally televised spectacular with 200 floats, bands, horses, and clowns (☎ 619/444–8712).

DEC.➤ **Christmas on El Prado** is sponsored by the museums in Balboa Park. Attractions include carolers and a candlelight procession, and admission is free to all the museums (☎ 619/239–0512). **San Diego Harbor Parade of Lights** brings colorfully lit boats through the downtown harbor (☎ 619/236–1212).

2 Exploring San Diego

EXPLORING SAN DIEGO is an endless adventure, limited only by time and transportation constraints, which, if you don't have a car, can be considerable.

By Maribeth Mellin

Updated by Edie Jarolim

San Diego is more a chain of separate communities than a cohesive city. Many of the major attractions are at least 5 miles away from one another. The streets are fun for getting an up-close look at how San Diegans live, but true southern Californians use the freeways, which crisscross the county in a sensible fashion. Interstate 5 runs a direct north–south route through the county's coastal communities to the Mexican border. Interstates 805 and 15 do much the same inland, with I–8 as the main east–west route. Highways 163, 52, and 94 act as connectors.

If you are going to drive around San Diego, study your maps before you hit the road. The freeways are convenient and fast most of the time, but if you miss your turnoff or get caught in commuter traffic, you'll experience a none-too-pleasurable hallmark of southern California living—freeway madness. Southern California drivers rush around on a complex freeway system with the same fervor they use for jogging scores of marathons each year. They particularly enjoy speeding up at interchanges and entrance and exit ramps. Be sure you know where you're going before you join the freeway chase. Better yet, use public transportation or tour buses from your hotel and save your energy for walking in the sun.

If you stick with public transportation, plan on taking your time. San Diego's bus system covers almost all the county, but it does so slowly. Since many of the city's major attractions are clustered along the coast, you'll be best off staying there or in the Hotel Circle/Mission Valley hotel zone. Downtown and Fashion Valley Shopping Center in Mission Valley are the two major transfer points. Some buses have bicycle racks in the back, and a bike is a great mode of transportation here. The bike-path system, although never perfect, is extensive and well marked. Taxis are expensive, given the miles between various sights, and are best used for getting around once you're in a given area.

We have divided San Diego into seven exploring sections, organized around neighborhoods (*see* the Exploring San Diego map for the location of each tour). Downtown's main thoroughfares are Harbor Drive, running along the waterfront; Broadway, through the center of downtown; and 6th Avenue to Balboa Park. The numbered streets run roughly north–south; the lettered and named streets (Broadway, Market, Island, and Ash) run east–west. Only Broadway, Market Street, and Island Avenue have two-way traffic. The rest alternate one-way directions.

There are large, reasonably priced ($3–$7 per day) parking lots along Harbor Drive, Pacific Highway, and lower Broadway and Market Street. Meters cost 50¢ an hour and are usually good for two hours. Don't plan on beating a ticket by rushing back and throwing quarters in your meter every so often. The space is limited to two hours—if you stay longer, no matter how much money is in your meter, you can get a ticket.

Balboa Park, Sea World, Cabrillo National Monument, and Mission Bay all have huge parking lots, and it is rare not to find a space, though it may seem as if you've parked miles away from your destination. Parking is more of a problem in Old Town, where the free lots

Torrey Pines
State Beach

MIRAMAR

Tour 7

MIRAMAR
NAVAL AIR
STATION

Torrey Pines

Clairemont   Mesa   Blvd.

Aero Dr.

PACIFIC
BEACH

LINDA
VISTA

Tour 6

MISSION
BEACH

Mission
Bay

Tour 5

■ Sea World

OCEAN
BEACH

Tour 4

Balboa
Park

POINT
LOMA

North Island
U.S. NAVAL
AIR STATION

DOWNTOWN

Imperial

National   Ave.

N

Coronado
Beach

Tours 1–3

San Diego Bay

PACIFIC OCEAN

Silver Strand Blvd.

0   4 miles

0   6 km

Chula Vista
Wildlife
Reserve

Silver Strand
State Beach

fill up quickly, and in La Jolla and Coronado, where you generally need to rely on hard-to-find street spots or expensive, by-the-hour parking lots.

TOUR 1: DOWNTOWN AND THE EMBARCADERO

Numbers in the margin correspond to points of interest on the Tours 1–3: Central San Diego map.

Downtown San Diego, just 3 miles south of the international airport, is changing and growing rapidly, gaining status as a cultural and recreational center for the county's residents and visitors alike.

San Diego's politicians and business leaders have made a concerted effort to draw San Diegans to an area long ignored or avoided by the local populace. Thanks to a 15-year redevelopment effort, elegant hotels, upscale condominium complexes, and swank, trendy cafés now attract newcomers and natives to a newly developed center city that has retained an outdoor character. Mirrored office and banking towers reflect the nearly constant blue skies and sunshine.

Downtown's natural attributes were easily evident to its original booster, Alonzo Horton, who arrived in San Diego in 1867. Horton looked at the bay and the acres of flatland surrounded by hills and canyons and knew he had found San Diego's center. Though Old Town, under the Spanish fort at the Presidio, had been settled for years, Horton understood that it was too far away from the water to take hold as the commercial center of San Diego. He bought 960 acres along the bay at 27½ per acre and literally gave away the land to those who would develop it or build houses. Within months, he had sold or given away 226 city blocks of land; settlers camped on their land in tents as their houses and businesses rose.

The transcontinental train arrived in 1885, and the land boom was on. Although the railroad's status as a cross-country route was short-lived, the population soared from 5,000 to 35,000 in less than a decade—a foreshadowing of San Diego's future. In 1887, the Santa Fe Depot was constructed at the foot of Broadway, two blocks from the water. Freighters chugged in and out of the harbor, and by the early 1900s, the navy had moved in.

As downtown grew into San Diego's transportation and commercial hub, residential neighborhoods blossomed along the beaches and inland valleys. The business district gradually moved farther away from the original heart of downtown, at 5th Avenue and Market Street, past Broadway, up toward the park. Downtown's waterfront fell into bad times during World War I, when sailors, gamblers, and prostitutes were drawn to one another and the waterfront bars.

But Alonzo Horton's modern-day followers, city leaders intent on prospering while preserving San Diego's natural beauty, have reclaimed the downtown area. Replacing old shipyards and canneries are hotel towers and waterfront parks; the Martin Luther King, Jr., Promenade project is slated to put 12 acres of greenery along Harbor Drive from Seaport Village to the convention center by the end of 1996. Nineteen ninety-two saw the completion of the part of the park near the $160 million, 760,000-square-foot San Diego Convention Center, which hosted its first events in early 1990. And a few blocks inland, the hugely successful Horton Plaza shopping center led the way for the hotels, restau-

14

Tours 1–3

rants, shopping centers, and housing developments that are now rising on every square inch of available space in downtown San Diego.

Your first view of downtown, regardless of your mode of transportation, will probably include the **Embarcadero,** a waterfront walkway on Harbor Drive lined with restaurants, sea vessels of every variety—cruise ships, ferries, tour boats, houseboats, and naval destroyers—and a fair share of seals and sea gulls. Many boats along the Embarcadero have been converted into floating gift shops, and others are awaiting restoration. If you plan to spend a good portion of your day in the area, either strolling or taking a harbor excursion, it's a good idea to park at the huge municipal lot ($3 per day) along the south side of the B Street Pier building; much of the parking along Harbor Drive is limited to two-hour meters.

To get some historical perspective, begin your tour two blocks north of the parking lot at the foot of Ash Street, where the *Berkeley,* an 1898 riverboat, is moored. It's headquarters for the **Maritime Museum,** a collection of three restored ships that may be toured for one admission price. The *Berkeley,* which served the Southern Pacific Railroad at San Francisco Bay until 1953, had its most important days during the great earthquake of 1906, when it carried thousands of passengers across San Francisco Bay to Oakland. Its carved wood paneling, stained-glass windows, and plate-glass mirrors have been restored, and its main deck serves as a floating museum, with exhibits on oceanography and naval history; permanent displays on the background of the America's Cup Race were recently installed. Anchored next to the *Berkeley,* the small Scottish steam yacht *Medea,* launched in 1904, may be boarded but has no interpretive displays.

The most interesting of the three ships is the ***Star of India,*** a beautiful windjammer built in 1863 and docked at the foot of Grape Street. The ship's high wooden masts and white sails flapping in the wind have been a harbor landmark since 1926. Built at Ramsey on the Isle of Man, the *Star of India* made 21 trips around the world in the late 1800s, when she traveled the East Indian trade route, shuttled immigrants from England to Australia, and served the Alaskan salmon trade. The ship languished after she was retired to San Diego Harbor, virtually ignored until 1959. Then a group of volunteers, organized by the Maritime Museum, stripped the wooden decks, polished the figurehead, and mended the sails. On July 4, 1976, the *Star of India* commemorated the bicentennial by setting sail in the harbor. The oldest iron sailing ship afloat in the world, she has made short excursions five times since then but for the most part stays moored at the pier and open to visitors. *1306 N. Harbor Dr.,* ☎ *619/234–9153.* ☛ *$6 adults, $4 senior citizens and students 13–17, $2 children 6–12, $12 families.* ☉ *Ships: daily 9–8.*

A cement pathway runs south from the *Star of India* along the waterfront to the pastel **B Street Pier,** used by ships from major cruise lines as both a port of call and a departure point. The cavernous pier building has a cruise-information center and a small, cool bar and gift shop.

Another two blocks south on Harbor Drive brings you to the foot of Broadway and **Broadway Pier** (also known as the "excursion pier"), a gathering spot for day-trippers ready to set sail. A cluster of storefront windows sell tickets for the harbor tours and whale-watching trips that leave from the dock in January and February, when the gray whales migrate from the Pacific Northwest to southern Baja. One of the most traditional, and delightful, boat trips to take from the pier is the **Bay Ferry** to Coronado Island (*see* Tour 2, *below,* for details).

TIME OUT   Those waiting for their boats can grab a beer or ice cream at the diner-style **Bay Cafe** and sit on the upstairs patio or on benches along the busy pathway; it's a good vantage point for watching the sailboats, paddle wheelers, and yachts vie for space. Another option is to buy some fish-and-chips and perch on an outdoor stool at **Anthony's Fish Grotto and Fishette,** the most casual of the three Embarcadero restaurants owned by the Anthony Ghio family.

The navy's Eleventh Naval District has control of the next few waterfront blocks to the south, and a series of destroyers, submarines, and carriers cruise in and out, some staying for weeks at a time. On weekends, the navy usually offers tours of these floating cities (☎ 619/532–1431 for recorded information on hours and types of ships). A steady stream of joggers, bicyclists, and serious walkers on the Embarcadero pathway picks up speed at **Tuna Harbor,** the hub of San Diego's commercial tuna fishing, one of the city's earliest industries.

★ ❹   **Seaport Village** (☎ 619/235–4013 for recorded events information or 619/235–4014) is the next attraction you'll reach if you continue south on Harbor Drive. It was a wise developer who saw the good fortune in this stretch of prime waterfront that now connects the harbor with the hotel towers and convention center. Spread out across 14 acres are three connected shopping plazas, designed to reflect the architectural styles of early California, especially New England clapboard and Spanish Mission. A ¼-mile wooden boardwalk that runs along the bay, as well as 4 miles of simulated dirt-road and cobblestone paths, leads to a bustling array of specialty shops, snack bars, and restaurants—more than 75 in all. You can browse through a shell shop, a rubber-stamp shop, and a shop devoted to left-handed people and nosh to your heart's delight on everything from fast Greek, Mexican, and French fare to seafood in nautical-style indoor restaurants. Seaport Village's shops are open daily 10–9 (10–10 in summer); a few eateries open early for breakfast, and many have extended nighttime hours, especially in summer.

Almost as many adults as children enjoy riding the hand-carved, hand-painted steeds on the **Broadway Flying Horses Carousel,** created by I.D. Looff in Coney Island in 1890. The ride was moved from its next home, Salisbury Beach in Massachusetts, and faithfully restored for Seaport Village, where it began operating in the West Plaza on the July 4 weekend of 1980; tickets are $1. Strolling clowns, mimes, musicians, and magicians are also on hand throughout the village to entertain kids; those not impressed by such pretechnological displays can duck into the Time Out entertainment center near the carousel and play video games.

TIME OUT   In the Central Plaza, **Upstart Crow & Co.,** a combination bookstore and coffeehouse, serves good cappuccino and espresso with great pastries and cakes.

Seaport Village's center reaches out onto **Embarcadero Marine Park North,** an 8-acre grassy point into the harbor where kite-fliers, roller-skaters, and picnickers hang out in the sun. Seasonal celebrations with live music and fireworks are held here throughout the year.

The mirrored towers of the San Diego Marriott Hotel and Marina mark the end of Seaport Village, but the waterfront walkway continues past the hotel's marina, where hotel guests moor their enormous, extravagant yachts. Just beyond the Marriott is the striking **San Diego Convention Center,** designed by Arthur Erickson; its nautical lines are complemented by the backdrop of blue sky and sea. The center often holds trade shows that are open to the public, and tours of the building are available.

Just south of the convention center, at the **Embarcadero Marina Park South,** the San Diego Symphony (☎ 619/699–4205) presents its annual Summer Pops concert series, complete with fireworks finales that light up the bay. These musical extravaganzas, increasingly popular in recent years, have gone upscale, offering cabaret seating as well as food and bar service.

One way to reach the heart of downtown is to walk up Market Street from Seaport Village. The **Olde Cracker Factory,** at Market and State streets, houses antiques and collectibles shops. Continue two blocks to Front Street and turn south one block to Island to reach the new facility of the **Children's Museum of San Diego** (*see* Chapter 3, San Diego for Children).

Another way to approach the central business district is to walk up Broadway from the Broadway Pier. Two blocks to the west of Harbor Drive, at Kettner Boulevard, you'll come to the Mission Revival–style **❻** **Santa Fe Depot,** built in 1915 on the site of the original 1887 station. The terminal for north- and south-bound Amtrak passengers, the graceful, tile-domed depot hosts an unattended tourist information booth with bus schedules, maps, and brochures. Formerly an easily spotted area landmark, the depot is now overshadowed by **1 America Plaza** next door. At the base of this massive 34-story office tower, designed by architect Helmut Jahn, is a transit center that links the train, trolley, and city bus systems. (The Greyhound bus station is just a few blocks away at 120 West Broadway.) The building's signature crescent-shaped glass-and-steel canopy arching out over the trolley tracks calls attention to the new Sculpture Plaza that fronts the downtown branch of the **San Diego Museum of Contemporary Art,** opened in early 1993. The two-story building adjoining the transit center, with four small galleries, is the main locus for contemporary art exhibits in San Diego while the original facility in La Jolla undergoes expansion. *1001 Kettner Blvd.,* ☎ *619/234–1001.* ☛ *$3 adults, $1 students and senior citizens, children under 13 free; free general admission Fri. 5:30–8 PM.* ☺ *Tues.–Thurs. and weekends 10:30 AM–5:30 PM, Fri. 10:30 AM–8 PM.*

❼ Six blocks farther east, at the corner of 1st Avenue and Broadway, downtown begins to come alive. Here you'll pass the **Spreckels Theater,** a grand old stage that presents pop concerts and touring plays these days. **❽** Another block down and across the street, the **U.S. Grant Hotel,** built in 1910, is far more formal than most other San Diego lodgings; the massive marble lobby, gleaming chandeliers, and white-gloved doormen hark back to the more gracious time when it was built.

★ ❾ The theme of shopping in adventureland carries over from Seaport Village to downtown San Diego's centerpiece, **Horton Plaza** (☎ 619/238–1596). This shopping, dining, and entertainment mall fronts Broadway and G Street from 1st to 4th avenues and covers more than six city blocks. The **International Visitor Information Center,** operated in the complex by the San Diego Convention and Visitors Bureau, is the traveler's best resource for information on the city. The staff members and volunteers who run the center speak an amazing array of languages and are well acquainted with the myriad needs and requests of tourists. They dispense information on hotels, restaurants, and tourist attractions, including Tijuana. *11 Horton Plaza, street level at corner of 1st*

Ave. and F St., ☎ *619/236–1212.* ⊘ *Year-round, Mon.–Sat. 8:30–5; June–Aug., also open Sun. 11–5.*

Designed by Jon Jerde and completed in 1985, Horton Plaza is far from what one would imagine a shopping center—or city center—to be. A collage of pastels with elaborate, colorful tile work on benches and stairways, cloth banners waving in the air, and modern sculptures marking the entrances, Horton Plaza rises in uneven, staggered levels to six floors, offering great views of downtown from the harbor to Balboa Park and beyond. The complex's innovative architecture has strongly affected the rest of downtown's development, and new apartment and condominium complexes along G and Market streets mimic its brightly colored towers and cupolas.

Horton Plaza has a large, multilevel parking garage; the long lines of cars in search of a place to land show just how successful the complex has become. The first three hours of parking are free with validation; after that, it's $1 for every half hour. If you use this garage, be sure to remember where you leave your car. The lot is notoriously confusing, and the various levels, coded by fruits and vegetables, don't quite match up with the levels the shops are on.

Robinson's, Nordstrom, the Broadway, and Mervyn's department stores anchor the shopping sections, with an eclectic assortment of 140 clothing, sporting goods, jewelry, book, and gift shops flanking them. A movie complex, restaurants, and a long row of take-out ethnic food shops and dining patios line the uppermost tier. On the lowest level, facing 1st Avenue, is the Farmers Market, an upscale grocery with fresh gourmet meats, seafood, and produce. The San Diego Repertory Theater, one of the longest-burning and brightest lights in San Diego's explosive theater scene, has two stages below ground level. Most of the shops close weekdays at 9 PM and weekends at 6 PM, but the restaurants and theaters stay open later.

TIME OUT   Dining options at Horton Plaza are extensive—everything from pungent burritos to Peking duck. **La Salsa,** on the uppermost dining level, has wonderful marinated pork tacos. Also on the top level, **Galaxy Grill** is a '50s-style diner with great burgers and shakes.

Opened in 1992 across from Horton Plaza at 777 Front Street between G and F streets, the **Paladion** (☎ 619/232–1627) is the most recent addition to the thriving downtown retail scene. This ultrahaute complex features a collection of toney boutiques such as Cartier, Tiffany, and Gucci.

Before Horton Plaza became the bright star on downtown's redevelopment horizon, the nearby **Gaslamp Quarter** was gaining attention and respect. A 16-block National Historic District, centered on 5th and 4th avenues from Broadway to Market Street, the quarter contains most of San Diego's Victorian-style commercial buildings from the late 1800s, when Market Street was the center of early downtown. At the farthest end of the redeveloped quarter, the **Gaslamp Quarter Association** is headquartered in the William Heath Davis House (410 Island Ave., ☎ 619/233–5227), one of the first residences in town. Davis was a San Franciscan whose ill-fated attempt to develop the waterfront area preceded the more successful one of Alonzo Horton. In 1850, Davis had this prefab saltbox-style house shipped around Cape Horn and assembled in San Diego. Walking tours of the historic district leave from here on Saturday at 11; the suggested donation is $5 for those over

12. If you can't make the tour, stop by the house between 10 and 2:30 Monday through Friday and pick up a self-guiding brochure and map.

In the latter part of the 19th century, businesses thrived in this area, but at the turn of the century, downtown's commercial district moved farther west toward Broadway, and many of San Diego's first buildings fell into disrepair. During the early 1900s, the quarter became known as the Stingaree district. Prostitutes picked up sailors in lively area taverns, and dance halls and crime flourished here; the blocks between Market Street and the waterfront were best avoided.

As the move for downtown redevelopment emerged, there was talk of destroying the buildings in the quarter, literally bulldozing them and starting from scratch. In 1974, history buffs, developers, architects, and artists formed the Gaslamp Quarter Council. Bent on preserving the district, they gathered funds from the government and private benefactors and began the painstaking, expensive task of cleaning up the quarter, restoring the finest old buildings, and attracting businesses and the public back to the heart of New Town. Some two decades later, their efforts have paid off. Former flophouses have become choice office buildings, and the area is dotted with characterful shops and restaurants.

⑪ Across the street from the Gaslamp Quarter Association's headquarters, at the corner of Island and 3rd avenues, is the **Horton Grand Hotel.** In the mid-1980s, this ornate, quintessentially Victorian hostelry was created by joining together two historic hotels, the Kahle Saddlery and the Grand Hotel, built in the boom days of the 1880s; Wyatt Earp stayed at the Kahle Saddlery (then called the Brooklyn Hotel) while he was in town speculating on real estate ventures and opening gambling halls. Doomed to demolition and purchased from the city for $1 each, the two hotels were dismantled and painstakingly reconstructed on a new site, about four blocks from their original locations. A small Chinese Museum serves as a tribute to the surrounding Chinatown district, a collection of modest homes that once housed Chinese laborers and their families.

Many of the quarter's landmark buildings are located on 4th and 5th avenues, between Island Avenue and Broadway. Among the nicest are the Backesto Building, the Louis Bank of Commerce, and the Mercantile Building, all on 5th Avenue, and the Keating Building on F Street. Johnny M's 801, at the corner of 4th Avenue and F Street, is a magnificently restored turn-of-the-century tavern with a 12-foot mahogany bar and a spectacular stained-glass domed ceiling.

As more and more artists—and art entrepreneurs—move to the area, the section of G Street between 6th and 9th avenues has become a haven for galleries; stop in at any one of them to pick up a map of the downtown arts district. For information about openings and other current events in the district, call the **Gaslamp Quarter Hot Line** (☎ 619/233–4691).

TIME OUT   Fifth Avenue between F and G streets is lined with restaurants, a number of them offering outdoor patios; **Trattoria La Strada** (702 5th Ave.) is a good place to sit out on a fine afternoon with a glass of wine and an antipasto. Many hip coffeehouses have also sprung up in the Gaslamp Quarter; you can nurse a double espresso at **Café LuLu** (419 F St.) for hours.

TOUR 2: CORONADO

Coronado Island, an incorporated city unto itself, is a charming, peaceful community. The Spaniards called the island Los Coronados, or "the Crowned Ones," in the late 1500s and the name stuck. Today's residents, many of whom live in grand Victorian homes handed down for generations, tend to consider their island to be a sort of royal encampment, safe from the hassles and hustle of San Diego proper.

North Island Naval Air Station was established in 1911 on the island's north end, across from Point Loma, and was the site of Charles Lindbergh's departure on his flight around the world. Today high-tech air- and seacraft arrive and depart continually from North Island, providing a real-life education in military armament. Coronado's long relationship with the navy has made it an enclave of sorts for retired military personnel.

The streets of the island are wide, quiet, and friendly, with lots of neighborhood parks where young families mingle with the island's many senior citizens. Grand old homes face the waterfront and the Coronado Municipal Golf Course, with its lovely setting under the bridge, at the north end of Glorietta Bay; it's the site of the annual Fourth of July fireworks. Community celebrations and live-band concerts take place in Spreckels' Park on Orange Avenue.

Coronado is visible from downtown and Point Loma and accessible via the arching blue 2.2-mile-long San Diego–Coronado Bridge, a landmark just beyond downtown's skyline. There is a $1 toll for crossing the bridge into Coronado, but cars carrying two or more passengers may enter through the free car-pool lane. The bridge handles more than 20,000 cars each day, and rush hour tends to be slow, which is fine, since the view of the harbor, downtown, and the island is breathtaking, day and night. Until the bridge was completed in 1969, visitors and residents relied on the Coronado Ferry, which ran across the harbor from downtown. When the bridge was opened, the ferry closed down, much to the chagrin of those who were fond of traveling at a leisurely pace. In 1987, the ferry returned, and with it came the island's most ambitious development in decades. Coronado's residents and commuting workers have quickly adapted to this traditional mode of transportation, and the ferry has become quite popular with bicyclists, who shuttle their bikes across the harbor and ride the island's wide, flat boulevards for hours.

You can board the Bay Ferry (☎ 619/234–4111) at downtown San Diego's Embarcadero from the Broadway Pier, at Broadway and Harbor Drive. Boats depart every hour on the hour from San Diego and every hour on the half hour from Coronado from 9 AM to 9:30 PM Sunday through Thursday, until 10:30 PM Friday and Saturday; the fare is $2 each way (50¢ extra for bicycles). San Diego Harbor Excursion (☎ 619/235–TAXI) has recently instituted water taxi service from Seaport Village to Ferry Landing Marketplace, Le Meridien Resort, and Hotel Del Coronado; the fare is $5. Call for the exact schedules.

⑫ The Bay Ferry's point of disembarkation is the **Ferry Landing Marketplace** (1st St. and B Ave., ☎ 619/435–8895), which is actually a new development on an old site. Its buildings resemble the gingerbread domes of the Hotel Del Coronado, long the island's main attraction. On a smaller scale, the Ferry Landing Marketplace is similar to Seaport Village, with little shops and restaurants and lots of benches facing the water. Nearby, the elegant Le Meridien Hotel accommodates many wedding receptions and gala banquets.

⓭ An electric trolley runs from the landing down **Orange Avenue,** the island's version of a downtown. It's easy to imagine you're on a street in Cape Cod when you stroll along this thoroughfare: The clapboard houses, small restaurants, and boutiques—many of them selling nautical paraphernalia—are in some ways more characteristic of New England than they are of California. But the East Coast illusion tends to dissipate as quickly as a winter fog here when you catch sight of one of the avenue's many citrus trees—or realize it's February and the sun is warming your face. The friendly volunteers at the Coronado Visitor Information center (1111 Orange Ave., ☎ 619/437–8788 or 800/622–8300) can answer your questions and provide you with an array of maps and brochures.

★ **⓮** At the end of Orange Avenue, the **Hotel Del Coronado** is the island's most prominent landmark. Selected as a National Historic Site in 1977, the Del (as natives say) celebrated its 100th anniversary in 1988. Celebrities, royalty, and politicians marked the anniversary with a weekend-long party that highlighted the hotel's colorful history, integrally connected with that of the island itself.

The Del was the brainchild of wealthy financiers Elisha Spurr Babcock, Jr., and H. L. Story, who, in 1884, saw the potential of the island's virgin beaches and its view of San Diego's emerging harbor. The next year, they purchased a 4,100-acre parcel of land for $110,000 and threw a lavish Fourth of July bash for prospective investors in their hunting and fishing resort. By the end of the year, they had roused public interest—and had an ample return on their investment. The hotel was completed in 1888, and Thomas Edison himself threw the switch as the Del became the world's first electrically lighted hotel. It has been a dazzler ever since.

The Del's ornate Victorian gingerbread architecture is recognized all over the world because the hotel has served as a set for many movies, political meetings, and extravagant social happenings. It is said that the Duke of Windsor first met Wallis Simpson here. Eight presidents have been guests of the Del, and the film *Some Like It Hot,* starring Marilyn Monroe, was filmed at the hotel. Today, lower-level corridors are lined with historic photos from the Del's early days.

A red carpet leads up the front stairs to the main lobby, with its grand oak pillars and ceiling, and out to the central courtyard and gazebo. To the right is the Crown Room, a cavernous room with an arched ceiling made of notched sugar pine and constructed without nails. You can tell by looking at this space that the hotel's architect, James Reed, had previously designed railroad stations.

TIME OUT The most popular meal on the island is the lavish Sunday brunch in the **Crown Room.** Pianists and harpists play soothing melodies from the curved balconies. The room can seat more than 1,000 diners, but it would be wise to make reservations in advance if you're dining with a group, particularly on holidays. Brunch is served from 9 to 2 and costs $23.95 for adults, $16.95 children 6–10, and $5.95 for children 2–5.

The Grand Ballroom overlooks the ocean and the hotel's long white beach. The patio surrounding the sky-blue swimming pool is a great place for just sitting back and imagining what the bathers looked like during the '20s, when the hotel rocked with good times. More rooms have been added in high-rise towers beside the original 400-room building, which is still the most charming place to stay. *1500 Orange Ave.,* ☎ *619/435–6611. 1-hr guided tours ($10) from lobby Thurs.–Sat. 10 and 11* AM. *Headsets for self-guided tours ($5) can be rented at the Signature Lobby across from concierge desk.*

⑮ Coronado's other main attraction is its 86 historic homes—many of them turn-of-the-century mansions—and sites. The **Glorietta Bay Inn,** across the street from the Del, was the residence of John Spreckels, the original owner of North Island and the property on which the Hotel Del Coronado now stands. On Tuesday, Thursday, and Saturday morning at 11, the inn is the departure point for a fun and informative 1½-hour walking tour of the area's historical homes. Sponsored by the Coronado Historical Association, the tour focuses on the Glorietta Bay Inn and the Hotel Del but also includes—from the outside only—some spectacular mansions along with the Meade House, where L. Frank Baum wrote *The Wizard of Oz* (some claim that Emerald City might be based on Coronado). The cost is $5; call 619/435–5892 or 619/435–5444 for more information.

⑯ You can start your own tour at nearby **Star Park** on Loma Avenue, the hub for five streets that have been designated historic sites. But before you set out, stop in at the **Coronado Beach Historical Museum,** opened by the Coronado Historical Association in April 1993. Housed in a beautifully restored Cape Cod–style cottage built by an East Coast family in 1898, the museum illustrates the island's history with photographs and displays of its major formative events and sites: the Hotel del Coronado (including an original chamber pot from one of the rooms); Tent City, a summer resort just south of the Del developed by John Spreckels at the turn of the century; the early ferry boats; and the North Island Naval Air Station. It also hosts a small gift shop and a cozy sun porch. *1126 Loma Ave.,* ☎ *619/435–7242.* ☛ *Free (donations accepted).* ☼ *Wed.–Sat. 10–4, Sun. noon–4.*

⑰ **Silver Strand Beach State Park** runs along Silver Strand Boulevard from the Del to Imperial Beach. The view from the shore to Point Loma is lovely, and the long, clean beach is a perfect family gathering spot, with fire rings, rest rooms, and lifeguards. Across from the strand is the Coronado Cays, an exclusive community, popular with yacht owners and celebrities, and the Loews Coronado Bay Resort, which opened in 1991.

TOUR 3: POINT LOMA, SHELTER ISLAND, AND HARBOR ISLAND

Point Loma curves around the San Diego Bay west of downtown and the airport, protecting the center city from the Pacific's tides and waves. Although a number of military installations are based here and some main streets are cluttered with motels and fast-food shacks, Point Loma is an old and wealthy enclave of stately family homes for military officers, successful Portuguese fishermen, and political and professional leaders. Its bayside shores front huge estates, with sailboats and yachts packed tightly in private marinas.

★ ⑱ Take Catalina Drive all the way down to the tip of Point Loma to reach **Cabrillo National Monument,** named after the Portuguese explorer Juan Rodríguez Cabrillo. Cabrillo, who had earlier gone on voyages with Cortés, was the first European to come to San Diego, which he called San Miguel, in 1542. In 1913, government grounds were set aside to commemorate his discovery. Today his monument, a 144-acre preserve of rugged cliffs and shores and outstanding overlooks, is one of the most frequently visited of all National Park Service sites.

Begin your tour at the visitor center, where films and lectures about Cabrillo's voyage, the sea-level tidal pools, and the gray whales migrating offshore are presented frequently. The center has an excellent shop with an interesting selection of books about nature, San Diego, and the sea; maps of the region, posters of whales, flowers, shells, and the requisite postcards, slides, and film are also on sale. Rest rooms and water fountains are plentiful along the paths that climb to the monument's various viewpoints, but, except for a few vending machines at the visitor center, there are no food facilities. Exploring the grounds consumes time and calories; bring a picnic and rest on a bench overlooking the sailboats headed to sea.

Signs along the walkways that edge the cliffs explain the views, with posters depicting the various navy, fishing, and pleasure craft that sail into and fly over the bay. Directly south across the bay from the visitor center is the North Island Naval Air Station on the west end of Coronado Island. Directly left on the shores of Point Loma is the Naval Ocean Systems Center and Ballast Point; nuclear-powered submarines are now docked where Cabrillo's small ships anchored in 1542.

A statue of Cabrillo overlooks downtown from the next windy promontory, where visitors gather to admire the stunning panorama over the bay, from the snowcapped San Bernardino Mountains, some 200 miles northeast, to the hills surrounding Tijuana. The stone figure standing on the bluff looks rugged and dashing, but he is a creation of an artist's imagination—no portraits of Cabrillo are known to exist.

The 2-mile Bayside Trail winds through cliffside chaparral, curving under the clifftop lookouts and bringing you ever closer to the bayfront scenery. You cannot reach the beach from this trail and must stick to the path to protect the cliffs from erosion and yourself from poisonous plants. Along the way, you'll see prickly pear cactus and yucca, black-eyed Susans, fragrant sage, and maybe a lizard or a hummingbird. The climb back is long but gradual, leading up to the old lighthouse.

The oil lamp of the **Old Point Loma Lighthouse** was first lit in 1855. The light, sitting in a brass-and-iron housing above a painstakingly refurbished white wooden house, shone through a state-of-the-art lens from France and was visible from the sea for 25 miles. Unfortunately, it was too high above the cliffs to guide navigators trapped in southern California's thick offshore fog and low clouds. In 1891, a new lighthouse was built on the small shore under the slowly eroding 400-foot cliffs. The old lighthouse is open to visitors, and the coast guard still uses the newer lighthouse and a mighty foghorn to guide boaters through the narrow channel leading into the bay.

The western and southern cliffs of Cabrillo Monument are prime whale-watching territory. A sheltered viewing station offers a tape-recorded lecture describing the great gray whales' migration from the Bering Sea to Baja, and high-powered viewers help you focus on the whales' water spouts. The whales are visible on clear days in January and February, mostly in early morning.

More accessible sea creatures can be seen in the tidal pools at the foot of the monument's western cliffs. Drive north from the visitor center to the first road on the left, which winds down to the coast guard station and the shore. When the tide is low (check with the ranger), you can walk on the rocks around saltwater pools filled with starfish, crabs, anemones, octopuses, and hundreds of other sea creatures and plants. The pools are protected by law, so the creatures are off-limits. *1800 Cabrillo Memorial Dr.,* ☎ *619/557–5450.* ☛ *$4 per car, $2 per person entering on foot or by bicycle; free for Golden Age Passport holders, people with disabilities, and children under 17.* ☼ *Park daily 9–5:15, Old Lighthouse 9–5, Bayside Trail 9–4, tidal-pool areas 9– 4:30 in winter; in summer, the park is open until sunset and other areas have extended hrs.*

⑲ More than 40,000 white headstones in **Fort Rosecrans National Cemetery** overlook both sides of the point just north of the monument as you head back into the neighborhoods of Point Loma. The navy has various centers along Rosecrans Street, which also leads to the U.S. Marine Corps Recruit Depot.

Continue north on Catalina Boulevard to Hill Street and turn left to ⑳ reach **Sunset Cliffs Park,** at the western side of Point Loma near Ocean Beach. The cliffs are aptly named, since their main attraction is their vantage point as a fine sunset-watching spot. The dramatic coastline here seems to have been carved out of ancient rock. Certainly the waves make their impact, and each year more sections of the cliffs sport caution signs. Don't ignore these warnings: It's easy to lose your footing and slip in the crumbling sandstone, and the surf can get very rough. Small coves and beaches dot the coastline and are popular with surfers drawn to the pounding waves and locals from the neighborhood who name and claim their special spots. The homes along Sunset Cliffs Boulevard are lovely examples of southern California luxury, with pink stucco mansions beside shingle Cape Cod–style cottages.

Return to Catalina Boulevard and backtrack south for a few blocks to reach Canon Street, which leads toward the peninsula's eastern ㉑ (bay) side. Almost at the shore, you'll see **Scott Street,** which runs along Point Loma's waterfront from Shelter Island to the Marine Corps Recruiting Center on Harbor Drive. Lined with deep-sea fishing charters and whale-watching boats, this is a good spot from which to watch fishermen (and women) haul marlin, tuna, and puny mackerel off their boats.

TIME OUT The freshest and tastiest fish to be found along Point Loma's shores comes from **Point Loma Sea Foods,** off Scott Street at Emerson Street, behind the Vagabond Inn. A fish market sells specialties fresh from the boat, and locals and tourists alike crowd the adjacent take-out counter for seafood cocktails and salads, great seviche, and wonderful crab and shrimp sandwiches made with freshly baked sourdough bread. There are a couple of places to sit outside, but most folks squeeze into tables in the small dining area behind the store.

㉒ Scott Street is bisected by Shelter Island Drive, which leads to **Shelter Island,** actually a peninsula that sits in the narrow channel between Point Loma's eastern shore and the west coast of Coronado. In 1950, the port director thought there should be some use for the soil dredged to deepen the ship channel. Why not build an island?

His hunch paid off. Shelter Island's shores now support towering mature palms, a cluster of mid-range resorts, restaurants, and side-by-side marinas. It is the center of San Diego's yacht-building industry, and boats in every stage of construction are visible in the yacht yards. A long sidewalk runs from the landscaped lawns of the **San Diego Yacht Club** (tucked down Anchorage Street off Shelter Island Drive), past boat brokerages to the hotels and marinas, which line the inner shore, facing Point Loma. On the bay side, fishermen launch their boats or simply stand on shore and cast. Families relax at picnic tables along the grass, where there are fire rings and permanent barbecue grills, while strollers wander to the huge Friendship Bell, given to San Diegans by the people of Yokohama in 1960.

㉓ Go back up Shelter Island Drive, turn right on Rosecrans Street, and make another right on North Harbor Drive to reach **Harbor Island,** a peninsula adjacent to the airport that was created out of 3.5 million tons of rock and soil from the San Diego Bay. Again, hotels and restaurants line the inner shores, but here, the buildings are many stories high, and the views from the bayside rooms are spectacular. The bay shore has pathways, gardens, and picnic spots for sightseeing or working off the calories from the island restaurants' fine meals. On the west point, Tom Ham's Lighthouse restaurant has a coast guard–approved beacon shining from its tower.

TOUR 4: BALBOA PARK

Numbers in the margin correspond to points of interest on the Tour 4: Balboa Park map.

★ Straddling two mesas overlooking downtown and the Pacific Ocean, **Balboa Park** is set on 1,400 beautifully landscaped acres. Hosting the majority of San Diego's museums and a world-famous zoo, the park serves as the cultural center of the city, as well as a recreational paradise for animal lovers and folks who want to spend a day picnicking or strolling in a lush green space.

Many of the park's ornate Spanish-Moorish buildings were intended to be temporary structures housing exhibits for the Panama–California International Exposition of 1915. Fortunately, city leaders realized the buildings' value and incorporated them in their plans for Balboa Park's acreage, which had been set aside by the city founders in 1868. The Spanish theme first instituted in the early 1900s was carried through in new buildings designed for the California Pacific International Exposition of 1935–36. El Prado, the courtyard and walkway first created for the 1915 exposition, now passes through San Diego's central museum district, with pathways forking off to other attractions.

The Laurel Street Bridge, also known as Cabrillo Bridge, is the park's official gateway; it leads over a vast canyon, filled with downtown commuter traffic on Highway 163, to El Prado, which, beyond the art museum, becomes the park's central pedestrian mall. At Christmas the bridge is lined with colored lights; bright pink blossoms on rows of peach trees herald the coming of spring. The 100-bell carillon in the California Tower tolls the hour. Figures of California's historic personages decorate the base of the 200-foot spire, and a magnificent blue-tiled dome shines in the sun.

Parking near Balboa Park's museums is no mean accomplishment, especially on fine summer days when the lots fill up quickly. If you're driving in via the Laurel Street Bridge, the first parking area you'll come to is off the Prado to the left, going toward Pan American Plaza. Don't despair if there are no spaces here; you'll see more lots as you continue down along the same road. If you end up parking a bit far from your destination, just consider the stroll back through the greenery part of the day's recreational activities.

Most of the park's museums are open daily 10–4; during the summer, a number have extended hours—phone ahead to ask. It's impossible

Tour 4: Balboa Park

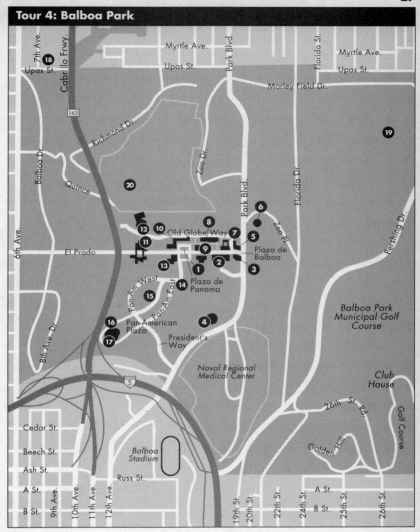

Balboa Park Visitors Center, **1**

Botanical Building, **8**

Casa de Balboa, **2**

Casa del Prado, **7**

Centro Cultural de la Raza, **4**

House of Charm, **13**

House of Pacific Relations, **15**

The Marston House, **18**

The Morley Field Sports Complex, **19**

The Museum of Man, **11**

Reuben H. Fleet Space Theater and Science Center, **3**

San Diego Aerospace Museum and International Aerospace Hall of Fame, **17**

San Diego Automotive Museum, **16**

San Diego Museum of Art, **10**

San Diego Natural History Museum, **5**

San Diego Zoo, **20**

Simon Edison Center for the Performing Arts, **12**

Spanish Village Art Center, **6**

Spreckels Organ Pavilion, **14**

Timken Museum of Art, **9**

to cover the entire park in one day, so decide before you head out what you'd like your focus to be. If your interests run to the aesthetic, the Museum of Photographic Arts and the San Diego Museum of Art are must-sees. Those with a penchant for natural and cultural history shouldn't miss the San Diego Natural History Museum or the Museum of Man; those oriented toward space and technology should visit the Reuben H. Fleet Space Theater and Science Center and the San Diego Aerospace Museum. If you don't choose to go inside, you'll be entertained by the street performers who gather along the Prado and delighted by the park's many gardens, representing a variety of natural landscapes. What follows are some highlights of the park's attractions, rather than a complete rundown of the sights and activities available here.

❶ A good place to begin a visit is at the **Balboa Park Visitors Center.** Maps and pamphlets—as well as the friendly volunteers who run the center—can help you decide what you'd like to see. The office sells the Passport to Balboa Park, which affords entry to nine museums for $18; it's worthwhile if you want to visit a number of them and aren't entitled to the other discounts that many give to children, senior citizens, and military personnel. On Tuesdays, the museums offer free admission on a rotating basis; inquire here about the schedule. Also available at the office is a schedule and route map for the free trams that operate around the park, giving you an alternative way to get back to your car or bus if all that culture has tired you. From April through October (Daylight Saving Time), trams run 9:30–5:30, approximately every 8–12 minutes; the rest of the year, service is 11–5 and frequency is 12–24 minutes. Restoration of the center's usual home, the House of Hospitality, began in January 1995 and should take two years to complete. For the time being, the information facility is set up on the Plaza de Panama, adjacent to its old site. ☎ *619/239–0512.* ◔ *Daily 9–4.*

❷ Next door to the House of Hospitality, the **Casa de Balboa** houses four museums: the San Diego Hall of Champions–Sports Museum, the Museum of Photographic Arts, the San Diego Historical Society–Museum of San Diego History, and the San Diego Model Railroad Museum. Starting from the left as you enter, the **Museum of San Diego History** features rotating exhibits on local urban history after 1850, when California became part of the United States. The society's research library is in the building's basement. ☎ *619/232–6203.* ☛ *$4 adults; $3 senior citizens, military personnel, and students; $1.50 children 5–12.* ◔ *Wed.–Sun. 10–4.*

Down the hall, the **San Diego Hall of Champions–Sports Museum** celebrates local heroes with a vast collection of memorabilia, uniforms, paintings, photographs, and computer and video displays. An amusing bloopers film is screened at the Sports Theater. ☎ *619/234–2544.* ☛ *$3 adults, $2 senior citizens, $1 children 6–17.* ◔ *Daily 10–4:30.*

The **Museum of Photographic Arts,** opened in 1983, is one of the few in the country dedicated solely to photography. World-renowned photographers, such as Ansel Adams, Imogen Cunningham, Henri Cartier-Bresson, and Edward Weston, are represented in the museum's collection, along with relatively obscure contemporary artists. Volunteers lead tours through the exhibits, which change every six weeks. Gallery talks by artists are given on weekends at 1 PM. ☎ *619/239–5262.* ☛ *$3, children under 12 free.* ◔ *Daily 10–5; closed national holidays and during installations.*

Below MOPA, in the basement of the Casa de Balboa, is the **San Diego Model Railroad Museum.** The room is filled with the sounds of chugging engines, screeching brakes, and shrill whistles when the six model-train exhibits are in operation. If you come in on Tuesday and Friday evenings, 7:30–11, you can watch model train layouts being created (free). ☎ 619/696–0199. ☛ *$3 adults; $2.50 senior citizens, students, and military personnel; children under 15 free.* ☉ *Wed.–Fri. 11–4, weekends 11–5.*

If you continue walking down El Prado, you'll come to the Plaza de Balboa and a large central fountain. Just past the fountain, El Prado ends in a bridge that crosses over Park Boulevard to a perfectly tended rose garden and a seemingly wild cactus grove. From here, you can see across the canyon to even more parkland, with picnic groves, sports facilities, and acres of ranging chaparral.

★ ❸ To the right of the Plaza de Balboa fountain, on the same side of the road as the Casa de Balboa, the **Reuben H. Fleet Space Theater and Science Center** features clever interactive exhibits that teach children and adults about scientific principles. The huge screen of the world's first IMAX Dome Theater premieres such exhilarating nature and science films as "Destiny in Space" (1994), which makes viewers feel as though they'd gone along on the 1993 expedition that fixed the ailing Hubble Space Telescope. The center's gift shop is akin to a museum, with toys and gadgets that inspire the imagination. At night, the Laserium presents laser shows set to rock music. ☎ 619/238–1233. ☛ *Science Center: $2.50 adults, $1.25 children 5–15 or included with price of theater ticket. Space Theater tickets: $6 adults, $4.50 senior citizens, $3.50 children 5–15; laser shows: $7.50 adults, $6 senior citizens, $5 children 5–15.* ☉ *Mon.–Tues. 9:30–6; Sun., Wed., and Thurs. 9:30–9; Fri.–Sat. 9:30 AM–10 PM.*

❹ To the south, past the parking lots of the Reuben H. Fleet Space Theater, is the **Centro Cultural de la Raza,** an old water tower converted into a cultural center focusing on Mexican, Native American, and Chicano arts. Attractions include a gallery with rotating exhibits and a theater, as well as a permanent collection of mural art, a fine example of which may be seen on the tower's exterior. ☎ 619/235–6135. ☛ *Free.* ☉ *Wed.–Sun. noon–5.*

❺ Across the Plaza de Balboa fountain from the Reuben H. Fleet Space Theater and Science Center, a short flight of steps will take you up to the **San Diego Natural History Museum,** which features displays on the plants and animals of southern California and Mexico. Children seem particularly impressed by the dinosaur bones and the live-insect zoo. The Hall of Mineralogy hosts an impressive collection of gems. Near the museum entrance, the 185-pound brass Foucault Pendulum, suspended on a 43-foot cable, demonstrates the earth's rotation. The museum frequently schedules nature walks, films, and lectures. ☎ 619/232–3821. ☛ *$4 adults, $3 senior citizens and military personnel, $2 children 6–17.* ☉ *Daily 9:30–4:30, until 6:30 Thurs.*

❻ North of the natural history museum, on the way to the zoo, is the **Spanish Village Art Center.** Built for the 1935–36 exposition, the village houses are now used as arts-and-crafts studios. The sculptors, photographers, jewelers, and other artists who rent space here demonstrate their skills and their wares—most available for sale—to the public. ☎ 619/233–9050. ☛ *Free.* ☉ *Daily 11–4.*

Behind the village, a 48-passenger **miniature train** runs a half-mile loop through eucalyptus groves. Nearby, riders on the antique **carousel** stretch from their seats to grab the brass rings suspended an arm's length away and earn a free ride. ☎ 619/239–4748. ☛ *$1 for railroad, $1 for carousel.* ◎ *Mid-June–Labor Day, daily 11–5:30; rest of yr, weekends, and school holidays 11–4:30.*

❼ If you head back east along the Prado from the San Diego Natural History Museum, you'll come to the **Casa del Prado,** which houses drama classes, group meetings, and special events. The San Diego Floral Association (☎ 619/232–5762) has a small gift shop, research library, and offices here. Be sure to wander through—you may chance upon a show of orchids, bonsai, or ikebana, the Japanese art of flower arranging. Several local theatrical companies perform at the adjoining Casa del Prado Theater.

❽ The action gets lively in the next section of El Prado, where mimes, jugglers, and musicians perform on long lawns beside the Lily Pond in front of the graceful **Botanical Building.** Built for the 1915 exposition, the latticed, open-air nursery houses more than 500 types of tropical and subtropical plants. The orchid collection is stunning, and there are benches beside cool, miniature waterfalls for resting in the shade. The Lily Pond, filled with giant koi fish and blooming water lilies, is popular with photographers. ☎ 619/235–1116. ☛ *Free.* ◎ *Fri.–Wed. 10–4.*

❾ On the other side of the Lily Pond is the only privately owned building in the park, operated by the Putnam Foundation. The small **Timken Museum of Art** houses a selection of minor works by major European and American artists, as well as a fine collection of Russian icons. ☎ 619/239–5548. ☛ *Free.* ◎ *Oct.–Aug., Tues.–Sat. 10–4:30, Sun. 1:30–4:30.*

❿ Just behind the Timken on the Plaza de Panama, the **San Diego Museum of Art** is known primarily for its Spanish Baroque and Renaissance paintings, including works by El Greco, Goya, Rubens, and Van Ruisdale. The museum also has strong holdings of Southeast Asian art and Indian miniatures, and its Baldwin M. Baldwin wing displays more than 100 pieces by Toulouse-Lautrec. The museum's latest acquisition is a large collection of contemporary California art. Opened in October 1994, an exciting new interactive computer gallery lets you locate the highlights of the museum's holdings on screen and custom-design a tour based on your interests. Among the other features of this unique, extremely user-friendly system—the first to be installed in the U.S. and similar to that in London's National Gallery—are historical information on the works and artists, magnification of details, and excellent color reproductions ($5 per print for adults, $3 for students). An outdoor Sculpture Garden exhibits both traditional and modern pieces in a striking natural setting. ☎ 619/232–7931. ☛ *$6 adults, $5 senior citizens, $2 students and children 6–17.* ◎ *Tues.–Sun. 10–4:30.*

TIME OUT Take a break from museum-hopping with a cup of freshly brewed coffee or a glass of California chardonnay in the San Diego Museum of Art's **Sculpture Garden Café,** which also offers a small selection of tasty—if rather pricey—gourmet lunches (Tues.–Sun. 11:30 AM–1:30 PM).

⓫ If you get back on El Prado and continue east, you'll come to the **Museum of Man,** located under the California Tower. One of the finest anthropological museums in the country, it houses an extensive collection first assembled for the 1915 exposition and amplified over the years. Exhibits focus on southwestern, Mexican, and South American cultures; the latest acquisition, in 1993, was a collection of ancient Egyptian artifacts. In the "Lifestyles and Ceremonies" section, high-tech gadgetry is employed in displays on biology, reproduction, and culture, offering a fascinating look at the costumes and rituals of San Diego's many ethnic communities. Weddings are sometimes held at the Chapel of St. Francis, a model of a typical early California hacienda chapel (viewed by appointment only). ☎ *619/239–2001.* ☛ *$4 adults, $2 children 13–18, $1 children 6–12.* ☉ *Daily 10–4:30.*

⓬ The **Simon Edison Centre for the Performing Arts** (☎ 619/239–2255 or 619/23–GLOBE), including the Cassius Carter Centre Stage, the Lowell Davies Festival Theatre, and the Old Globe Theatre, sits beside the Museum of Man under the California Tower. Originally devoted to Shakespearean theater, the Globe now also holds first-rate productions by other playwrights, too. All three theaters are small and intimate, and evening performances on the outdoor stages are particularly enjoyable during the summer.

⓭ Across the Prado and back toward the Museum of Art, the **House of Charm** has been closed for a massive, two-year renovation, but by November 1995 should be the new home for the Mingei International Museum of Folk Art (*see* Tour 7, *below*). The Mingei will share the space with rehearsal halls for the Old Globe Theater, and with the House of Charm's original tenant, the San Diego Art Institute, currently holding its shows in Mission Valley Shopping Center (1640 Camino del Rio N, Suite 1368, ☎ 619/220–4800 for hrs information).

Next to the House of Charm, the **Alcazar Garden** was designed to replicate the gardens surrounding the Alcazar Castle in Seville. The flower beds are ever-changing horticultural exhibits, with bright orange and yellow poppies blooming in the spring and deep rust and crimson chrysanthemums appearing in the fall. The benches by the tiled fountains are nice spots to rest.

At the Plaza de Panama parking lot, west of the Art Institute, another road heads south from El Prado. It's divided by a long island of flowers as it curves around the **Spreckels Organ Pavilion** and the 4,445-pipe Spreckels Organ, believed to be the largest outdoor pipe organ in the world. You can hear this impressive instrument at one of the concerts offered at 2 PM on Sunday afternoons year-round. On summer evenings, local military bands, gospel groups, and barbershop quartets hold concerts, and at Christmas, the park's massive Christmas tree and life-size nativity display turn the pavilion into a seasonal wonderland. ☎ *619/226–0819.* ☛ *Free.* ☉ *Fri.–Sun. 10–4.*

Northeast of the Organ Pavilion, the first phase of a new **Japanese Friendship Garden** includes an exhibit house, a traditional sand-and-stone garden, and a picnic area with a view of the canyon below. There is also a snack bar and a small gift shop. ☎ *619/232–2780.* ☛ *$2 adults; $1 senior citizens, military personnel, visitors with disabilities, students, and ages 7–18.* ☉ *Fri.–Sun. and Tues. 10–4.*

To the right of the organ pavilion, on Pan American West Road, the ⓯ **House of Pacific Relations** (☎ 619/234–0739) is really a cluster of stucco cottages representing 31 foreign countries. The buildings are open on Sunday from 12:30 to 4:30 PM; from March through October, ethnic song and dance performances are held on the outdoor stage at 2 PM (check the schedule at the park information center).

Farther west, in the building used as the Palace of Transportation for ⓰ the 1935–36 exposition, the **San Diego Automotive Museum** maintains a large collection of vintage cars and motorcycles and has an ongoing automobile restoration program. ☎ *619/231–2886.* ☞ *$5 adults, $4 senior citizens and active military, $2 children 6–17.* ☉ *Daily 10–4:30.*

⑰ The southern road ends at the Pan American Plaza and the **San Diego Aerospace Museum and International Aerospace Hall of Fame.** Looking unlike any other structure in the park, the sleek, streamlined edifice was commissioned by the Ford Motor Company for the 1935–36 exposition; at night, with a line of blue neon outlining it, the round building looks like a landlocked UFO. Exhibits about aviation and aerospace pioneers line the rotunda, and a collection of real and replicated aircraft fills the center. ☎ *619/234–8291.* ☞ *$5 adults, $4.50 senior citizens, $1 children 6–17.* ☉ *Daily 10–4:30.*

Next to the aerospace center, the **Starlight Bowl** (☎ 619/544–7800 or 619/544–STAR) presents live musicals during the summer on its outdoor stage; actors freeze in their places when planes roar overhead on their way to Lindbergh Field. The Federal Building, also in the Pan American Plaza, is the home of the U.S. Olympic Volleyball Team, and the Municipal Gymnasium is used by amateur basketball and volleyball teams.

President's Way leads from the plaza to Park Boulevard, the main thoroughfare from the park to downtown. **Pepper Grove,** along the boulevard, has lots of picnic tables and a playground.

The parklands across the Cabrillo Bridge, at the west end of El Prado, have been set aside for picnics and athletics. Roller skaters perform along Balboa Drive, leading to **Marston Point,** overlooking downtown. Ladies and gents in spotless white outfits meet regularly on summer afternoons for lawn-bowling tournaments at the green beside the bridge. Dirt trails lead into pine groves with secluded picnic areas.

The point's name commemorates businessman George W. Marston, a San Diego pioneer and philanthropist who financed the architectural landscaping of Balboa Park. At the northwest edge of the park his 16-
⑱ room residence, **the Marston House,** is now maintained by the San Diego Historical Society. It's a classic example of the American Craftsman style, built in 1905 by Irving Gill's architectural firm. The lovely 4½-acre grounds are landscaped in the English Romantic tradition. *3525 7th Ave.,* ☎ *619/298–3142.* ☞ *$3.* ☉ *Weekends noon–4:30.*

The far-east end of Balboa Park, across Park Boulevard and Florida
⑲ Canyon on Morley Field Drive, is the park's athletic center. **The Morley Field Sports Complex** (☎ 619/692–4919) has an unusual Frisbee Golf Course, with challenging "holes" (wire baskets hung from metal poles) where players toss their Frisbees over canyons and treetops to reach their goal. Morley Field also boasts a public pool, boccie, badminton, and tennis courts, an archery range, a pool, playgrounds, and a velodrome used for bicycle races.

Fronting Park Boulevard is Balboa Park's most famous attraction, the
★ **⑳** 100-acre **San Diego Zoo.** More than 3,200 animals of 777 species roam in expertly crafted habitats that spread down into, around, and above the natural canyons. Equal attention has been paid to the flora and the fauna, and the zoo is an enormous botanical garden with one of the world's largest collections of subtropical plants.

From the moment you walk through the entrance and face the swarm of bright pink flamingos and blue peacocks, you know you've entered a rare pocket of natural harmony. Exploring the zoo fully requires the stamina of a healthy hiker, but open-air trams that run throughout the day allow visitors to see 80% of the exhibits on their 3-mile tour. The animals are attuned to the buses and many like to show off; the bears are particularly fine performers, waving and bowing to their admirers. The Skyfari ride, which soars 170 feet above ground, gives a good overview of the zoo's layout and a marvelous panorama of the park, downtown San Diego, the bay, and the ocean, far past the Coronado Bridge.

Still, the zoo is at its best when you can wander the paths that climb through the huge enclosed Scripps Aviary, where brightly colored tropical birds swoop between branches just inches from your face. The Gorilla Tropics exhibit, beside the aviary, is one of the zoo's latest ventures into bioclimatic zone exhibits, where animals live in enclosed environments modeled on their native habitats. Throughout the zoo, walkways wind over bridges and past waterfalls ringed with tropical ferns; giant elephants in a sandy plateau roam so close you're tempted to pet them. The San Diego Zoo houses the only koalas outside Australia, and three rare golden monkeys number among its impressive collection of endangered species; a small two-headed snake named Thelma and Louise holds court in the reptile house.

The Children's Zoo is worth a visit, no matter what your age. Goats and sheep beg to be petted and are particularly adept at snatching bag lunches, while bunnies and guinea pigs seem willing to be fondled endlessly. In the nursery windows, you can see baby lemurs and spider monkeys playing with Cabbage Patch kids, looking much like the human babies peering from strollers through the glass. The exhibits are designed in size and style for four-year-olds, but that doesn't deter children of all ages from having fun. Even the rest rooms are child-size. The hardest part of being in the Children's Zoo will be getting your family to move on.

The Wedgeforth Bowl, a 3,000-seat amphitheater, holds various animal shows throughout the day, occasionally hosted by the zoo's ambassador of goodwill, Joan Embery, called "the most widely known inhabitant of the zoo." Embery's frequent appearances on Johnny Carson's *Tonight Show,* usually with some charming critter to entertain the host, made the San Diego Zoo a household name among late-night viewers.

The zoo's simulated Asian rain forest, Tiger River, brings together 10 exhibits with more than 35 species of animals. As spectacular as the tigers, pythons, and water dragons are, they seem almost inconsequential among the $500,000 collection of exotic trees and plants. The mist-shrouded trails winding down a canyon into Tiger River pass by fragrant jasmine, ginger lilies, and orchids, giving the visitor the feeling of descending into a South American jungle. In Sun Bear Forest, playful cubs constantly claw apart the trees and shrubs that serve as a natural playground for climbing, jumping, and general rowdiness. At the zoo's newest habitat, Hippo Canyon—a 2-acre African rain forest opened at the base of Tiger River in 1995—you can watch the huge but surprisingly graceful beasts frolicking underwater. However, these newcomers, along with the other zoo locals, are likely to be overshadowed for a while by two glamorous overseas visitors who arrived in the spring: Shi Shi and Bay Yun, a pair of giant pandas on 12-year loan from the People's Republic of China.

TIME OUT   The zoo is not known for its culinary wonders, though there are plenty of food stands selling popcorn, pizza, and enormous ice-cream cones. The best restaurant in the zoo is the **Peacock and Raven,** just inside the main entrance, serving sandwiches, salads, and light meals. The views are rather better than the food at the **Treehouse Cafe** at Gorilla Tropics, but the restaurant's Swiss Family Robinson perspective is fun. The **Safari Kitchen,** left of the Flamingo Lagoon, offers reasonably good fried chicken and warm chocolate chip cookies.

In many ways also a self-sustaining habitat for humans, the zoo rents strollers, wheelchairs, and cameras; it also has a first-aid office, a lost-and-found, and an ATM. It's best to avert your eyes from the zoo's two main gift shops until the end of your visit; you can spend a half-day just poking through the wonderful animal-related posters, crafts, dishes, clothing, and toys. ☎ 619/234–3153. ☛ *Zoo, including unlimited access to Skyfari ride and Children's Zoo: $13 adults, $6 children 3–11; bus tour: $3 adults, $2.50 children; senior citizens deluxe (includes bus tour) $14.40; children under 12 free during Oct.; free to all on Founder's Day, Oct. 3. D, MC, V. �---©�---ฺ Fall–spring, daily 9–4 (visitors may remain until 5); summer, daily 9–9 (visitors may remain until 10).*

TOUR 5: OLD TOWN

Numbers in the margin correspond to points of interest on the Tour 5: Old Town San Diego map.

San Diego's Spanish and Mexican history and heritage are most evident in Old Town, just north of downtown at Juan Street, near the intersection of I–5 and I–8. Old Town didn't become a state historic park until 1968, but fortunately, private efforts kept the area's history alive until then, and a number of San Diego's oldest structures remain in good shape.

Although Old Town is often credited as being the first European settlement in southern California, the true beginnings took place overlooking Old Town from atop Presidio Park (*see below*). There, Father Junípero Serra established the first of California's missions, San Diego de Alcalá, in 1769. Some of San Diego's Native Americans, called the San Diegueños by the Spaniards, were forced to abandon their seminomadic lifestyle and live at the mission. They were expected to follow Spanish customs and adopt Christianity as their religion, but they resisted these impositions fiercely; of all the California missions, San Diego de Alcalá was the least successful in carrying out conversions. For security reasons, the mission was built on a hill, but it didn't have an adequate water supply, and food became scarce as the number of Native Americans and Spanish soldiers occupying the site increased.

In 1774, the hilltop was declared a Royal Presidio, or fortress, and the mission was moved to its current location along the San Diego River, 6 miles east of the original site. Losing more of their traditional grounds and ranches as the mission grew along the riverbed, the Native Americans attacked and burned it in 1775, destroying religious objects and killing Franciscan Padre Luis Jayme. Their later attack on the presidio was less successful, and their revolt was short-lived. By 1800, about 1,500 Native Americans were living on the mission's grounds, receiving religious instruction and adapting to Spanish ways.

The pioneers living within the presidio's walls were mostly Spanish soldiers, poor Mexicans, and mestizos of Spanish and Native American ancestry, many of whom were unaccustomed to farming San Diego's arid land. They existed marginally until 1821, when Mexico gained independence from Spain, claimed its lands in California, and flew the

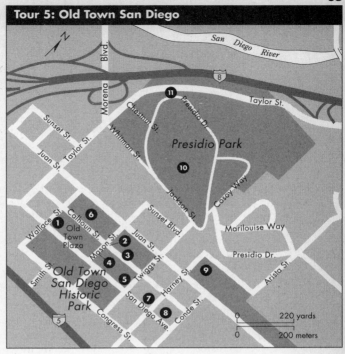

Tour 5: Old Town San Diego

Mexican flag over the presidio. The Mexican government, centered some 2,000 miles away in Monterrey, stripped the missions of their landholdings, and an aristocracy of landholders began to emerge. At the same time, settlers were beginning to move down from the presidio to what is now called Old Town.

A rectangular plaza was laid out along today's San Diego Avenue to serve as the settlement's center. In 1846, during the war between Mexico and the United States, a detachment of marines raised the U.S. flag over the plaza on a pole said to have been a mainmast. The flag was torn down once or twice, but by early 1848, Mexico had surrendered California, and the U.S. flag remained. In 1850, San Diego became an incorporated city, with Old Town as its center.

Old Town's historic buildings are clustered around **Old Town Plaza,** bounded by Wallace Street on the west, Calhoun Street on the north, Mason Street on the east, and San Diego Avenue on the south; you can see the presidio from behind the cannon by the flagpole. These days, the plaza is a pleasant place for resting and regrouping as you plan your tour of Old Town and watch other visitors stroll by; art shows often fill the lawns around the plaza. San Diego Avenue is closed to traffic here, and the cars are diverted to Juan and Congress streets, both of which are lined with shops and restaurants. There are a number of free parking lots on the outskirts of Old Town, but they fill quickly. By the summer of 1996, the San Diego trolley should stop here; in the meantime, if you plan to visit on the weekend, come early to find a spot.

★ ❶ The **Old Town San Diego State Historic Park** office is in the **Robinson-Rose House,** on the west (Wallace Street) side of the plaza. This was the original commercial center of old San Diego, housing railroad offices, law offices, and the first newspaper press; one room has been restored and outfitted with period furnishings. Park rangers now show films and distribute information from the living room. An excellent free walking tour of the park leaves from here daily at 2 PM, weather permitting. From 10 to 1 every Wednesday and the first Saturday of the month, park staff and volunteers in period costume give cooking and crafts demonstrations at the Machado y Stewart adobe; adjacent to the Bandini House near Juan Street, you can watch a blacksmith hammering away at his anvil, starting at 10 every Wednesday and Saturday. *4002 Wallace St.,* ☎ *619/220–5422.* ⊗ *Daily 10–5. Closed Thanksgiving, Dec. 25, Jan. 1.*

Many of Old Town's buildings were destroyed in a huge fire in 1872, but after the site became a state historic park in 1968, efforts were begun to reconstruct or restore the structures that remained. Eight of the original adobes are still intact. The tour map available at the Robinson-Rose House gives details on all of the historic houses on the plaza and in its vicinity; a few of the more interesting ones are noted below. Most of the houses are open to visitors daily 10–4 and most do not charge admission.

❷ On Mason Street, at the corner of Calhoun Street, **La Casa de Bandini** is one of the loveliest haciendas in San Diego. Built in 1829 by a Peruvian, Juan Bandini, the house served as Old Town's social center during Mexican rule. Albert Seeley, a stagecoach entrepreneur, purchased the home in 1869, built a second story, and turned it into the Cosmopolitan Hotel, a comfortable way station for travelers on the day-long trip south from Los Angeles. These days, Casa Bandini's colorful gardens and main-floor dining rooms house a popular Mexican restaurant.

❸ Next door on Calhoun Street, the **Seeley Stables** became San Diego's stagecoach stop in 1867 and were the transportation hub of Old Town until near the turn of the century, when the Southern Pacific Railroad became the favored mode of travel. The stables now house a collection of horse-drawn vehicles, western memorabilia, and Native American artifacts. There is a $2 admission fee for adults, $1 for children 6–17.

❹ This fee also covers admittance to **La Casa de Estudillo,** built on Mason Street in 1827 by the commander of the San Diego Presidio, Jose Maria Estudillo. The largest and most elaborate of the original adobe homes, it was occupied by members of the Estudillo family until 1887. After being left to deteriorate for some time, it was purchased and restored in 1910 by sugar magnate and developer John D. Spreckels, who advertised it in bold lettering on the side as "Ramona's Marriage Place"; the small chapel in the house was believed to be the setting for the wedding in Helen Hunt Jackson's popular novel.

❺ On Twigg Street and San Diego Avenue, the **San Diego Union Newspaper Historical Museum** is in the Casa de Altamirano, a New England–style wood-frame house prefabricated in Maine and shipped around Cape Horn in 1851. The building has been restored to replicate the newspaper's offices of 1868, when the first edition of the *San Diego Union* was printed.

Also worth exploring in the plaza area are the **Dental Museum, Mason Street School, Wells Fargo Museum,** and the **San Diego Courthouse.** Ask at the visitor center for locations.

6 Northwest of the plaza lies the unofficial center of Old Town, the **Bazaar del Mundo** (☎ 619/296–3161), a shopping and dining enclave built to represent a colonial Mexican square. The central courtyard is always in blossom, with magenta bougainvillea, scarlet hibiscus, and irises, poppies, and petunias in season. Ballet Folklorico and flamenco dancers perform on weekend afternoons, and the bazaar frequently holds arts-and-crafts exhibits and Mexican festivals in the courtyard. Colorful shops specializing in Latin American crafts and unusual gift items border the square. Although many of the shops here have high-quality wares, prices can be considerably higher than those at shops on the other side of Old Town plaza; it's a good idea to do some comparative shopping before you make any purchases.

TIME OUT The margarita is Old Town's premier drink, and **Casa de Pico** in the Bazaar del Mundo is one of Old Town's most popular spots to indulge in one. The excellent *antijitos,* or Mexican appetizers, including flavorful guacamole and nachos, are good accompaniments. Also in the bazaar, **La Panaderia** bakery sells fresh, hot *churros*—long sticks of fried dough coated with cinnamon and sugar.

Old Town's boundaries and reputation as a historic attraction and shopping-dining center have spread in the past few years. Opened in late 1992 on San Diego Avenue beside the state park headquarters, **Dodson's Corner** is a modern retailer in a mid-19th-century setting; two of the shops in the complex, which sells everything from quilts and western clothing to pottery and jewelry, are reconstructions of homes that stood on the spot in 1848. Farther away from the plaza, art galleries and expensive gift shops are interspersed with curio shops, restaurants, and open-air stands selling inexpensive Mexican pottery, jewelry, and blankets. San Diego Avenue continues as Old Town's main drag, with an ever-changing array of shopping plazas constructed in mock Mexican-plaza style. The best of these is the **Old Town Esplanade,** between Harney and Conde streets. Several shops display Mexican and South American folk art.

Historic sites punctuate the lineup of ice-cream and souvenir shops on
7 San Diego Avenue, including the **Thomas Whaley Museum,** built in 1856. This was southern California's first two-story brick structure, and it served as the county courthouse and government seat during the 1870s. An array of historical artifacts, including one of the six life masks that exist of Abraham Lincoln, is on display here. The place is most famed, however, for the ghost that is said to inhabit it; this is one of the few houses authenticated by the United States Department of Commerce as being haunted. *2482 San Diego Ave.,* ☎ *619/298–2482.* ☛ *$4 adults, $3 senior citizens, $2 children 5–16.* ⊙ *Daily 10–5. Closed national holidays.*

8 Farther down San Diego Avenue, **El Campo Santo,** an old adobe-walled cemetery established in 1849, was the burial place for many members of Old Town's founding families, as well as for a number of the gamblers and bandits who passed through town until 1880. Antonio Garra, a chief who led an uprising of the San Luis Rey Indians, was executed at El Campo Santo in front of the open grave he was forced to dig for himself. These days a peaceful spot for visitors to contemplate, the small cemetery was cleaned up in the early 1990s, its monuments straightened, and wrought-iron gates reconstructed around some of the plots.

9 **Heritage Park,** up the Juan Street hill near Harney Street, is the site of several grand Victorian homes and the town's first synagogue, all moved by the Save Our Heritage Organization (SOHO) from other parts of San Diego and restored. Some of the ornate houses may seem surprisingly colorful, but they are accurate representations of the bright tones of the era. The homes are now used for offices, shops, restaurants, and, in one case, a bed-and-breakfast inn. The climb up to the park is a bit steep, but the view of the harbor is great.

⑩ The rolling hillsides of the 40-acre **Presidio Park,** overlooking Old Town from the north end of Taylor Street, are popular with picnickers, and many couples have taken their wedding vows on the park's long stretches of lawn, some of the greenest in San Diego. You may encounter enthusiasts of a new sport, grass skiing, gliding over the grass and down the hills on wheels. Unless you love to climb, drive to the top of Presidio Park and then wander around on foot. At the north end, near
⑪ Taylor Street, the **Junípero Serra Museum** is perched atop a 160-foot hill overlooking Mission Valley and the site of the original Spanish presidio and mission. The museum houses an interesting collection of artifacts from San Diego's earliest days. *2727 Presidio Dr.,* ☎ *619/297–3258.* ☛ *$3 adults, children under 13 free.* ☉ *Tues.–Sat. 10– 4:30, Sun. noon–4:30.*

TOUR 6: MISSION BAY AND SEA WORLD

Numbers in the margin correspond to points of interest on the Tour 6: Mission Bay Area map.

San Diego's monument to sports and fitness, Mission Bay is a 4,600-acre aquatic park dedicated to action and leisure. Admission to its 27 miles of bayfront beaches and 17 miles of ocean frontage is free. All you need for a perfect day is a bathing suit, shorts, and the right selection of playthings. Above the lawns facing I–5, the sky is flooded with the bright colors of huge, intricately made kites.

When explorer Juan Rodríguez Cabrillo first spotted the bay in 1542, he called it Baja Falso (False Bay) because the ocean-facing inlet led to acres of swampland inhospitable to boats and inhabitants. In the 1960s the city planners decided to dredge the swamp and build a bay with acres of beaches and lawns for play. Only 25% of the land was permitted to be commercially developed, and, as a result, only a handful of resort hotels break up the striking natural landscape.

❶ The **Visitor Information Center,** at the East Mission Bay Drive exit from I–5, is an excellent tourist resource for the bay and all San Diego. On a glassed-in patio overlooking Mission Bay, you can peruse a free map while enjoying a cold drink from the snack bar. The center is a gathering spot for the runners, walkers, and exercisers who take part in group activities in the area. There's also a small gift shop here. *2688 E. Mission Bay Dr.,* ☎ *619/276–8200.* ☉ *Mon.–Sat. 9–5 (until 6 or 7 in summer), Sun. 9:30–4:30 (until 5:30 in summer).*

A 5-mile-long pathway runs through this section of the bay from the trailer park and miniature golf course, south past the high-rise Hilton Hotel to Sea World Drive. Playgrounds and picnic areas abound on the beach and low grassy hills of the park. Group gatherings, company picnics, and birthday parties are common along this stretch, where huge parking lots seem to expand to serve the swelling crowds on sunny days. On weekday evenings, a steady stream of joggers, bikers, and skaters releasing the stress from a day at the office line the path. In the daytime, swimmers, water-skiers, fishers, and boaters—some in single-person kayaks, others in crowded powerboats—vie for space in the water.

Tour 6: Mission Bay Area

The San Diego Crew Classic, which takes place in April, fills this section of the bay with teams from all over the country and college reunions, complete with flying school colors and keg beer. Swimmers should note signs warning about water pollution; certain areas of the bay are chronically polluted, and bathing is strongly discouraged.

2 **Fiesta Island,** off East Mission Bay Drive and Sea World Drive, is a smaller, man-made playground popular with jet- and waterskiers. In July, the annual Over-the-Line Tournament, a competition involving a local variety of softball, attracts thousands of players and oglers, drawn by the teams' raunchy names and outrageous behavior.

Ingraham Street is another main drag through the bay, from the shores of Pacific Beach to Sea World Drive. The focal point of this part of the bay is **Vacation Isle.** You don't have to stay at the island's Princess Resort to visit its lushly landscaped grounds and bayfront restaurants. Ducks are as common as tourists here, and Vacation Isle's village is a great family playground. Powerboats take off from Ski Beach, across Ingraham Street, which is also the site of the Texaco Star Mart Cup hydroplane races, held in September. The noise from these boats is deafening, and the beach is packed from dawn till dark.

West Mission Bay Drive runs from the ocean beyond Mission Boulevard to Sea World Drive. The pathways along the Mission Beach side of the bay are lined with vacation homes, many of which can be rented by the month. Those who are fortunate enough to live here year-round have the bay as their front yards, with wide sandy beaches, volleyball courts, and—less of an advantage—an endless stream of sightseers on the sidewalk. **Belmont Park,** once an abandoned amusement park at the corner of Mission Boulevard and West Mission Bay Drive, is now a shopping, dining, and recreation area between the bay and the Mission Beach boardwalk. Twinkling lights outline the refurbished old Belmont Park roller coaster on which screaming thrill-seekers ride. Nearby, younger riders enjoy the antique carousel, as well as the fresh cotton candy sold at the stand just next to it. The Plunge, an indoor freshwater swimming pool, has also been renovated and is open to the public, making Belmont Park a focal point for the ocean beach area.

⑤ At the dock of the Bahia Hotel (998 W. Mission Bay Dr., ☎ 619/488–0551), on the eastern shores of West Mission Bay Drive, you can board the *Bahia Belle* for a sunset cruise of the bay. From September through November and from January through June, the restored paddle boat departs Friday and Saturday every hour on the half hour from 7:30 PM to 1:30 AM; in July and August, it sails Wednesday through Sunday on the same schedule. Owned and operated by the hotel, the boat is free for guests of the Bahia or its sister hotel, the Catamaran. All other adults pay $5 for unlimited cruising; children under 12 pay $3. Those who cruise at 9:30 PM or later must be at least 21.

⑥ **Ventura Cove,** opposite the Bahia, is a good, quiet picnic spot. The frontage road past the sport fishing marina leads to **Marina Village,** the only shopping center on the bay, with specialty shops and bayview restaurants.

⑦ **Hospitality Point,** at the end of the frontage road, is another pretty, secluded spot for a picnic with a view of sailboats and yachts entering the open sea. At the entrance to Hospitality Point, the Mission Bay Park Headquarters offers area maps and other recreational information. It's also the place to pick up a permit if you decide to throw a wedding in the park. *2581 Quivira Ct.,* ☎ *619/221–8900.* ☉ *Weekdays 8–5.*

TIME OUT The **Hyatt Islandia** (1441 Quivira Rd.) spreads out a copious brunch on Sunday for $19. **Sportsmen's Sea Foods** (1617 Quivira Rd.) serves good fish-and-chips to eat on the inelegant but scenic patio (by the marina, where sportfishing boats depart daily) or to take out to your chosen picnic spot. Many folks prefer to bring their own food: Picnics and barbecues are popular at the bay, where many picnic areas have stationary barbecue grills.

★ ⑧ Spread over 100 tropically landscaped bayfront acres, where a cool breeze always seems to rise from the water, **Sea World** is one of the world's largest marine-life amusement parks. A hospitality center to the right of the entrance reminds visitors that this popular attraction is owned by Anheuser-Busch: Adults can get two small free cups of beer in the building, which also houses a deli restaurant. Next door are stables for the huge Clydesdale horses that are hitched daily near the Penguin Encounter (*see below*).

The traditional favorite exhibit at Sea World is the Shamu show, with giant killer whales entertaining the crowds in a recently constructed stadium, but performing dolphins, sea lions, and otters at other shows also delight audiences with their antics. At another popular exhibit, the Penguin Encounter, a moving sidewalk passes through a glass-enclosed arctic environment, in which hundreds of emperor penguins slide over glaciers into icy waters (the penguins like it cold, so you may consider bringing a light sweater along for this one). Imaginative youngsters are especially fond of the Shark Encounter, which features a variety of species of the fierce-looking predators. The hands-on California Tide Pool exhibit gives visitors a chance to explore San Diego's indigenous marine life with a guide well versed in the habits of these creatures. At Forbidden Reef, you can feed bat rays and come nose to nose with creepy moray eels. Visitors to Rocky Point Preserve can interact with bottlenose dolphins and Alaskan sea otters that were treated after the 1989 *Exxon-Valdez* oil spill. The newest attraction, Mission: Bermuda Triangle (unveiled Memorial Day weekend, 1994), replicates the thrills of a submersible dive to the ocean bottom via a sophisticated motion-based film.

Not all the exhibits are water oriented. Children are entranced by Cap'n Kids' World, an enclosed playground with trampolines, swinging wood bridges, towers for climbing, and giant tubs filled with plastic balls. The Wings of the World show features a large assemblage of free-flying exotic birds. Those who want to head aloft themselves may consider the park's Sky Tower, a glass elevator that ascends 265 feet; the views of San Diego County from the ocean to the mountains are especially pleasing in early morning and late evening. A six-minute sky-tram ride that leaves from the same spot travels between Sea World and the Atlantis Hotel across Mission Bay. Admission for the Sky Tower and the tram is $2 apiece or $3 for both.

Sea World is filled with souvenir shops and refreshment stands; it's difficult to come away from here without spending a lot of money on top of the hefty entrance and parking fees. Many hotels, especially those in the Mission Bay area, offer Sea World specials; some include price reductions, while others allow two days of entry for a single admission price—a good way to spread out what can otherwise be a very full day of activities. *Sea World Dr., at the west end of I–8,* ☎ *619/226–3901 for recorded information or 619/226–3815.* ☛ *$28.95 adults, $20.95 children 3–11; parking $5; 90-min behind-the-scenes walking tours: $5 adults, $4 children 3–11, $3.50 senior citizens. D, MC, V.* ☺ *Daily 10–dusk; extended hrs during summer. Call ahead to inquire about park hrs for the day you intend to visit.*

TOUR 7: LA JOLLA

Numbers in the margin correspond to points of interest on the Tour 7: La Jolla map.

La Jollans have long considered their village to be the Monte Carlo of California, and with good cause. Its coastline curves into natural coves backed by verdant hillsides and covered with lavish homes worth millions. Though La Jolla is considered part of San Diego, it has its own postal zone and a coveted sense of class; old-monied residents mingle here with visiting film stars and royalty who frequent established hotels and private clubs. If development and construction have radically altered the once-serene and private character of the village, it has gained a cosmopolitan air that makes it a popular vacation resort for the international set.

The Native Americans called the site La Hoya, meaning "the cave," referring to the grottos dotting the shoreline. The Spaniards changed the name to La Jolla, meaning "the jewel," and its residents have cherished the name and its allusions ever since.

To reach La Jolla from I–5, take the Ardath Road exit if you're traveling north and drive slowly down Prospect Street so you can appreciate the breathtaking view. If you're heading south, get off at the La Jolla Village Drive exit, which will lead into Torrey Pines Road. For those who enjoy meandering, the best way to approach La Jolla from

Tour 7: La Jolla

N
0   1 mile
0   1 km

PACIFIC OCEAN

Ellen Browning
Scripps Park, **4**
La Jolla Caves, **5**
La Jolla Shores, **7**
La Valencia Hotel, **6**
Mingei International
Museum of World
Folk Art, **14**
Mount Soledad, **2**
Salk Institute, **9**
San Diego Museum of
Contemporary Art, **3**

Stephen Birch
Aquarium-
Museum, **8**
Torrey Pines City
Park Beach, **11**
Torrey Pines Glider
Port, **10**
Torrey Pines State
Reserve, **13**
University of
California at San
Diego, **12**
Windansea Beach, **1**

the south is to drive through Mission and Pacific beaches on Mission Boulevard, past the crowds of roller skaters, bicyclists, and sunbathers. The clutter and congestion ease up as the street becomes La Jolla Boulevard, where quiet neighborhoods with winding streets lead down to some of the best surfing beaches in San Diego. The boulevard here is lined with expensive restaurants and cafés, as well as a few take-out spots.

❶ At the intersection of La Jolla Boulevard and Nautilus Street, turn toward the sea to reach **Windansea Beach,** made famous by Tom Wolfe's *The Pump House Gang,* which pokes fun at the So-Cal surfing culture. The surfing here is said to be as good as that in Hawaii. As you head north, streets curve past other neighborhood beaches where local surfers jealously guard their watery turf. Road signs along La Jolla Boulevard and Camino de la Costa direct drivers and bicyclists past some of La Jolla's loveliest homes—many designed by such famous architects as Frank Lloyd Wright and Irving Gill—toward the village.

TIME OUT A breakfast of the excellent buttery croissants or brioches at the **French Pastry Shop** (5550 La Jolla Blvd.) will fortify you for some serious tanning at Windansea Beach. The health-conscious may want to stop in at **Windansea Natural Grocery** (6903 La Jolla Blvd.) and pick up a smoothie or hummus sandwich to bring along to the shore.

❷ Nautilus Street east leads up to **Mount Soledad,** the highest spot in La Jolla. The cross on top of the mountain is an excellent vantage point from which to get a sense of San Diego's geography: Looking down from here, you can see the coast from the county's northern border to the south far beyond downtown—barring smog and haze. Sunrise services are held here on Easter Sunday.

As you approach the village, La Jolla Boulevard turns into Prospect Street, one of La Jolla's two main drags. The town's cultural center, **❸** the **San Diego Museum of Contemporary Art** (700 Prospect St., ☎ 619/454–3541), lies on the less trafficked southern end of Prospect. Housed in a remodeled Irving Gill home, the museum has a fine permanent collection of post-1950 art. Since early 1994, the facility has been undergoing expansion and renovation by architect Robert Venturi; it is slated to reopen in early 1996. In the meantime, those interested in contemporary art must be content with visiting the much smaller downtown facility, opened in 1993 in the America Plaza complex (*see* Tour 1, *above*). As we went to press, new hours and admission prices were not yet available for the La Jolla museum; call ahead for information.

❹
★ Continue north on Prospect and turn west onto Coast Boulevard to reach La Jolla's great natural coastal attraction, **Ellen Browning Scripps Park** at **La Jolla Cove.** Towering palms line the sidewalk along Coast Boulevard, where strollers in evening dress are as common as Frisbee-throwers. The **Children's Pool,** at the south end of the park, is aptly named for its curving beach and shallow waters protected by a seawall from strong currents and waves.

Smaller beaches appear and disappear with the tides, which carve small private coves in cliffs covered with ice plants. Some of these cliffs are unstable, but there are plenty of pathways leading down to the beaches. Just be sure to keep an eye on the tide to keep from getting trapped once the waves come in. A long layer of sandstone stretching out above the waves provides a perfect sunset-watching spot, with plenty of tiny tidal pools formed in eroded pockets in the rocks; starfish, sea anemones, and hermit crabs cluster here when the tide is in. Again, keep an eye on the waves because these rocks can get mighty slippery.

At the north end of La Jolla Cove, an underwater preserve makes the adjoining beach the most popular one in the area. On summer days, when the water visibility reaches 20 feet deep or so, the sea seems almost to disappear under the mass of bodies floating face down, snorkels poking up out of the water. The small beach is literally covered with blankets, towels, and umbrellas, and the lawns at the top of the stairs leading down to the cove are staked out by groups of scuba divers putting on wet suits and tanks. If you're not here by noon, forget about finding a parking spot or a small square of sand for your towel. But no matter what time you arrive, be sure to walk through the park, past the groves of twisted junipers to the cliff's edge. Perhaps one of the open-air shelters overlooking the sea will be free, and you can spread your picnic out on a table and watch the scene and the scenery.

5 Just past the far northern point of the cove, in front of the La Jolla Cave and Shell Shop, a trail leads down to **La Jolla Caves;** it's some 133 steps down to the largest one, Sunny Jim Cave. For claustrophobic types, there are photos of the watery grottoes in the shop, along with a good selection of shells and coral jewelry. *1325 Coast Blvd.,* ☎ *619/454–6080.* ☛ *Caves: $1.25 adults, 50¢ children 3–11.* ☉ *Mon.–Sat. 10–5, Sun. 11–5, sometimes later in summer.*

One block inland from the cove, Prospect Street is lined with toney restaurants and expensive boutiques; in recent years, a number of low-level office buildings and two-story shopping complexes have also cropped up here. At the intersection of Prospect and Girard Avenue,
6 La Jolla's other main drag, sits the pink Art Deco–style **La Valencia Hotel.** Operating as a luxury hotel since 1928, La Valencia has long been a gathering spot for Hollywood celebrities, who came down to escape from the Los Angeles bustle at this lovely hideaway; in the 1940s, Gregory Peck would invite friends to La Valencia's Whaling Bar to try to convince them to participate in one of his favorite projects, the La Jolla Theater. Today, the hotel's grand lobby with floor-to-ceiling windows overlooking the cove is a popular wedding spot, and the Whaling Bar is still a favorite meeting place for La Jolla's power brokers.

Like Prospect Street, Girard Avenue is lined with expensive shops and office buildings; it also hosts the village's only movie house, which tends to show nonmainstream films. The shopping and dining district has spread to Pearl and other side streets, where a steady parade of amblers and sightseers stroll about, chatting in many languages. Wall Street, a quiet tree-lined boulevard, was once the financial heart of La Jolla, but banks and investment houses can now be found throughout town. The La Jolla nightlife scene is an active one, with jazz clubs, piano bars, and watering holes for the elite younger set coming and going with the trends.

TIME OUT **Alfonso's** (1251 Prospect St.) is La Jolla's original sidewalk café, with tables crowded together under a shady awning. The margaritas here are excellent, as are the chips, salsa, and huge carne asada burritos. Another favorite gathering spot is the **Pannikin** (7467 Girard Ave.), where locals chat over cups of steaming fresh coffee and flaky croissants. The front-porch patio is great for people-watching.

If you continue north of the cove on La Jolla Shores Drive, you'll come to the La Jolla Beach and Tennis Club, host of many tennis tourna-
7 ments. **La Jolla Shores'** beaches are some of the finest in San Diego,

with long stretches allotted to surfers or swimmers. Just beyond the beaches is the campus of the Scripps Institute of Oceanography, formerly the site of the marine institute's aquarium.

The largest oceanographic exhibit in the United States, Scripps' **Stephen Birch Aquarium-Museum** reopened in late 1992 about 1½ miles northwest of its original site, on a signed drive leading off North Torrey Pines Road just south of La Jolla Village Drive. More than 30 huge tanks are filled with colorful saltwater fish, and a spectacular 70,000-gallon tank simulates a La Jolla kelp forest. Next to the fish themselves, the most interesting attraction is the 12-minute simulated submarine ride (children under 3 discouraged); the ocean noises and marine-life visuals are realistic almost to the point of inducing seasickness. *2300 Expedition Way,* ☎ *619/534–3474.* ☛ *$6.50 adults, $5.50 senior citizens 60 and older, $4.50 ages 13–17 and students with current ID, $3.50 children 3–12, active military free; parking $2.50.* ☉ *Daily 9–5. Closed Thanksgiving, Dec. 25.*

As La Jolla Shores Drive goes north, it curves onto Torrey Pines Road, off which you'll soon glimpse the world-famous **Salk Institute,** designed by Louis Kahn. The same road that lead to the institute ends at the **Torrey Pines Glider Port.** On days when the winds are just right, gliders line the clifftops, waiting for the perfect gust to carry them into the sky. Seasoned hang gliders with a good command of the current can soar over the sea for hours, then ride the winds back to the cliffs. Less-experienced fliers sometimes land on the beach below, to the cheers and applause of the sunbathers who scoot out of their way. The view from atop the cliffs with the colorful gliders in the sky is spectacular.

The beach at the foot of the cliffs is officially named **Torrey Pines City Park Beach,** but locals call it Black's Beach. For many years, Black's was widely accepted as being clothing-optional; although nudity is now prohibited by law, it is practiced whenever the authorities are out of sight. This is one of the most beautiful and secluded beaches in San Diego, with long stretches of pale sand backed by steep cliffs whose colors change with the light from the sun. There are no rest rooms, showers, or snack shops, though some hardy entrepreneurs do lug ice chests filled with sodas and beer down the cliffs to sell to the unprepared. The paths leading down to the beach are steep, and the cliffs are very unstable. Cliff rescues are not uncommon, particularly when daring explorers ignore the safety signs and strike out on uncharted trails. Stick to the well-traveled paths.

At the intersection of Torrey Pines Road and Genessee Avenue is the northern entrance to the **University of California at San Diego.** The massive campus spreads over canyons and eucalyptus groves, where students and faculty jog, bike, and roller-skate to class. If you're interested in contemporary art, ask at one of the two information booths for a map of the Stuart Collection, a thought-provoking group of sculptures located at different points around campus; Nam June Paik and Jenny Holtzer are among the artists whose works are displayed. UCSD's Price Center features both an excellent two-level bookstore and a good coffeehouse, Roma. Look for the postmodern Central Library, which resembles a large spaceship.

A bit farther north is **Torrey Pines State Reserve,** a 1,750-acre sanctuary for the United States' rarest pine tree, the Pinus torreyana. About 6,000 of these unusual trees, some as tall as 60 feet, grow on the clifftops above one of San Diego County's loveliest beaches. This park is one of only two places where the torrey pine can be found—the other is Santa Rosa Island, about 175 miles to the northwest. The reserve has several hiking trails leading to the cliffs, 300 feet above the ocean; trail maps are available at the park station. Picnic areas are scattered in pine groves, and wildflowers grow profusely in the spring. The beach below the reserve, called Torrey Pines State Beach, is another of the loveliest in the county. If you walk south past the lifeguard towers, you can find a secluded spot under the golden brown cliffs and feel as if there is no one on the beach but you. When the tide is out, it's possible to walk south all the way to Black's Beach through arches and over rocky promontories carved by the waves. *North Torrey Pines Rd. (also known as Old Hwy. 101),* ☎ *619/755–2063. From I–5, take Genessee Ave. west exit, then turn right (north) on Old Hwy. 101.* ☉ *Daily 8–sunset.* ☛ *Parking: $4. There is a large parking lot by the beach and another up the hill by the park station.*

La Jolla's newest enclave is the Golden Triangle, spreading through the Sorrento Valley east of I–5. High-tech research-and-development companies, attracted to the area in part by the facilities of UCSD, Scripps, and Salk, have developed huge state-of-the-art compounds in areas that were populated solely by coyotes and jays not so long ago. The area along La Jolla Village Drive and Genessee Avenue has become an architectural wonderland full of futuristic buildings. The most striking are those in Michael Graves's Aventine complex, visible from I–5 at the La Jolla Village Drive exit. About half a mile south (just off the Nobel exit) and equally eye-catching, the huge, white Mormon Temple is reminiscent of a medieval castle; completed in 1993, it still startles drivers heading up the freeway.

The first major establishment in the Golden Triangle was University Towne Center (UTC), a huge shopping mall with an indoor ice-skating rink. The delightful **Mingei International Museum of World Folk Art,** one of only five facilities in the world devoted to this subject, is located here among the shops and restaurants. The museum has some wonderfully creative shows featuring toys, pottery, textiles, costumes, and gadgets from all over. Not on any of UTC's maps, the Mingei is a bit hard to find (it's on the upper level, adjacent to the foot bridge next to Forum Hall), but in late 1995 the museum will move into Balboa Park's House of Charm (*see* Tour 4, *above*). You should be able to get up-to-date information on the new facility by calling the museum's current number. *4405 La Jolla Village Dr.,* ☎ *619/453–5300.* ☛ *$3 adults, $1 children 5–12.* ☉ *Tues.–Sat. 11–5, Sun. 2–5. Closed Mon. and national holidays.*

SIGHTSEEING CHECKLISTS

Museums and Historic Sites

Children's Museum of San Diego. *See* Chapter 3, San Diego for Children.

Junípero Serra Museum. *See* Tour 5: Old Town, *above.*

Maritime Museum. *See* Tour 1: Downtown and the Embarcadero, *above.*

The Marston House. *See* Tour 4: Balboa Park, *above.*

Mingei International Museum of World Folk Art. *See* Tour 7: La Jolla, *above.*

Mission San Diego de Alcala. Established by Father Junipero Serra in 1769 on Presidio Hill, this mission—the first of a chain of 21 stretching northward along the California coast—moved to its present location in 1774. Padre Luis Jayme, California's first Catholic martyr, killed by Native Americans in 1775, is buried in the mission sanctuary; a small museum named for him features relics of early mission days. You can also visit the original mission chapel. The schedule of religious services includes a folk music mass at 9 AM every Sunday. *10818 San Diego Mission Rd.,* ☎ *619/281–8449.* ☛ *$2 adults, $1 senior citizens over 55, 50¢ children under 12.* ☉ *Daily 9–5. Closed Thanksgiving, Dec. 25, Jan. 1.*

Mission San Luis Rey. Father Fermin Lasuen, a successor to Father Junipero Serra, established the "King of the Missions." The most extensive collection of old Spanish vestments in the United States is on display in the museum. *4050 Mission Ave., San Luis Rey, 4 mi east of I–5 in Oceanside,* ☎ *619/757–3651.* ☛ *$3 adults, $1 children under 12.* ☉ *Mon.–Sat. 10–4:30, Sun. noon–4:30 (gift shop 9–4:30 daily).*

Museum of Man. *See* Tour 4: Balboa Park, *above.*

Museum of Photographic Arts. *See* Tour 4: Balboa Park, *above.*

Museum of San Diego History. *See* Tour 4: Balboa Park, *above.*

Reuben H. Fleet Space Theater and Science Center. *See* Tour 4: Balboa Park, *above.*

San Diego Aerospace Museum. *See* Tour 4: Balboa Park, *above.*

San Diego Automotive Museum. *See* Tour 4, Balboa Park, *above.*

San Diego Model Railroad Museum. *See* Tour 4, Balboa Park, *above.*

San Diego Museum of Art. *See* Tour 4: Balboa Park, *above.*

San Diego Museum of Contemporary Art. *See* Tour 1: Downtown *and* Tour 7: La Jolla, *above.*

San Diego Natural History Museum. *See* Tour 4: Balboa Park, *above.*

San Diego Hall of Champions–Sports Museum. *See* Tour 4: Balboa Park, *above.*

Timken Museum of Art. *See* Tour 4: Balboa Park, *above.*

Villa Montezuma. The Jesse Shepard House, built in 1887, is a fine example of Queen Anne Victorian architecture with a California flair. The house has stained-glass windows with portraits of Shakespeare, Beethoven, Mozart, and Goethe. Redwood paneling and massive fireplaces decorate the living quarters, which have been restored by the San Diego Historical Society. *1925 K St.,* ☎ *619/239–2211.* ☛ *$3 adults.* ☉ *Weekends noon–4:30 PM.*

Parks and Gardens

With its huge urban green spaces and vast expanses of wilderness, San Diego County is in many ways one big park. The flowers bloom year-round here, with red and white poinsettias popping up everywhere at Christmas and candy-colored pink and yellow flowered ice plants edging the roads year-round. The dry climate, which seems inhospitable to growing things, actually nurtures some amazing flora. The golden, bushy stalks of pampas grass grow in wild patches near Sea World. Birds of paradise poke up straight and tall, tropical testimonials to San Diego's temperate climate. Bougainvillea covers roofs and hillsides in

La Jolla, spreading magenta blankets over whitewashed adobe walls. Towering palms and twisted junipers are far more common than maples or oaks, and fields of wild daisies and chamomile cover dry, dusty lots.

Citrus groves pop up in unlikely places, along the freeways and back roads. When the orange, lemon, and lime trees blossom in spring, the fragrance of their tiny white blossoms is nearly overpowering. Be sure to drive with your windows down—you'll be amazed at the sweet, hypnotic scent. Jasmine seems to be the city's flower, blooming on bushes and vines in front yards and parking lots.

Balboa Park is really a series of botanical gardens, with a verdant, tropical oasis in its midst at the San Diego Zoo. The animals are fascinating, for sure, but the zoo's real charm and fame come from its tradition of creating hospitable environments that replicate natural habitats as closely as possible. Botanists will particularly enjoy Tiger River, a $500,000 collection of endangered tropical plants.

Cultivated and wild gardens are an integral part of all Balboa Park, thanks to the "Mother of Balboa Park," Kate Sessions, who made sure both the park's developed and undeveloped acreage bloomed with the purple blossoms of the jacaranda tree and planted thousands of palms and other trees throughout the park. Left alone, Balboa Park would look like **Florida Canyon,** which lies between the main park and Morley Field, along Park Boulevard. Volunteers from the **San Diego Natural History Museum** give free guided nature walks throughout the county on weekends. For information on tours and special activities, call 619/232–3821.

The **Rose Garden,** along Park Boulevard overlooking Florida Canyon, has more than 2,000 rose plants. In the adjacent **Cactus Garden,** trails wind around prickly cacti and soft green succulents, many indigenous to the area. The **Alcazar Garden,** off El Prado across from the Museum of Man, blooms with colorful, seemingly perennial, flower beds. The **Palm Arboretum,** near the Organ Pavilion, has more than 60 varieties of palm trees along a shady bridge. East of the pavilion, the rocks and trees of the **Japanese Friendship Garden** are arranged to inspire contemplation. The redwood-lathed **Botanical Building,** built in 1915, houses a beautiful selection of tropical flowers and plants, with ceiling-high tree ferns shading tiny, fragile orchids and feathery bamboos.

Mission Bay Park is more of a playground than a botanical wonder, but its grassy lawns are a soothing sight for displaced East Coasters. **Old Town San Diego State Park,** though historic in focus, has some lovely small, grassy spots for resting and picnicking. The lawns between the historic district and Bazaar del Mundo, by the plaza, are particularly inviting and often hold arts-and-crafts shows. **Presidio Park** has a beautiful private canyon surrounded by palms at the bottom of the hill, off Taylor Street just before it intersects with I–8. At **Torrey Pines States Reserve,** north of La Jolla atop an oceanside cliff, beautiful trails wind amid the profusion of unusual twisted trees.

Other Places of Interest

The **San Diego Wild Animal Park,** about 30 miles northeast of downtown San Diego, is an extension of the San Diego Zoo. The 2,200-acre preserve in the San Pasqual Valley is designed to protect endangered species of animals from around the world. Five exhibit areas have been carved out of the dry, dusty canyons and mesas to represent the animals' natural habitats in North Africa, South Africa, East Africa, Asian swamps, and Asian plains.

The best way to see these preserves is on the 50-minute, 5-mile Wgasa Bushline Monorail ride (included in the price of admission). As you pass in front of the large, naturally landscaped enclosures, you'll see animals bounding through prairies and mesas as they would in the wild. More than 3,000 animals from some 450 species roam or fly through the expansive grounds. Enemy species are separated from each other by deep moats, but only the truly predatory tigers, lions, and cheetahs are kept in isolation. Photographers with zoom lenses can get spectacular shots of zebras, gazelles, and rhinos (a seat on the right-hand side of the monorail is best for viewing the majority of the animals). The trip is especially enjoyable in the early evening when the heat has subsided and the animals are active and feeding. On summer nights, the monorail travels through the park after dark, when soft amber sodium-vapor lamps highlight the animals in action. The setting, seemingly far from civilization, with clear starry skies, is enthralling and nearly as exciting as the real thing.

The park is as much a botanical garden as a zoo, and botanists collect rare and endangered plants for preservation. For example, the 5-foot-tall desert cypress found here is native to the Sahara; only six such trees are still in existence there.

The 1¼-mile-long Kilimanjaro Hiking Trail winds through some of the park's hilliest terrain in the East Africa section, with observation decks overlooking the elephants and lions. A 70-foot suspension bridge, made of Douglas fir poles, spans a steep ravine, leading to the final observation point and a panorama of the San Pasqual Valley and the Wild Animal Park.

The park's center is called Nairobi Village, where the sound of African drums provides a constant background of safari noise. The ticket booths are designed to resemble the tomb of an ancient king of Uganda, and dancers regularly perform complex African tribal dances in the center of the village. In the Petting Kraal, deer, sheep, and goats affectionately tolerate tugs and pats and are quite adept at posing for pictures with struggling toddlers on their backs. At the Congo River Fishing Village, 10,000 gallons of water pour each minute over a huge waterfall into a large lagoon. The park's latest (1993) addition, the Hidden Jungle, features creatures that creep, flutter, or just hang out in a tropical habitat: Gigantic cockroaches and bird-eating spiders share the turf with colorful butterflies and hummingbirds and oh-so-slow-moving two-toed sloths.

Ravens, vultures, hawks, and a great horned owl perform throughout the day at the Bird Show Amphitheater. All the park's animal shows are entertainingly educational. The gift shops have a wide assortment of African crafts and animal-oriented souvenirs, and free-loan cameras are available. Serious shutterbugs might consider joining one of the park's special photo caravans ($60–$85, including admission).

To reach the San Diego Wild Animal Park, take I–15 north to Via Rancho Pkwy. in Escondido, then follow signs (6 mi) to park, ☎ *619/234-6541 or 619/480–0100 (both recordings).* ☛ *$17.45 adults, $15.70 senior citizens, $10.45 children 3–11. A combination pass ($24 adults, $13 children) affords entry, within 5 days of purchase, to both the San Diego Zoo and the San Diego Wild Animal Park. Parking: $3. AE, D, MC, V.* ☉ *Daily 9 AM; closing time (generally 4 PM in winter, 5 PM in*

*summer) may be extended for special events; call ahead for informa-
tion.*

Scenic Drives

Unless you're on the freeway, it's hard *not* to find a scenic drive in San
Diego, but an officially designated 52-mile **Scenic Drive** over much of
central San Diego begins at the foot of Broadway. Road signs with a
white sea gull on a yellow-and-blue background direct the way through
the Embarcadero to Harbor and Shelter islands, Point Loma and
Cabrillo Monument, Mission Bay, Old Town, Balboa Park, Soledad
Mountain, and La Jolla. It's best to take this three-hour drive, outlined
on some local maps, on the weekend, when the commuters are off the
road.

Off the Beaten Track

Don't think you've finished seeing San Diego once you've hit all the
main attractions. The real character of the place doesn't shine through
until you've visited a few neighborhoods and mingled with the locals.
Then you can say you've seen San Diego.

Mission Hills is an older neighborhood near downtown that has the charm
and wealth of La Jolla and Point Loma without the crowds. The prettiest streets are above Presidio Park and Old Town, where huge mansions with rolling lawns resemble eastern estates; to see them, head up
Fort Stockton Drive from the Presidio or Juan Street past Heritage Park
in Old Town to Sunset Boulevard. Washington Street runs up a steep
hill from I–8 through the center of Mission Hills. At 4015 Goldfinch,
visit the Gathering, a neighborhood restaurant with great breakfasts
and outdoor tables for reading the Sunday paper in the sun.

Hillcrest, farther up Washington Street beginning at 1st Avenue, is San
Diego's Castro Street, the center for the gay community and artists of
all types. University, 4th, and 5th avenues are filled with cafés, boutiques, and excellent bookstores. The Guild Theater and Hillcrest Cinemas, both on 5th Avenue, show first-run foreign films. The Blue
Door, next to the Guild, is one of San Diego's best small bookstores.
The '50s retro-style Corvette Diner, on 4th Avenue between University Avenue and Washington Street, features burgers and shakes and
campy waitresses. Quel Fromage, a coffeehouse on University Avenue
between 5th and 6th avenues, has long been the place to go to discuss
philosophical or romantic matters over espresso.

Like most of San Diego, Hillcrest has been undergoing massive redevelopment. The largest project is the **Uptown District,** on University Avenue at 8th Avenue. This self-contained residential-commercial center
was built to resemble an inner-city neighborhood, with shops and
restaurants within easy walking distance of high-price town houses.
Restaurants include Cane's, a trendy pasta café, and La Salsa, part of
a chain of excellent Mexican take-out stands.

Washington Street eventually becomes Adams Avenue, San Diego's Antiques Row, with shops displaying an odd array of antiques and collectibles. Adams Avenue leads into **Kensington** and **Talmadge,** two lovely
old neighborhoods overlooking Mission Valley. The Ken Cinema (4061
Adams Ave.) shows older cult movies and current art films.

Ocean Beach, the westernmost point of the continental United States,
is a holdover from the radical days in the '60s and still considered something of a hippie haven. Of all the mainland beach towns, OB is the

most self-contained, with a mixed populace of young families, long-time residents, and drifters. The OB Pier is the best spot for getting a real feel for the place, though you may find the crowd a bit unsavory. For the bikinied beauties on roller skates, visit the Mission Beach boardwalk, where the parade is never-ending.

San Diego's large Vietnamese, Cambodian, and Korean communities congregate in **Linda Vista** and **North Park.** There are wonderful neighborhood restaurants in these relatively nondescript areas. The Mexican-American community is centered in **Barrio Logan,** under the Coronado Bridge. Chicano Park, just under the bridge supports, has huge murals depicting Mexican history, painted by artists from all over California.

3 San Diego for Children

IT'S HARD TO OVERSTATE San Diego's qualifications as a kid-friendly place to visit. For starters, it has an abundance of some of the best natural playgrounds for children of all ages: beaches. But if the weather is not cooperative or you've always found beaches to be just too filled with sand, San Diego also boasts one of the world's great zoos; a splashy marine park; an excellent group of museums covering everything from ancient civilization to outer space; train rides; ships; indoor fun zones; and the famous Palomar Observatory.

By Lori
Chamberlain

Because of the relaxed southern California culture, San Diego is an easy place to be with kids in general. Few restaurants, for example, make children unwelcome—and some are specifically designed for those traveling with children at the restaurant-unfriendly age. In addition, intense competition by hotels for the lucrative family market means low rates or special programs for youngsters at many places. There are also plenty of sources in town for kiddie supplies, including some great stores for books, toys, or clothing, as well as a number of arts venues specifically geared toward children.

EXPLORING

The well-known sights in San Diego live up to their reputations and shouldn't be missed. But consider, too, some of the lower-key attractions, which may prove less crowded and equally well suited to your children's interests.

The Major Sights

The San Diego Zoological Society maintains two excellent zoos in the San Diego area. If you have time, visit both; otherwise, you'll have to make a tough choice. The **San Diego Zoo** (*see* Tour 4 *in* Chapter 2, Exploring San Diego) has an extensive Children's Zoo, with exhibits at kid-height and a petting area with well-behaved goats and sheep. The 50-minute monorail ride through Africa and Asia at the **Wild Animal Park** (*see* Other Places of Interest *in* Chapter 2, Exploring San Diego), about 45 minutes from town, is best for kids old enough to sit for that period of time. Younger ones should enjoy stroking the exotic hoofed animals in the Petting Kraal or feeding the ducks and other waterfowl in the lagoon surrounding Nairobi Village, near the entrance to the park. Both the San Diego Zoo and the Wild Animal Park hold excellent informational presentations about animals, including sea lion shows at the zoo, and bird and elephant shows at the Wild Animal Park.

Sea World (*see* Tour 6 *in* Chapter 2, Exploring San Diego) is another popular place for kids, although for the price of entry you'll want to be sure your children are old enough (at least 3) to enjoy it. Not to be missed here are the Shamu show (sit up front if you *want* to get very wet), the dolphin exhibit (they'll eat little fish tidbits right out of your hand), the bat ray exhibit (you can pet them as they swim by), and the Penguin Encounter (no touching, but these guys are endlessly amusing). Cap'n Kids' World, an imaginative, no-holds-barred playground, will captivate youngsters and focus their energy for hours. The play equipment is designed for a variety of ages—the younger ones like tumbling in huge pools of plastic balls, while older children enjoy racing all over the rope swings and balconies.

The **Stephen Birch Aquarium-Museum** (*see* Tour 7 *in* Chapter 2, Exploring San Diego) offers another marine experience. Kids 5 and older should enjoy the simulated submarine ride (the cutoff age is 3, but the experience may be a bit scary for little ones), and a tidal pool gives younger children a chance to hold and pet starfish and sea anemones.

Tidal pools in their natural setting may be seen at **Cabrillo National Monument** (*see* Tour 3 *in* Chapter 2, Exploring San Diego), where kids can also climb up into an old lighthouse and, outside the visitor center, look through viewers at the surrounding cityscape and naval installations.

You may follow a visit to the San Diego Maritime Museum (*see below*) with a **harbor excursion** or, for a real bargain, a **ferry trip to Coronado** (*see* Sightseeing *in* The Gold Guide for both).

At **Seaport Village** (*see* Tour 1 *in* Chapter 2, Exploring San Diego), the Flying Horses Carousel should temporarily divert kids who are less keen on shopping than their parents.

Museums

Many of Balboa Park's museums (*see* Tour 4 *in* Chapter 2, Exploring San Diego) are geared toward, or have exhibits designed for, children. The Omnimax theater at the **Reuben H. Fleet Space Theater and Science Center,** for example, screens first-rate nature and science films, and the science center offers a wide variety of imaginative hands-on exhibits illustrating the laws of physics in ways you'll wish you'd learned in school. The **Natural History Museum** has a solid collection that includes a large dinosaur skeleton, as well as excellent seasonal shows: Recent displays starred robotic whales and—a kid's dream—a huge array of robotic insects. The **Model Railroad Museum,** also a winner, houses one of the world's largest collections of minigauge trains. For artistically oriented children, the **San Diego Museum of Art** offers special programs.

At the **San Diego Maritime Museum** (*see* Tour 1 *in* Chapter 2, Exploring San Diego), you can climb aboard the 1863 clipper ship *Star of India,* as well as an 1898 ferryboat and a World War I vintage steam yacht.

The **Mingei International Museum** (*see* Tour 7 *in* Chapter 2, Exploring San Diego) has colorful folk art exhibits from all parts of the world—often more interesting to kids than "high art."

The **Children's Museum of San Diego,** in the downtown area near the Convention Center, has approximately 30,000 square feet of space devoted to interactive, experiential environments for kids. Included are an art zone, where children can work on group projects or their own projects to take home, and a toddler area. In 1995, the "If I Had a Hammer" exhibit allowed children over the age of 8 to build an 8′ × 11′ house, and in "Virtual Hoops," children could play—you guessed it—virtual basketball. *200 W. Island Ave.,* ☎ *619/233–5437.* ☛ *$4 adults and children 2 and older, $2 senior citizens.* ☉ *Tues.–Sat. 10–4:30, Sun. 11–4:30.*

Fire-fighting artifacts of all sorts fill the **Firehouse Museum**: motorized, and horse- and hand-drawn fire engines, extinguishers, an extensive collection of helmets, and other memorabilia. *1572 Columbia St.,* ☎ *619/232–3473.* ☛ *Free; $1 donation requested.* ☉ *Wed.–Fri. 10–2, weekends 10–4.*

Fun Parks

The jewel in the crown of Belmont Park (*see* Tour 6 *in* Chapter 2, Exploring San Diego) is the classic **Giant Dipper Roller Coaster,** with more than 2,600 feet of tracks and 13 hills. Riders must be at least 4′2″. ☎ *619/488–1549.* ☛ *$2.50.* ☉ *Sun.–Thurs. 11–6, Fri. and Sat. 11–10.*

Also in Belmont Park, **Pirate's Cove** is a fantastic maze of brightly colored tunnels, slides, an obstacle course, and more, all with a pirate theme. Socks are required. ☎ *619/539–7474.* ☛ *Children 2–18, $4.50 weekdays, $6.50 weekends; adults, $2.50 daily.* ☉ *Mon.–Thurs. 11–8, Fri. 11–9, Sat. 10–9, Sun. 10–7, extended hrs on holidays.*

In the Pt. Loma area, the **Discovery Zone** has similar facilities for kids to 12 years. A Mini Zone will entertain those under 2 (or 40″). *3625 Midway Dr.* ☎ *619/523–9005 (other locations in El Cajon, Solana Beach, and Oceanside).* ☛ *Children 2–12, $5.99 weekdays, $6.99 weekends; children under 2, $3.99 weekdays, $4.99 weekends.* ☉ *Sun.–Thurs. 10 AM–8 PM, Fri.–Sat. 10 AM–9 PM.*

The **Family Fun Center** has three miniature-golf courses, batting cages, boats, go-carts, tank tag, and video-game rooms. *6999 Claremont Mesa Blvd.,* ☎ *619/560–4211.* ☛ *Free.* ☉ *Mon.–Thurs. and Sun. 9 AM–midnight, Fri.–Sat. 9 AM–2 AM; outside attractions may close earlier.*

Off the Beaten Track

You can pet bat rays at the low-key **Chula Vista Nature Interpretive Center,** a wetland preserve about 15 minutes south of downtown. Hands-on exhibits focus on marine life as well as other animal life typical of salt marshes. Take I–5 south to E Street and park in the lot at E Street and Bay Boulevard; a shuttle will take you across the salt marsh to the museum. *1000 Gunpowder Point Dr.,* ☎ *619/422–2481.* ☛ *$3.50 adults, $2.50 senior citizens, $1 children 6–17; includes round-trip shuttle.* ☉ *Tues.–Sun. 10–5.*

Under the aegis of the **San Diego Railroad Museum,** the Campo Depot, built in 1915, operates a scenic 1½-hour train trip through the San Diego backcountry on weekends. Included is an optional walking tour of the museum's approximately 90 pieces of vintage railroad equipment, in various stages of restoration. *50 mi east of San Diego (take I–8 east, exit at Buckman Springs Rd., and follow signs),* ☎ *619/595–3030 for general information or 619/478–9937 for Campo Depot.* ☛ *Depot free; train ride $10 adults, $8 senior citizens, $3 children 6–12.* ☉ *Trains depart at 12:01 PM and 2:30 PM on weekends only.*

For a well-rounded day trip with children, consider heading out to the **Palomar Observatory,** an hour or so outside San Diego. You can't actually look through the 200-inch Hale telescope, but there are lots of exhibits here on stars and the universe. Then visit the **Palomar Mountain State Park** or the **Cuyamaca Rancho State Park,** where you can hike and picnic. Top this off with a drive through the mountains to the old mining town of **Julian** to visit a gold mine and get some excellent apple pie. For details on all these attractions, *see* Inland North County *in* Chapter 10, Excursions from San Diego.

If you're in San Diego in June or early July, don't miss the **Del Mar Fair** (*see* The San Diego North Coast *in* Chapter 10, Excursions from San

Diego), a *big* exposition with lots of rides, livestock, hundreds of exhibits, food, entertainment, and contests.

SHOPPING

If you've brought the wrong clothes for your kids or find yourself without enough toys or other amusements, no problem: San Diego is an easy place to get any supplies that you may need—or that your children decide they have to have.

Books

In La Jolla, the **White Rabbit** has a great selection of reading material for children (*see* Bookstores *in* Chapter 4, Shopping). Among the many places to pick up comics are **Amazing Comix** (3555 Rosecrans, Pt. Loma, ☎ 619/225–0279; other locations) and the **Comic Gallery** (4224 Balboa Ave., Claremont Mesa, ☎ 619/483–4853; other locations).

Clothing

Gap Kids, in Horton Plaza, University Town Centre, and La Jolla (7835 Girard Ave., ☎ 619/454–2052), is probably the best bet for children's togs. **Nordstrom,** also located in several of the area shopping malls, carries good-quality lines of kids' clothing. For slightly less pricey attire, try **Mervyn's** in Horton Plaza. **Gymboree,** in the Horton Plaza and the Fashion Valley malls, is good for baby gear. (*See* Chapter 4, Shopping, for mall locations.)

Toys and Gadgets

In addition to the toy stores listed in Chapter 4, Shopping, **Whistle Stop Model Trains** (3834 4th Ave., downtown, ☎ 619/295–7340) carries books on trains and railroads, in addition to model trains. **Brad Burt's Magic Shop** (4690 Convoy, Claremont Mesa, ☎ 619/571–4749) offers a good selection of tricks and clown supplies. If you want to join the fun at Mission Beach, you can pick up a kite at **Kite Country** in Horton Plaza (☎ 619/233–9495), **All About Kites** (3689 Midway Dr., Pt. Loma Loma, ☎ 619/224–1610), and **Homer's** (4871 Newport Ave., Ocean Beach, ☎ 619/222–5834). The **Nature Company** (7840 Girard Ave., La Jolla, ☎ 619/459–0871; branches in Horton Plaza and Fashion Valley) carries books and gizmos of interest to kids and also sponsors nature programs for children.

BEACHES, PARKS, AND PLAYGROUNDS

San Diego itself is a huge outdoor playground, its beaches and parks unrivaled in quantity and quality by those of any other U.S. city. Specially designated children's play areas, many with excellent equipment, just add to the town's myriad outdoor kiddie options.

Beaches

A number of the San Diego beaches described in Chapter 5, Beaches, are particularly attractive for children. Try the **Children's Pool** in La Jolla and **La Jolla Cove,** which also features tidal pools and a large grassy area for picnicking. Wide and well-guarded **La Jolla Shores** beach is nicely suited for families. Other good bets include **Silver Strand State Beach** in Coronado, with its light action on the waves, and **Del Mar Beach,** a guarded spread of sand near a playground, shops, and restaurants.

If you're visiting in July, you may want to visit the Imperial Beach Pier to admire the sand castles built during Sand Castle Days (*see* Festivals and Seasonal Events *in* Chapter 1, Destination: San Diego).

Parks

Balboa Park is a must-see for those traveling with children of any age (*see* Tour 4 *in* Chapter 2, Exploring San Diego). In addition to the San Diego Zoo and museums, noted above, the park has a restored wooden carousel, a miniature train ride, a somewhat old-fashioned playground, *plenty* of grass, and, on weekends, an interesting variety of street performers.

Mission Bay Park (*see* Tour 6 *in* Chapter 2, Exploring San Diego) is another sure thing for those toting tots and older kids. The east side of the park has a series of well-equipped playgrounds and good space for flying kites. For those with slightly older children, the sidewalks around the bay are perfect for roller-blading. Belmont Park, which borders Mission Bay Park on the west, has both a restored giant roller coaster (*see* Fun Parks, *above*) and the city's most beautiful swimming pool. (Don't venture here on a sunny Saturday, however, unless you're willing to fight the crowds for a parking spot.) In addition to the sand, there's plenty of grass for lounging and picnicking. And, of course, there's the water.

Playgrounds

The high price of real estate in San Diego means not everyone has a house with a huge backyard; in addition, as in most other places, parents here use playgrounds as a guilt-free way to socialize with other parents. There are a number of well-equipped, well-maintained playgrounds in town; the **Community Parks and Recreation Department** (☎ 619/685–1300) can tell you which one is nearest your hotel.

Though there are some playgrounds in the downtown area, better ones can be found close by on the west side of Mission Bay. Doyle Community Park, near University Towne Center on Regents Road at Berino Court, has an impressive collection of new and progressive playground equipment. The playground at Kate O. Sessions Memorial Park (Pacific Beach, on Soledad Road and Loring Street) is small, but there's lots of grass for flying kites and beautiful views of the city and bay. In La Jolla, the La Jolla Recreation Center (615 Prospect St.) has both new and traditional playground equipment within smelling distance of the ocean. In Del Mar, you can push your child on the swings and watch the waves breaking down below at a small playground at the foot of 15th Street; adjacent to the park is a grassy area suitable for picnicking.

DINING

In the relaxed atmosphere for which San Diego is famous, kids are almost always welcome in restaurants, and most places make at least some accommodation for them: child-size portions; seats for children; or, at a minimum, friendliness. Generally, the only places you may wish to avoid are upscale restaurants listed in Chapter 8 in the expensive ($$$) and very expensive ($$$$) price ranges.

Restaurants

Of the places reviewed in Chapter 7, Dining, the bustling **Piatti's, California Café, The Fish Market, Hob Nob Hill, Hard Rock Cafe, Old Town Mexico Cafe, SamSon's,** and **El Indio** are particularly suited for families; your children's din will blend right in.

Other non-fast-food options for families include **Baja Grill** (1342 Camino Del Mar, Del Mar, ☎ 619/792–6551), where a fish pond will entertain your kids while you finish eating your seafood dinner in an outdoor setting; **Pizza Nova** (Costa Verde Shopping Center, on Genessee across from University Towne Center, ☎ 619/458–9525); and the **Old Spaghetti Factory** (275 5th Ave., downtown, ☎ 619/233–4323). If your children are not restaurant-trained, or if you want takeout for a nice picnic, try the terrific chicken at **Saffron** (3731 India St., downtown, ☎ 619/574–0177).

Fast-Food Outlets

Chuck E Cheese (3146 Sports Arena Blvd., Pt. Loma, ☎ 619/523–4385; other locations in Mira Mesa, La Mesa, Escondido, Oceanside, and National City) offers mediocre food in an environment given over to kids, including toys, games, and those big ball enclosures. In Del Mar, **McDonald's** (2705 Via de la Valle, ☎ 619/481–8595) and **Burger King** (12847 El Camino Real, ☎ 619/792–4011) both have playgrounds on the premises.

Sweets and Treats

There are plenty of good ice cream parlors in town, but for the full-on experience, try **Farrell's** (136 Fashion Valley, ☎ 619/291–1887), a loud, lively, and very popular sit-down place with more ice cream delights than you can eat comfortably.

LODGING

Virtually all tourist-oriented sections of San Diego have lodgings suited to a family pocketbook and/or recreational needs. The top area for all-around child appeal, however, would have to be Mission Bay, near beaches, parks, the Belmont roller coaster, and, of course, Sea World (many Mission Bay hotels offer Sea World packages or discounts). Conversely, although downtown has attractions for all ages, it's still generally desolate at night; accommodations in the lively Embarcadero section are the only ones that can be recommended.

Some of the more expensive hotels and resorts in San Diego have special activity programs and camps to keep their guests' offspring occupied; many places offer excellent family discounts, and a number of lodgings are well suited to those traveling with children because they have kitchen and laundry facilities. Unless otherwise indicated, full reviews of the following hotels are found in Chapter 8, Lodging.

Children's Programs

Loew's Coronado Bay Resort has year-round day and evening programs for children ages 4–12. Programs depend on the age of the children enrolled and include arts and crafts as well as a variety of outdoor activities. Prices are $17 per child for half-day programs, $12 for evening programs, and $30 for a full day of events. There is a discount for the second child enrolled.

During the summer, the **Hotel Del Coronado** offers a wide variety of activities, such as sand-castle-building, scavenger hunts, and educational bike rides; egg hunts are organized at spring break. There's a youth tennis program for ages 3 and up during the summer, and, for children ages 13–17, instruction in wind-surfing and sailing. Prices for the programs vary.

From Memorial Day through Labor Day, **San Diego Hilton Beach and Tennis Resort** organizes daytime and evening activities designed for children ages 6–12, including indoor and outdoor games, arts and crafts, and movies. Those under 6 may enjoy the activities, though they must be accompanied by an adult. The program is free, but parents must stay on the property. There's also a small playground on the premises and one close by with play equipment for children with disabilities.

On Friday and Saturday from Memorial Day through Labor Day, children ages 3 through 15 can take part in an evening (4–10 PM) program at the **Hyatt Islandia**; the cost for supervised activities, such as games, videos, and arts and crafts, is $5 per child per hour, $2.50 for the second child in the same family. Parents must stay on the hotel property.

The **San Diego Princess Resort** runs a Kid Camp from June through Labor Day weekend and organizes activities for children during winter and spring breaks, as well as during the Memorial Day weekend. There is also a program for teens two nights a week.

Rancho Bernardo Inn (*see* Inland North County *in* Chapter 10, Excursions from San Diego) also has a children's program during spring break, Memorial Day weekend, July 4th weekend, and the month of August.

Family Rates

Many hotels and motels run family specials or allow children to stay free in the same room with their parents, with nominal charges for cribs and $5–$10 charges for extra beds; inquire when making reservations. For example, at the sister **Catamaran** and **Bahia** hotels in Mission Bay, there's no charge for children 12 and under; at the **Hotel del Coronado,** children 15 and under stay in their parents' room gratis. Some of the **Days Inn** hotels (☎ 800/325–2525; six locations in San Diego) charge only a small fee for children under 18; all allow children 12 and under to stay in their parents' room at no extra charge. Children of any age stay free with their parents at the **San Diego Mission Valley Hilton.** Meals for children under 12 are only $1.99 at **Holiday Inn on the Bay** in the Embarcadero area.

Facilities

Although cooking and doing laundry don't play a large part in most parents' dream vacations, many like to know that the option for those activities is there—if only to ignore it. The **La Jolla Cove Motel** has kitchenettes and laundry facilities, as well as lower room rates than most hotels in the La Jolla Cove area. Farther north, **La Jolla Palms Inn** has even lower rates and offers many remarkably large rooms with huge closets; some rooms have kitchenettes, and three suites feature separate eat-in kitchens.

Embassy Suites San Diego Bay, in the Embarcadero area, has in-room refrigerators, microwaves, and separate sleeping areas. At the **Best Western Shelter Island Marina Inn,** you can book reasonably priced two-bedroom suites with eat-in kitchens. Full or partial kitchens are also available at the **Bahia** and **Catamaran** hotels in Mission Beach. In the Embarcadero section, **Holiday Inn on the Bay** has laundry facilities.

Baby-Sitting

Agencies
Many of the concierges at San Diego's best hotels recommend **Marion's Child Care** (☎ 619/582–5029) and **Reliable Baby Sitter Agency** (☎ 619/296–0856) for baby-sitting services.

THE ARTS

San Diego offers a nice range of cultural entertainment for all types of kids, whether your child is a budding violinist or thinks Yo Yo Ma is a type of string toy.

Theater

San Diego Junior Theatre (Casa del Prado, Balboa Park, ☎ 619/239–1311) puts on five productions each year, featuring student actors ages 4–18, under the direction of theater professionals.

San Diego Children's Theatre (☎ 619/675–0463) stages a few musicals each year at the Poway Center for the Performing Arts (15500 Espola Rd. , Poway, ☎ 619/748–0505), starring children 4 years of age and up.

Christian Youth Theater (☎ 619/696–1929 or 619/588–0206 for camp information), a nondenominational theater program, presents many productions by and for youths in various locations around San Diego County. Performances in 1995 included *Beauty and the Beast, The Little Mermaid,* and *Robin Hood.* It also runs classes and camps for children ages 6–18.

The **San Diego Actors Theatre** (☎ 619/268–4494) sponsors the Children's Classics series of fairy tales and children's stories adapted for the stage at L'Auberge Del Mar Garden Amphitheater (1540 Camino Del Mar, ☎ 619/259–1515). Performances of such stories as the *Mad Hatter's Tea Party, Little Red Riding Hood,* and *Rapunzel* are held on various Saturday mornings throughout the year (call ahead for schedules); child volunteers perform with the group.

For the younger set, the San Diego Guild of Puppetry operates a **Puppetry Hotline** (☎ 619/685–5045). Many of the performances are staged at the Marie Hitchcock Puppet Theater (Palisades Building, Balboa Park), which is celebrating more than 30 years of puppetry.

The oldest theater in San Diego, located in the heart of downtown, the **Spreckles Theater** (*see* Theater *in* Chapter 9, The Arts and Nightlife) has a Children's Series that includes major productions by the National Theatre for Children, the San Diego Children's Theatre, and the American Ballet Ensemble.

Music

At Copley Symphony Hall (*see* Concerts *in* Chapter 9, The Arts and Nightlife), the **San Diego Symphony** has family concerts on selected Sunday afternoons during its regular season. During the summer, the symphony sponsors outdoor Pops concerts near Seaport Village that the whole family can also enjoy.

Budding musicians will enjoy the Discovery series for rising stars put on at 3 PM on selected Sundays by the **La Jolla Chamber Music Society** (☎ 619/459–3728); concerts are held at the Sherwood Auditorium (*see* Concerts *in* Chapter 9, The Arts and Nightlife) throughout the regular season.

Art

If your kids are at least 2½ years old, you can drop them off at **Artworks** (437 S. Hwy. 101, Suite 121, Solana Beach, ☎ 619/481–2738) and let them do their thing in a variety of different art media ($10 per hour). The center also features such classes as printmaking, sculpture, drawing, painting, and woodworking; fees vary.

4 Shopping

MOST SAN DIEGO SHOPS are open daily 10–6; department stores and shops within the larger malls stay open until 9 PM on weekdays. Sales are advertised in the daily *San Diego Union–Tribune* and in the *Reader*, a free weekly that comes out on Thursday.

By Marael Johnson

Updated by Albert M. Columbo

Shopping Districts

San Diego's shopping areas are a mélange of self-contained mega-malls, historic districts, quaint villages, funky neighborhoods, and chic suburbs.

Coronado

Across the bay, Coronado is accessible by car or ferry. **Orange Avenue,** in the center of town, has six blocks of ritzy boutiques and galleries. The elegant Hotel del Coronado, also on Orange Avenue, houses exclusive (and costly) specialty shops. **Old Ferry Landing,** where the San Diego ferry lands, is a waterfront center similar to Seaport Village.

Downtown

Horton Plaza, in the heart of center city, is a shopper's Disneyland—visually exciting, multilevel department stores; one-of-a-kind shops; fast-food counters; classy restaurants; a farmers' market; live theater; and cinemas. Surrounding Horton Plaza is the Gaslamp Quarter, a redevelopment area that features art galleries, antiques, and specialty shops housed in Victorian buildings and renovated warehouses.

The Paladion, just across 1st Avenue from Horton Plaza, is San Diego's answer to Rodeo Drive. This posh complex, opened in 1992, houses a collection of upscale boutiques—including Cartier, Tiffany, Gucci, Alfred Dunhill, Gianni Versace, and Salvatore Ferragamo.

Hotel Circle

The Hotel Circle area, northeast of downtown near I–8 and Freeway 163, has two major shopping centers. **Fashion Valley** and **Mission Valley Center** contain hundreds of shops, as well as restaurants, cinemas, and branches of almost every San Diego department store.

Kensington/Hillcrest

These are two of San Diego's older, established neighborhoods, situated several miles north and east of downtown. **Adams Avenue,** in Kensington, is Antiques Row. More than 20 dealers sell everything from postcards and kitchen utensils to cut glass and porcelain. The vicinity surrounding **University Avenue** at 5th Avenue (near the neon Hillcrest sign) is populated with designer clothes shops, specialty gift shops, bookstores, and music stores. **International Male** and the **Gap** are the anchor stores among boutiques like **California Man, Gamma Gamma, London Underground,** and **Tredair UK.** University Avenue is crossed 1 mile east by **Park Boulevard,** where you'll find **Babette Schwartz's** zany pop culture store and many "nostalgia" shops featuring clothing, accessories, furnishings, and bric-a-brac of the 1920s–'60s. **Uptown District,** a shopping center on University Avenue, has the neighborhood's massive Ralph's grocery store, as well as several specialty shops.

La Jolla/Golden Triangle

La Jolla, about 15 miles northwest of downtown on the coast, is an ultra-chic, ultra-exclusive resort community. High-end and trendy bou-

64

San Diego Shopping

tiques line Girard Avenue and Prospect Street. Coast Walk, nestled along the cliffside of Prospect Street, offers several levels of sophisticated shops, galleries, and restaurants, as well as a spectacular ocean view. The Golden Triangle area, several miles east of coastal La Jolla, is served by **University Towne Centre,** between I–5 and Highway 805. This megamall features the usual range of department stores, specialty shops, sportswear chains, restaurants, and cinemas. Nearby **Costa Verde Centre,** on the corner of Genessee and La Jolla Village Drive, is an enormous strip mall of convenience stores and inexpensive eateries.

North County

This rapidly expanding area boasts an array of high-range shopping districts. One of the most attractive retail centers in the area, **Del Mar Plaza** (15th St. and Camino Del Mar) boasts a spectacular view of the Pacific and many excellent restaurants, boutiques, and specialty stores. Farther north in Encinitas is the **Lumberyard** (1st St. and Old Hwy. 1), an upscale strip mall where one can find everything from yogurt shops and stationery to sportswear and sushi. Inland from Del Mar in Escondido, one of the area's newest enclosed malls, **North County Fair** (Via Rancho Pkwy., east of Hwy. 15), is anchored by Nordstrom, Robinsons-May, and The Broadway.

Old Town

North of downtown, off I–5, this popular historic district is reminiscent of a colorful Mexican marketplace. Adobe architecture, flower-filled plazas, fountains, and courtyards highlight the shopping areas of **Bazaar del Mundo, La Esplanade,** and **Old Town Mercado,** where you will find international goods, toys, souvenirs, and arts and crafts.

Seaport Village

On the waterfront, a few minutes from downtown, **Seaport Village** offers quaint theme shops, restaurants, arts-and-crafts galleries, and commanding views of Coronado, the bridge, and passing ships.

Department Stores

The Broadway (Fashion Valley, ☎ 619/291–6011; Horton Plaza, ☎ 619/231–4747; La Jolla, ☎ 619/453–2060). This dependable emporium sells moderate to expensive name-brand contemporary clothing, accessories, gifts, and furnishings for the whole family.

Bullock's (Mission Valley Center, ☎ 619/299–9811). A division of the Federated department stores group, Bullock's offers designer apparel, fragrances, accessories, and furnishings for men, women, and teens.

Neiman-Marcus (Fashion Valley, ☎ 619/692–9100). This Texas-based department store is world-famous for fine apparel, couture, furs, jewels, accessories, and gifts.

Nordstrom (Fashion Valley, ☎ 619/295–4441; Horton Plaza, ☎ 619/239–1700; University Towne Centre, ☎ 619/457–4575). Up-to-the-minute, moderate to expensive clothing and accessories for men, women, and teens are found at these stores, noted for their extensive shoe departments and customized service.

Robinsons-May (Fashion Valley, ☎ 619/291–5800; Mission Valley Center, ☎ 619/297–2511; University Towne Centre, ☎ 619/455–5650). This chain is known for good service and frequent sales on contemporary clothing, fragrances, and accessories for the whole family.

Specialty Stores

Accessories
Bags, Belts and Beyond (7886 Girard Ave., La Jolla, ☎ 619/459–3536). Here there are discounted designer handbags, belts, costume jewelry, accessories, and collectible gift items.

Pomegranate (1152 Prospect Ave., La Jolla, ☎ 619/459–0629). Come to this store for fine accessories and exceptional antique jewelry.

Antiques
Maidhof Bros. (1891 San Diego Ave., Old Town, ☎ 619/574–1891) is one of California's oldest and largest dealers in nautical and brass items.

The OB Attic (4921 Newport Ave., Ocean Beach, ☎ 619/223–5048) features an assortment of antique and used furniture along with collectible items.

The **Olde Cracker Factory** (448 W. Market St., Gaslamp Quarter, ☎ 619/233–1669) houses three floors of specialty shops in a converted brick warehouse.

The **Private Collector** (800 W. Washington St., Mission Hills, ☎ 619/296–5553) has an extensive variety of antiques, both large and small.

Unicorn Company Arts & Antiques Mall (704 J St., Gaslamp Quarter, ☎ 619/232–1696) is the largest antiques complex in San Diego.

Art Galleries
Africa and Beyond (1250 Prospect Ave., La Jolla, ☎ 619/454–9983) has a splendid collection of ethnic art, crafts, masks, jewelry, and beads.

Porter Randall Gallery (5624 La Jolla Blvd., La Jolla, ☎ 619/551–8884) has become a major venue for contemporary art. The gallery also hosts literary events and poetry readings.

Sue Tushingham McNary Art Gallery (Hotel Del Coronado Arcade, Coronado, ☎ 619/435–1819) displays paintings, lithographs, etchings, miniatures, and prints of San Diego scenes.

Tasende Gallery (820 Prospect St., La Jolla, ☎ 619/454–3691) specializes in modern European painting and sculpture.

Thomas Babeor and Company (7470 Girard Ave., La Jolla, ☎ 619/454–0345) carries the work of nationally recognized modern European and American artists.

Bargains
The Garment Center (1911 San Diego Ave., Old Town, ☎ 619/597–0788 or 619/453–6814). This is the place for manufacturers' end-of-season merchandise, discounted up to 60%.

Nordstrom Rack (Mission Valley Center, ☎ 619/296–0143). Top-of-the-line, end-of-season collections from Nordstrom department store, at about 50% off, are featured here.

San Diego Factory Outlet Center (Camino de la Plaza, San Ysidro, last exit off I–5 before the Mexican border, ☎ 619/690–2999). There are more than 25 discount factory outlets here, including Nike, Mikasa, Levi Strauss, and Eddie Bauer.

Beachwear

Hansen's (1105 1st St., Encinitas, ☎ 619/753–6595), one of San Diego's oldest surfboard manufacturers, now also features a full line of recreational clothing and casual wear.

La Jolla Surf Systems (2132 Avenida de la Playa, La Jolla, ☎ 619/456–2777) carries swimsuits and other resort wear.

Pilar's Beach Wear (3745 Mission Blvd., Mission Beach, ☎ 619/488–3056) has one of California's largest selections of imported and American major-label swimsuits, offering mix-and-match as well as split sizes.

Bookstores

Blue Door (3823 5th Ave., Hillcrest, ☎ 619/298–8610) has an extensive selection of hard-to-find literary paperbacks, poetry, and magazines.

Esmeralda Book Shop (1555 Camino Del Mar, Del Mar, ☎ 619/755–2707), which carries hard-to-find and unusual selections along with best-sellers, has a cappuccino bar and patio.

John Cole's Book Shop (780 Prospect St., La Jolla, ☎ 619/454–4766), in a 1904 cottage with loads of character, offers a fascinating selection of books on art and architecture.

Wahrenbrock's Book House (726 Broadway, San Diego, ☎ 619/232–0132) is one of San Diego's oldest and largest used-book stores.

The White Rabbit (7755 Girard Ave., La Jolla, ☎ 619/454–3518) features books for prereaders through junior high school age.

Boutiques for Men

Custom Shirts of La Jolla (7643 Girard Ave., La Jolla, ☎ 619/459–6147) stocks fine slacks, jackets, and sportswear. Shirts are made to order from more than 300 fabrics.

Durante's (1412 Camino Del Mar, Del Mar, ☎ 619/755–0116) offers a good selection of sportswear and beach attire.

Gentleman's Quarter (1224 Prospect St., La Jolla, ☎ 619/459–3351; Flower Hill Mall, 2690 Via de la Valle, Del Mar, ☎ 619/481–7124) specializes in European designer suits, shirts, and sportswear.

International Male (3964 5th St., San Diego, ☎ 619/294–8600) sells contemporary men's fashions at reasonable prices.

Boutiques for Women

Capriccio (6919 La Jolla Blvd., La Jolla, ☎ 619/459–4189) is a *Women's Wear Daily* recommendation for high-end European and designer ensembles and elegant evening wear.

Chico's (Del Mar Plaza, Del Mar, ☎ 619/792–7080), like its Santa Fe counterpart, specializes in brightly colored, natural-fiber clothing with a southwestern accent.

Distinctions (8650 Genesee Ave., Costa Verde Center, La Jolla, ☎ 619/550–1776) showcases women's fashions in sizes 12 and up; selections range from dresses to sportswear and swimwear to formal as well as accessories.

Sigi Boutique (788 Girard Ave., La Jolla, ☎ 619/454–7244) displays a range of European clothing and accessories.

Crafts Galleries

Brushworks Gallery (425 Market St., downtown, ☎ 619/238–4381) features contemporary crafts.

International Gallery (643 G St., Gaslamp Quarter, ☎ 619/235–8255) carries fine gifts; crafts; and folk, primitive, and native art from around the world.

Food

Greentree Grocers (3560 Mt. Acacia Blvd., San Diego, ☎ 619/560–1975) features excellent organic produce, meats, and health supplies.

Horton Plaza Farmers Market (Horton Plaza, ☎ 619/696–7766) has spectacular displays of gourmet foods, including cheeses, meats, produce, and deli specialties.

Ocean Beach People's Food Co-op (4765 Voltaire St., Ocean Beach, ☎ 619/224–1387) is where you'll find San Diego's largest selection of organic grains, beans, and produce.

Trader Joe's (1211 Garnet Ave., Pacific Beach, ☎ 619/272–7235; 8657 Villa La Jolla Dr., La Jolla, ☎ 619/546–8629), part of a California chain, stocks an affordable and eclectic selection of gourmet foods from around the world.

The Vegetable Shop (6123 Calzada del Bosque, Rancho Santa Fe, ☎ 619/756–3184) is one of San Diego's greatest culinary assets. The premium fruits and vegetables picked daily make their way into such famed eateries as Berkeley's Chez Panisse and Los Angeles's Spago, as well as into many of San Diego's finer restaurants.

Jewelry

Ben Bridge Jeweler (Horton Plaza, ☎ 619/696–8911; Mission Valley Center, ☎ 619/294–2808; University Towne Centre, ☎ 619/453–9996) offers fine watches, diamonds, repairs, and custom work.

The Collector (1274 Prospect St., La Jolla, ☎ 619/454–9763) is a world-renowned source for colored gemstones and contemporary pieces designed by international jewelers and resident goldsmiths.

Gary Gilmore Goldsmith (4919 Newport Ave., Ocean Beach, ☎ 619/225–1137) carries elegant, simple jewelry crafted by the owner; you may want to buy that engagement ring here.

J. Jessop & Sons (Horton Plaza, ☎ 619/239–9311) has been in business for nearly a century, specializing in diamonds, gems, and fine watches.

Luggage

John's Fifth Avenue Luggage (3833 4th Ave., Hillcrest, ☎ 619/298–0993; Fashion Valley, ☎ 619/574–0086) has a large selection of luggage, attaché cases, and travel accessories.

Le Travel Store (Horton Plaza, ☎ 619/544–0005) stocks luggage, totes, travel packs, luggage carts, and travel accessories.

Perfume

House of Versailles (Hotel del Coronado Arcade, Coronado, ☎ 619/435–1010) is a world-famous perfumery offering custom blending and pH and fragrance compatibility analysis.

Seashells

La Jolla Cave and Shell Shop (1325 Coast Blvd., La Jolla, ☎ 619/454–6080) stocks specimen and decorative shells, coral, and nautical gifts.

Seaport Village Shell Company (817-D W. Harbor Dr., ☎ 619/234–1004) has a unique collection of shells, coral, and jewelry.

Sporting Goods

Fit for Sports (1735 University Ave., Hillcrest, ☎ 619/299–9644) carries a large assortment of well-priced running shoes, clothing, and accessories.

Ocean Enterprises (7710 Balboa Ave., Clairemont, ☎ 619/565–6054) stocks high-quality wet suits, dry suits, and skin- and scuba-diving equipment.

Oshman's Sporting Goods (Mission Valley Center, ☎ 619/299–0701) has all types of athletic and camping equipment, including athletic shoes and sportswear.

Swap Meets

Bargain shoppers spend their weekend mornings at **Kobey's Swap Meet** (3500 Sports Arena Blvd., near Midway and Rosecrans, ☎ 619/226–0650). The open-air market seems to expand every week, with sellers displaying everything from futons to fresh strawberries from the farming communities. The back section with secondhand goods is a bargain-hunter's delight. Admission to the swap meet, open Thursday–Sunday 7 AM–3 PM, is $1.

Toys

Imaginarium (322 Horton Plaza, ☎ 619/237–0122; University Towne Centre, ☎ 619/755–4488) offers toys, dolls, and educational materials from all around the world.

Thinker Things (2670 Via de la Valle, Del Mar, ☎ 619/755–4488) carries an extensive collection of dolls and puppets in addition to its toys, crafts, and games.

Toys "R" Us (1240 W. Morena Blvd., Mission Bay area, ☎ 619/276–7094; 1240 Auto Pkwy., Escondido, ☎ 619/747–4975) is a supermarket of toys, stuffed animals, and games for all ages.

T-Shirts

Pacific Eyes & T's (1241 Prospect St., La Jolla, ☎ 619/454–7532; 2461 San Diego Ave., Old Town, ☎ 619/692–0059) has T-shirts in every price category.

5 Beaches

By Kevin Brass

Updated by
Albert M.
Columbo

SAN DIEGO'S BEACHES are one of its greatest natural attractions. In some places, the shorefront is wide and sandy; in others, it's narrow and rocky or backed by impressive sandstone cliffs. You'll find beaches teeming with activities and deserted spots for romantic sunset walks. San Diego is a prime destination for surfers; the variety of breaks and their exposure to ocean swells make the surf off this portion of the Pacific coast remarkably consistent and fun. For a surf and weather report, call 619/221–8884.

Overnight camping is not allowed on any San Diego city beaches, but there are campgrounds at some state beaches throughout the county; call 800/444–7275 for state beach camping reservations. Lifeguards are stationed at city beaches (from Sunset Cliffs to Black's Beach) in the summertime, but coverage in winter is provided by roving patrols only. Dogs are not permitted at most beaches in San Diego, and tickets for breaking the law can be very expensive. However, it is rarely a problem to bring your pet to isolated beaches during the winter.

Pay attention to all signs listing illegal activities; undercover police often patrol the beaches, carrying their ticket books in coolers. Glass is prohibited on all beaches, and fires are allowed only in fire rings or barbecues. Alcoholic beverages—including beer—are completely banned on some city beaches; others allow you to partake between 8 AM and 8 PM only. Check out the signs posted at the parking lots and lifeguard towers before you hit the shore with a six pack or some wine coolers. Imbibing in beach parking lots, on boardwalks, and in landscaped areas is always illegal; where drinking is permitted, stay on the sand. For more information on the beach-booze ban, call Pacific Beach Community Relations (☎ 619/581–9920) or Ocean Beach Community Relations (☎ 619/531–1540). For a general beach and weather report, phone 619/289–1212.

Beaches are listed from south to north. For information on Mission Bay, *see* Tour 6 *in* Chapter 2, Exploring San Diego.

South Bay

Border Field State Beach. The southernmost San Diego beach is different from the majority of California beaches. Located just north of the Mexican border, it is a marshy area with wide chaparrals and wildflowers, a favorite among horse riders and hikers. However, frequent sewage contamination from Tijuana makes the water dangerous for swimming. For this reason, the beach is often closed. There is ample parking, and there are rest rooms and fire rings. *Exit I–5 at Dairy Mart Rd. and head west along Monument Rd.*

South Beach. One of the few beaches where dogs are free to romp, this is a good spot for long, isolated walks. The often-contaminated water and rocky beach tend to discourage crowds. The downside: There are few facilities, such as rest rooms, and sewage contamination from Tijuana can create a health hazard at times. *Located at end of Seacoast Dr. Take I–5 to Coronado Ave. and head west on Imperial Beach Ave. Turn left onto Seacoast Dr.*

Imperial Beach. In July, this classic southern California beach is the site of one of the nation's largest annual sand-castle competitions. Surfers and swimmers flock here to enjoy the water, waves, and beach, which is an ideal playing field for the Frisbee games of the predominantly young crowd. There are lifeguards on duty during the summer, parking lots,

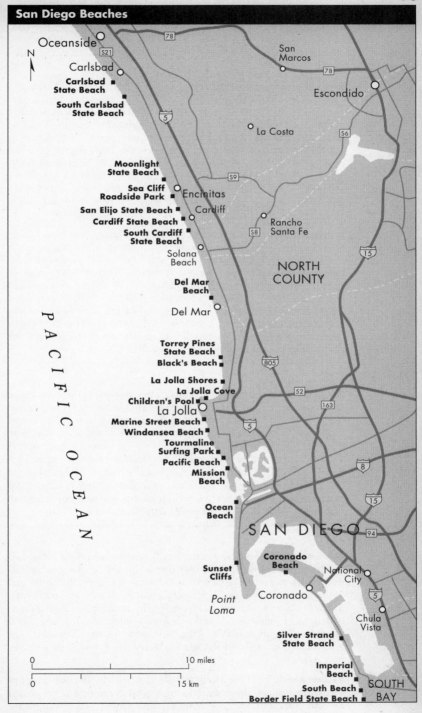

San Diego Beaches

Oceanside

Carlsbad

Carlsbad State Beach

South Carlsbad State Beach

San Marcos

Escondido

La Costa

Moonlight State Beach

Sea Cliff Roadside Park

Encinitas

Cardiff

San Elijo State Beach

Cardiff State Beach

South Cardiff State Beach

Solana Beach

Rancho Santa Fe

NORTH COUNTY

Del Mar Beach

Del Mar

Torrey Pines State Beach

Black's Beach

La Jolla Shores

La Jolla Cove

Children's Pool

La Jolla

Marine Street Beach

Windansea Beach

Tourmaline Surfing Park

Pacific Beach

Mission Beach

PACIFIC OCEAN

Ocean Beach

SAN DIEGO

Coronado Beach

National City

Sunset Cliffs

Point Loma

Coronado

Chula Vista

Silver Strand State Beach

Imperial Beach

0   10 miles

0   15 km

South Beach

Border Field State Beach

SOUTH BAY

food vendors nearby, and rest rooms. Note: Although the surf here can be excellent, this is another spot at which to be careful of sewage contamination. *Take Palm Ave. west from I–5 until it hits water.*

Coronado

Silver Strand State Beach. Farther north on the isthmus of Coronado (commonly mislabeled an island), Silver Strand was set aside as a state beach in 1932. The name is derived from the tiny silver seashells found in abundance near the water. The water is relatively calm, making this beach ideal for families. Four parking lots provide room for more than 1,500 cars. Parking is free from Labor Day through February; the rest of the year the cost is $4 per car. There is also an RV campground (cost: $14 per night) and a wide array of facilities but no hook-ups; spots are available on a first-come, first-served basis. ☎ 619/435–5184. *Take the Palm Ave. exit from I–5 west to Hwy. 75; turn right and follow signs.*

Coronado Beach. With the famous Hotel Del Coronado as a backdrop, this wide stretch of sandy beach is one of the largest and most picturesque in the county. It is surprisingly uncrowded on most days, since the locals go to the less touristy areas in the south or north. It's perfect for sunbathing or games of Frisbee and Smash Ball (played with paddles and a small ball). Parking can be a little difficult on the busiest days, but there are plenty of rest rooms and service facilities, as well as fire rings. The view (even for a brief moment) as you drive over the Coronado Bridge makes it a worthwhile excursion. *From bridge, turn left on Orange Ave. and follow signs.*

Point Loma

Sunset Cliffs. Beneath the jagged cliffs on the west side of the Point Loma peninsula is one of the more secluded beaches in the area, popular primarily with surfers and locals. The tide goes out each day to reveal tidal pools teeming with life at the south end of the peninsula, near Cabrillo Point. Farther north, the often-large waves attract surfers and the lonely coves attract sunbathers. Stairs are available at the foot of Bermuda and Santa Cruz avenues, but much of the access is limited to treacherous cliff trails. There are no facilities. Your visit here will be much more enjoyable at low tide; check the local newspaper for tide schedules. *Take I–8 west to Sunset Cliffs Blvd. and head south.*

San Diego

Ocean Beach. The north end of this beach, past the second jetty, is known as Dog Beach because it's the only one within the San Diego city limits that allows canines to romp around without a leash. The south end of Ocean Beach, near the pier, is a hangout for surfers and transients. Much of the area, though, is a haven for local volleyball players, sunbathers, and swimmers. You'll find food vendors and fire rings here; limited parking is available. *Take I–8 west to Sunset Cliffs Blvd. and head south. Turn right on Voltaire St., West Point Loma Blvd., or Newport Ave.*

Mission Beach. The boardwalk stretching along Mission Beach is popular with strollers, roller skaters, and bicyclists cruising at the posted 15-mph speed limit. Surfers, swimmers, and volleyball players congregate at the south end, which tends to get extremely crowded, especially on hot summer days. Toward the north end, near the Belmont Park roller coaster, the beach narrows and the water grows rougher—and the crowd gets even thicker. The refurbished Belmont Park is now a shopping and dining complex. Parking can be a challenge, but there are plenty of rest rooms and restaurants in the area. *Exit I–5 at Garnet Ave. and head west to Mission Blvd. Turn south and look for parking.*

Pacific Beach. The boardwalk turns into a sidewalk here, but there are still bike paths and picnic tables running along the beachfront. The beach is a favorite for families, teens, and surfers alike. Parking can be a problem, although there is a small lot at the foot of Ventura Place. *Exit I–5 at Garnet Ave. and head west to Mission Blvd. Turn north and look for parking.*

La Jolla

The beaches of La Jolla combine unusual beauty with good fishing, exciting scuba diving, and excellent surf. On the down side, they are very crowded and have limited parking facilities. Don't even think about bringing your pet—dogs are not even allowed on the sidewalks above some La Jolla beaches.

Tourmaline Surfing Park and **Windansea Beach.** These La Jolla beaches are two of the top surfing spots in the area. Tourmaline has the better parking area of the two and is more hospitable to tourists. The surf at Windansea is world-class, but the local crowd can be less than welcoming. *Take Mission Blvd. north (it turns into La Jolla Blvd.) and turn west on Tourmaline St. (for the surfing park) or Nautilus St. (for Windansea Beach).*

Marine Street Beach. This is an ideal stretch of sand for sunbathing and beach games. *Accessible from Marine St. off La Jolla Blvd.*

Children's Pool. For the tykes, a circular sea wall preserves this shallow lagoon. Small waves and no riptide provides a safe, if crowded, haven. *Follow La Jolla Blvd. north. When it forks, take the left, Coast Blvd.*

Shell Beach. Just north of the Children's Pool is a small cove, accessible by stairs, with a relatively secluded and beautiful beach. The exposed rocks just off the coast here have been designated a protected habitat for seals; you can watch them sun themselves and frolic in the water. *Continue along Coast Blvd. north from the Children's Pool.*

La Jolla Cove. Just north of Shell Beach is La Jolla Cove, one of the prettiest spots in the world. A beautiful, palm-tree-lined park sits on top of cliffs formed by the incessant pounding of the waves. At low tide the tidal pools and cliff caves provide an exciting destination for explorers. Divers explore the underwater delights of the San Diego–La Jolla Underwater Park, an ecological reserve. The cove is also a favorite of rough-water swimmers, for whom buoys mark distances. The beach below the cove is beautiful and great for kids over 8 years old. *Follow Coast Blvd. north to signs, or take the La Jolla Village Dr. exit from I–5, head west to Torrey Pines Rd., turn left and drive down hill to Girard Ave. Turn right and follow signs.*

La Jolla Shores. This is one of the most popular and overcrowded beaches in the county. On holidays, such as Memorial Day, all access routes are usually closed. The lures are a wide sandy beach; fun surf for boogie-boarders, body-surfers, and regular surfers alike; and a concrete boardwalk paralleling the beach. There is also a wide variety of facilities, from posh restaurants to snack shops, within walking distance. Go early to get a parking spot. *From I–5 take La Jolla Village Dr. west* *and turn left onto La Jolla Shores Dr. Head west to Camino del Oro or Vallecitos St. Turn right and look for parking.*

Black's Beach. The late 1970s prohibition against public nudity doesn't stop nudists from frequenting this isolated beach. The cliffs should be avoided because of recent weakening by storms. Access along the shore should coincide with low tides. The powerful waves attract surfers, and secluded trails attract nudist nature lovers. There are no lifeguards on duty, and strong ebb tides are common: Only experienced swimmers should take the plunge. *Take Genessee Ave. west from I–5 and follow signs to glider port; easier access, via a paved path, is available on La Jolla Farms Rd., but parking there is limited to 2 hrs.*

Del Mar

Torrey Pines State Beach. This is one of the easiest and most comfortable beaches to visit in the area. The large parking lot ($4) is rarely full. There is year-round lifeguard service, and fire rings are available for beach parties. Torrey Pines tends to get crowded during the summer, but more isolated spots under the cliffs are within a short walk in either direction. Exotic trails up into the hillside park offer lovely hikes. ☎ *619/755–2063. Take the Carmel Valley Rd. exit west from I–5. ☉ Daily 9–sunset.*

Del Mar Beach. The numbered streets of Del Mar, from 15th to 29th, end at a wide, sandy beach, popular with volleyball players, surfers, and sunbathers. Although parking can be a problem on nice summer days, access is relatively easy, and the beach and water are both extremely comfortable. The portions of Del Mar south of 15th Street are lined with beautiful cliffs and are rarely crowded. Leashed dogs are permitted on most sections of Del Mar Beach year-round; between October and May, dogs may run free at Rivermouth, Del Mar's northernmost beach. During the annual summer meeting of the Del Mar Thoroughbred Club, horse bettors can be seen sitting on the beach in the morning working on the *Daily Racing Form* before heading across the street to the track in the afternoon. *Take the Via de la Valle exit from I–5 west to Old Hwy. 101 (also known as Camino del Mar in Del Mar) and turn left.*

Solana Beach

Most of the beaches of this little city are tucked away under cliffs; access is limited to private stairways. But at the west end of Lomas Santa Fe Drive, at a beach area known to the locals as Pillbox because of the bunkerlike structures on top of the cliffs, you'll find a large parking lot, rest rooms, and easy access to a small cove beach. During low tide, it's an easy walk to the beaches under the cliffs. *From I–5 take Lomas Santa Fe Dr. west to its end.*

Cardiff

The area along Old Highway 101 north of Solana Beach is blessed with three state beaches. A small parking lot immediately to the north of the cliffs of Solana Beach marks **South Cardiff State Beach.** A reef break makes it extremely popular with surfers, which is also true of **Cardiff State Beach,** a mile to the north. A full campground with store and shower facilities can be found at **San Elijo State Beach,** a little farther to the north. Parking at state beaches is $4 per car. For camping reservations at San Elijo, call 800/444–7275. *From I–5, turn west on Lomas Santa Fe Dr. to Old Hwy. 101 and turn right.*

Encinitas

Undoubtedly one of the most picturesque spots in the county is **Sea Cliff Roadside Park,** off Old Highway 101 on the south end of Encinitas. Palm trees and the golden domes of the nearby Self Realization Fellowship earned the beach its local nickname, Swami's. It is also considered to be one of the top surfing spots in the area. The only access to the beach is by a long stairway leading down from the clifftop park. *Follow Old Hwy. 101 north from Cardiff, or exit I–5 at Encinitas Blvd., go west to Old Hwy. 101, and turn left.*

Tucked into a break in the cliffs a mile to the north is **Moonlight State Beach,** with large parking areas and full facilities. *Take the Encinitas Blvd. exit from I–5 and head west until you hit the Moonlight parking lot.*

Carlsbad

Winter storms badly erode the southern Carlsbad beaches, leaving them somewhat rockier than most other southern California beaches. This is particularly true of **South Carlsbad State Beach,** which has lost large amounts of sand over the years. Still, it's an excellent swimming spot, and there is overnight camping (☎ 800/444–7275). No overnight camping is allowed at **Carlsbad State Beach,** farther to the north, but there is a fishing area and a parking lot. In 1987, a boardwalk was built that runs below the cliffs a bit to the north and has eased access to the Carlsbad beaches. *Exit I–5 at La Costa Ave. and head west to Old Hwy. 101. Turn north and follow coastline.*

Oceanside

Two miles of wide, sandy beaches are extremely popular with swimmers, surfers, and marines from nearby Camp Pendleton. The surf is good around the Oceanside Pier at the foot of 6th Avenue and on either side of the two jetties. The exceptionally sandy beaches are ideal for almost all beach sports. *Take Vista Way west from I–5 to Hill St. (Old Hwy. 101) and turn right. Best access points are from Cassidy St. and the Oceanside Harbor area.*

6 Sports and the Outdoors

PARTICIPANT SPORTS

Updated by
Albert M.
Columbo

At least one stereotype of San Diego is true—it is an active, outdoors-oriented community. People recreate more than spectate. It's hard not to, with such a wide variety of choices available.

Ballooning

Enjoy the views of the Pacific Ocean, the mountains, and the coastline south to Mexico and north to San Clemente from a hot-air balloon at sunrise or sunset. The conditions are perfect: necessary winds and wide-open spaces. Ballooning companies operating in the San Diego area include **California Dreamin'** (2153 Woodland Heights Glen, Escondido, ☎ 619/471–1393 or 800/794–7599), **Pacific Horizons** (16236 San Dieguito Rd., Rancho Santa Fe, ☎ 619/756–1790 or 800/244–1790), and **Skysurfer Balloon Company** (1221 Camino Del Mar, Del Mar, ☎ 619/481–6800 or 800/660–6809).

Bicycling

On any given summer day, Old Highway 101, from La Jolla to Oceanside, looks like a freeway for cyclists. Never straying more than a quarter mile from the beach, it is easily the most popular and scenic bike route around. Although the roads are narrow and winding, experienced cyclists like to follow Lomas Santa Fe Drive in Solana Beach east into beautiful Rancho Santa Fe, perhaps even continuing east on Del Dios Highway, past Lake Hodges, to Escondido. For more leisurely rides, Mission Bay, San Diego Harbor, and the Mission Beach boardwalk are all flat and scenic. For those who like to race on a track, San Diego even has a velodrome in Balboa Park. Call the Velodrome Office (☎ 619/296–3345) for more information. San Diego County also offers challenging mountain-bike trails. Local bookstores and camping stores sell trail guides.

Bikes can be rented at any number of places, including **Bicycle Barn** in Pacific Beach (746 Emerald St., ☎ 619/581–3665) and **Hamel's Action Sports Center** in Mission Beach (704 Ventura Pl, ☎ 619/488–5050). **Performance Bicycle Shop** (3619 Midway Dr., ☎ 619/223–5415), known for its catalogue business, has an impressive supply of bicycles and bicycling accessories at its San Diego location. A free comprehensive map of all county bike paths is available from the local office of the **California Department of Transportation** (2829 Juan St., Old Town, ☎ 619/688–6699).

Bocce Ball

The popular Italian version of lawn bowling is played on Monday, Wednesday, and Friday, from 1 to 5 PM, on courts in the Morley Field section of Balboa Park. The games are open to the public, and there are usually bocce balls at the courts. Call 619/692–4919 for more information.

Diving

Enthusiasts from all over the world flock to San Diego to skin-dive and scuba-dive in the areas off La Jolla and Point Loma that are rich in ocean creatures and flora. At La Jolla Cove, you'll find the **San Diego–La Jolla Underwater Park,** an ecological preserve. Farther north, off the south end of Black's Beach, the rim of **Scripps Canyon** lies in about 60 feet of water. The canyon plummets to more than 900 feet in some sections. Another popular diving spot is Sunset Cliffs in Point Loma, where a wide variety of sea life is relatively close to shore. Strong rip currents make it an area best enjoyed by experienced divers.

Diving equipment and boat trips can be arranged through **San Diego Divers Supply** (☎ 619/224–3439), **Ocean Enterprises** (☎ 619/565–6054), **Del Mar Ocean Sports** (☎ 619/792–1903), or at the several **Diving Locker** locations throughout the area. It is illegal to take any wildlife from the ecological preserves in La Jolla or near Cabrillo Point. Spearfishing requires a license (available at most dive stores), and it is illegal to take out-of-season lobster and game fish out of the water. For general diving information, contact the San Diego City Lifeguards' Office (☎ 619/221–8884).

Fishing

Variety is the key. The Pacific Ocean is full of corbina, croaker, and halibut just itching to be your dinner. No license is required to fish from a public pier, such as the Ocean Beach pier. A fishing license from the state Department of Fish and Game (☎ 619/525–4215), available at most bait-and-tackle stores, is required for fishing from the shoreline, although children under 15 won't need one.

There is also a wealth of well-stocked freshwater lakes in the area. Lake Jennings and Lake San Vicente in the East County are popular spots for catching trout and bass. Lakes Morena and Jennings offer both fishing and camping facilities. For general information on lakes, call 619/465–3474. Three freshwater lakes—Dixon, Hodges, and Wohlford—surround the North County city of Escondido. Camping is allowed at Wohlford at the Oakvale R.V. Park (☎ 619/749–2895) and at Lyle's at Dixon Lake (☎ 619/741–3328; Dixon Lake ranger station, ☎ 619/741–4680). Boats can be rented at all the above-mentioned lakes; a state fishing license is required.

Several companies offer half-day, day, or multiday fishing expeditions in search of marlin, tuna, albacore, and other deep-water fish. **Fisherman's Landing** (☎ 619/221–8500), **H & M Landing** (☎ 619/222–1144), and **Seaforth Boat Rentals** (☎ 619/223–7584) are among the companies operating from San Diego. **Helgren's Sportfishing** (☎ 619/722–2133) offers trips from Oceanside Harbor.

Fitness

Several hotels offer full health clubs, at least with weight machines, stationary bicycles, and spas. These include, in the downtown area, the **Doubletree San Diego** (910 Broadway Circle, ☎ 619/239–2200) and the **Pan Pacific** (400 W. Broadway, ☎ 619/239–4500). Other hotels with health clubs are the **Hotel del Coronado** (1500 Orange Ave., Coronado, ☎ 619/435–6611); **La Costa Resort and Spa** (Costa del Mar Rd., Carlsbad, ☎ 619/438–9111); **Le Meridien** (2000 2nd St., Coronado, ☎ 619/435–3000); the **San Diego Hilton Beach and Tennis Resort** (1775 E. Mission Bay Dr., Mission Bay, ☎ 619/276–4010); and the **Sheratons on Harbor Island** (1380 Harbor Island Dr., Harbor Island, ☎ 619/291–6400).

Guests of the **Hanalei Hotel** (2270 Hotel Circle N, ☎ 619/297–1101) have access to the tennis and racquetball courts, weight room, saunas, and other facilities of the nearby **Mission Valley Health Club** (901 Hotel Circle S, ☎ 619/298–9321). Guests of the **Hyatt Regency** in La Jolla (3777 La Jolla Village Dr., ☎ 619/552–1234) can use the splendid facilities at the **Sporting Club at Aventine** (8930 University Center

La., ☎ 619/552–8000). The dozen **Family Fitness Centers** in the area (including centers in Mission Valley, ☎ 619/281–5543; Sports Arena/Point Loma area, ☎ 619/224–2902; and Golden Triangle/UTC, ☎ 619/457–3930) allow nonmembers to use the facilities for a small fee. Both **Gold's Gym** (249 Garnet Ave., ☎ 619/272–3400) in Mission Beach and the downtown **Bodyworks Health & Fitness** (1130 7th Ave., ☎ 619/232–5500) allow nonmembers to use the facilities for a small fee. If you just want a good old-fashioned workout, **Bodybuilders** (3647 India St., Middletown, ☎ 619/299–2639), a co-ed gym, has a daily rate for visitors ($7 per visit).

Frisbee Golf

This is just like golf, except it's played with Frisbees. A course, laid out at Morley Field in Balboa Park, is open seven days a week from dawn to dusk, and there is no charge to play. Rules are posted. Directions to the field are available from the always-genial Balboa Park Information Center (☎ 619/239–0512).

Golf

It would be difficult to find a better place to play golf year-round than San Diego. The climate—generally sunny, without a lot of wind—is perfect for the sport, and there are courses in the area to suit every level of expertise. Experienced golfers can play the same greens as PGA-tournament participants, while beginners or rusty players can book a week at a golf resort and benefit from expert instruction. You'd also be hard-pressed to find a locale that has more scenic courses, offering everything from sweeping views of the ocean to lovely, verdant hills inland.

As you may expect, these advantages make San Diego very popular with golfers; during busy vacation seasons, it can be difficult to get a good tee-off time. Call in advance to see if it's possible to make a reservation. You don't necessarily have to stay at a resort to play its course; check if the one you're interested in is open to nonguests. Most public courses in the area offer an inexpensive current list of fees and charges for all San Diego courses. The **Southern California Golf Association** (☎ 818/980–3630 or 213/877–0901) publishes an annual directory with detailed and valuable information on all member clubs. Another good resource for golfers is the **Southern California Public Links Information Service** (☎ 714/994–4747). The following is not intended to be a comprehensive list but offers suggestions on some of the best places to play in the area.

Public Courses

Carmel Mountain Ranch Country Club (14050 Carmel Ridge Rd., San Diego, ☎ 619/487–9224): 18 holes, driving range, equipment rentals. A challenging course with many difficult holes, Carmel Mountain Ranch is not particularly scenic: It's in a suburban area and runs through a housing development.

Coronado Golf Course (2000 Visalia Row, Coronado, ☎ 619/435–3121): 18 holes, driving range, equipment rentals, clubhouse. Views of San Diego Bay and the Coronado Bridge from the back nine holes on this good walking course make it very popular—and rather difficult to get on.

Eastlake Country Club (2375 Clubhouse Dr., Chula Vista, ☎ 619/482–5757): 18 holes, driving range, equipment rental, snack bar. This new facility is a fun course for golfers of almost all levels of expertise; it's not overly difficult, and features such as water hazards provide a challenge.

Four Seasons Resort–Aviara (7447 Batiquitos Dr., Carlsbad, ☎ 619/929–0077): 18 holes, driving range, equipment rental. The resort that Aviara was supposed to anchor has not yet materialized, but this well-maintained Arnold Palmer–designed course was ranked by *Golf Digest* as one of the five best new resort golf courses for 1992.

Mission Bay Golf Course (2702 N. Mission Bay Dr., San Diego, ☎ 619/490–3370): 18 holes, driving range, equipment rentals. A not-very-challenging executive (par 3 and 4) course, Mission Bay is lit for night play.

Mt. Woodson Country Club (16422 North Woodson, Ramona, ☎ 619/788–3555): 18 holes, equipment rentals, golf shop, snack bar. This heavily wooded course in the mountains outside San Diego offers scenic views and interesting wooden cart bridges.

Rancho San Diego Golf Course (3121 Willow Glen Rd., El Cajon, ☎ 619/442–9891): 36 holes, driving range, equipment rentals. A good walking course, Rancho San Diego has nice putting greens and lots of cottonwood trees.

Redhawk Golf Course (45100 Redhawk Pkwy., Temecula, ☎ 909/695–1424 or 800/451–HAWK in CA): 18 holes, driving range, golf shop, snack bar. The extremely difficult design of this course will prove frustrating to those who are not experienced golfers, but experts should enjoy Redhawk.

Steele Canyon Golf Course (3199 Stonefield Dr., Jamul, ☎ 619/441–6900): 27 holes, driving range, golf shop, and snack bar. Carts are a necessity at this very hilly, Gary Player–designed course with lovely views.

Torrey Pines Municipal Golf Course (11480 N. Torrey Pines Rd., La Jolla, ☎ 619/452–3226): 36 holes, driving range, equipment rentals. One of the best public golf courses in the United States, Torrey Pines offers stunning views of the Pacific from every hole and is sufficiently challenging to host the Buick Invitational in February. It's not easy to get a good tee time at this justly popular course, but every golfer visiting the area should try to play it at least once.

Resorts

Carlton Oaks Lodge and Country Club (9200 Inwood Dr., Santee, ☎ 619/448–4242): 18 holes, driving range, equipment rentals, clubhouse. Many local qualifying tournaments are held at this very difficult, Pete Dye–designed course, with lots of trees and water hazards.

Carmel Highland Doubletree Golf and Tennis Resort (14455 Penasquitos Dr., San Diego, ☎ 619/672–9100): 18 holes, driving range, equipment rental, clubhouse. This fairly hilly, well-maintained resort course is just across I–15 from the Carmel Mountain Ranch public course (*see above*).

Handlery Hotel & Country Club (950 Hotel Circle, San Diego, ☎ 619/298–0511): 27 holes, driving range, equipment rentals. Offering an excellent staff of professional instructors, Handlery resort also features nice putting greens on its challenging course. It's perfect for golfers who want a vacation with lessons.

La Costa Resort and Spa (Costa del Mar Rd., Carlsbad, ☎ 619/438–9111 or 800/854–5000): 36 holes, driving range, clubhouse, equipment rental, pro shop. One of the premier golf resorts in southern

California, La Costa hosts the annual PGA and Senior PGA Tournament of Champions in January. You'll find every golf amenity on the premises: a nice driving range, an excellent golf school, and a fabulous pro shop. All this doesn't come cheap, but, then again, how many courses will send a limo to pick you up at the airport?

Pala Mesa Resort (2001 Old Hwy. 395, Fallbrook, ☎ 619/728–5881): 18 holes, driving range, equipment rentals. Narrow fairways help make this a very challenging course, but it's well maintained and offers nice views of the inland mountains.

Rancho Bernardo Inn and Country Club (17550 Bernardo Oaks Dr., Rancho Bernardo, ☎ 800/542–6096): 18 holes, driving range, equipment rentals. The golf's fine here, and Rancho Bernardo Inn lays out one of the best Sunday brunches in the county.

Singing Hills Country Club (3007 Dehesa Rd., El Cajon, ☎ 619/442–3425): 54 holes, driving range, equipment rentals. Set in a canyon surrounded by small mountains, this lush, green course has lots of water hazards. One of *Golf Digest*'s favorites, Singing Hills comes very highly recommended by everyone who's played it. Hackers will love the executive par-3 course; seasoned golfers can play the championship courses.

Temecula Creek Inn Golf Resort (44501 Rainbow Canyon Rd., Temecula, ☎ 909/694–1000): 27 holes, golf shop. Not only does it have a picturesque, wooded course, but Temecula Creek also features one of the best restaurants in the county and is near a number of wineries.

Whispering Palms Country Club (5690 Concah del Golf, Rancho Santa Fe, ☎ 619/756–2471): 27 holes, driving range, equipment rental, pro shop. The well-maintained Whispering Palms, a nice walking course in a pretty area near polo grounds and stables, is one of the more popular places to play in the San Diego area.

Hang Gliding

The **Torrey Pines Glider Port,** perched on the cliffs overlooking the ocean just north of La Jolla, is one of the most spectacular—and easiest—spots to hang glide in the world. However, it is definitely for experienced pilots only. Hang-gliding lessons are available from **Hang Gliding Center** (☎ 619/450–9008) and **Ultimate High Aviation** (☎ 619/748–1739), among others. For general information about the gliderport, contact the Torrey Pines Hang Gliders Association (☎ 619/457–9093).

Horseback Riding

Expensive insurance has severely cut the number of stables that offer horses for rent in San Diego County. The businesses that remain have a wide variety of organized excursions. **Holidays on Horseback** (☎ 619/445–3997), in the East County town of Descanso, leads rides ranging from a few hours to a few days in the Cuyamaca Mountains. It rents special, easy-to-ride fox trotters to beginners. **Bright Valley Farm** (11990 Campo Rd., Spring Valley, ☎ 619/670–1861) is a wonderful place to ride. South of Imperial Beach, near the Mexican border, **Sandi's Rental Stables** (☎ 619/424–3124) leads rides through Border Field State Park.

Jet Skiing

Waveless Mission Bay and the small Snug Harbor Marina (☎ 619/434–3089), just east of the intersection of Tamarack Avenue and I–5 in Carlsbad, are favorite spots for this exhilarating sport. **California Water Sports** (☎ 619/434–3089) has information about equipment rentals and purchases. Jet Skis can be launched from most beaches, although they need to be ridden beyond surf lines, and some beaches have special regulations governing their use. **Seaforth Boat Rentals** (☎ 619/223–1681) rents Jet Skis for use in the South Bay Marina, and they are also available at Snug Harbor in Carlsbad.

Jogging

There is no truth to the rumor that San Diego was created to be one big jogging track, but it often seems that way. From downtown, the most popular run is along the Embarcadero, which stretches around the bay. There are nice, uncongested sidewalks through most of the area. The alternative for downtown visitors is to head east to Balboa Park, where a labyrinth of trails snake through the canyons. Mission Bay, renowned for its wide sidewalks and basically flat landscape, may be the most popular jogging spot in San Diego. Trails head west around Fiesta Island from Mission Bay, providing distance as well as a scenic route. Del Mar has the finest running trails along the bluff; park your car near 15th Street and run south along the cliffs for a gorgeous view of the ocean. There are organized runs almost every weekend. For more information, call *Competitor* magazine (☎ 619/793–2711) or the **San Diego Track Club** (☎ 800/450–7382). **The Tinley Store** (1229 Camino Del Mar, ☎ 619/755–8015) has all the supplies and information you'll need for running in San Diego. Some tips: Don't run in bike lanes, and check the local newspaper's tide charts before heading to the beach.

Off-Road Driving

The 40,000-acre Ocotillo Wells State Vehicular Recreation Area (☎ 619/767–5391) provides plenty of room to ride around in dune buggies and on motorcycles and three-wheel vehicles. It can be reached by following Highway 78 east from Julian.

Rollerblading

The sidewalks at Mission Bay are perfect for rollerblading; you can admire the sailboats and kites while you get some exercise. You can rent Rollerblades at **Hamel's Action Sports Center** in Mission Beach (☎ 619/488–5050) and at the **Bicycle Barn** in Pacific Beach (☎ 619/581–3665).

Sailing

The city that is hosting the 1995 America's Cup Races is perfect for sailing. The winds are consistent, especially during the winter. If you're bringing your boat to San Diego, there are several marinas that rent slips to the public, including the **Best Western Shelter Island Marina Inn** (2051 Shelter Island Dr., ☎ 619/223–0301); the **Dana Inn and Marina** (1710 W. Mission Bay Dr., ☎ 619/222–6440); **Hyatt Islandia** (1441 Quivira Rd., ☎ 619/224–1234); the **Kona Kai Club** (1551 Shelter Island Dr., ☎ 619/222–1191); the **San Diego Marriott** (333 W. Harbor Dr., ☎ 619/234–1500); and the **Sunroad Resort Marina** (955 Harbor Island Dr., ☎ 619/574–0736). Both the **San Diego Yacht Club** (1011 Anchorage La., ☎ 619/222–1103) and the **Southwestern Yacht Club** (2702 Qualtrough St., ☎ 619/222–0438) have reciprocal arrangements with other yacht clubs.

If you left your boat at home, vessels of various sizes and shapes, from small paddleboats to sleek 12-meters, can be rented from the **Bahia Resort Hotel** (998 W. Mission Bay Dr., ☎ 619/488–0551); the **Catamaran Resort Hotel** (3999 Mission Blvd., ☎ 619/488–1081); **Harbor Sailboats** (2040 Harbor Island Dr., ☎ 619/291–9570); the **Hotel Del Coronado** (1500 Orange Ave., Coronado, ☎ 619/435–6611); the **Hyatt Islandia** (1441 Quivira Rd., ☎ 619/224–1234); the **Mission Bay Sports Center** (1010 Santa Clara Pl., ☎ 619/488–1004); and **Seaforth Boat Rental** (1641 Quivira Rd., ☎ 619/223–1681).

If you'd rather leave the sailing to others, charters with full crews can be arranged through the **Charter Connection** (7045 Charmant Dr., No. 2, ☎ 619/224–8585); **Fraser Charters, Inc.** (2353 Shelter Island Dr., ☎ 619/225–0588); **Hornblower Dining Yachts** (2825 5th Ave., ☎ 619/238–1686); and **Interpac Yachts** (1050 Anchorage La., ☎ 619/222–0327). **Harbor Sailboats** (2040 Harbor Island Dr., Suite 104, ☎ 619/291–9570) and the **Mission Bay Sports Center** (1010 Santa Clara Pl., ☎ 619/488–1004) offer lessons. For general information, including tips on overnight anchoring, contact the Harbor Police (☎ 619/291–3900).

Skiing

Have breakfast on the beach and ski in the afternoon. Several ski resorts are within a two- to four-hour drive. In the Big Bear Lake area, in the San Bernardino Mountains east of Los Angeles, **Bear Mountain Ski Resort** (☎ 909/585–2517), **Snow Summit** (☎ 909/866–5766), and **Snow Valley** (☎ 909/867–2751) usually have good snow December–April. All are accessible by following I–15 north to I–10 east. Farther to the north, about an eight-hour drive away, **Mammoth Mountain** earns its name—it's one of the largest facilities in the west. Bus trips and junkets are constantly being organized to make the drive easier. Check with any of the local sporting-goods stores, most of which will also offer equipment for rent.

Surfing

In San Diego, surfing is a year-round sport (thanks to wet suits in the winter) for people of all ages, many of whom are addicted to this way of life. Beginners should paddle out at Mission, Pacific, Tourmaline, La Jolla Shores, Del Mar, or Oceanside beaches. Experienced surfers should hit Sunset Cliffs, the La Jolla reef breaks, Black's Beach, or Swami's (Sea Cliff Roadside Park) in Encinitas (*see* Chapter 5, Beaches, for directions). Most public beaches have separate areas for surfers. Those interested in devoting some time to learning how to surf may consider the seven-day sessions at the **Paskowitz Surfing Summer Camps** in San Onofre; call (☎ 310/276–5754) or write (Box 522, San Clemente 92674) for a brochure. For a shorter commitment, consider **Kahuna Bob's Surf School** (1058 Hermes Ave., Encinitas, ☎ 619/943–7009), for sessions seven days a week; a two-hour lesson costs $30, and all equipment is supplied.

Many local surf shops rent boards, including **Star Surfing Company** (☎ 619/273–7827) in Pacific Beach and **La Jolla Surf Systems** (☎ 619/456–2777) and **Hansen's** (☎ 619/753–6595) in Encinitas.

Swimming

If the ocean is too cold and salty, there are several public pools open for those interested in getting in a few laps. The most spectacular pool in town is the **Mission Beach Plunge** (3115 Ocean Front Walk, ☎ 619/488–3110), in Belmont Park, where the public can swim weekdays 6–8 AM, noon–1, and 3:30–8, weekends 8–4. Admission is $2.25. The **Copley Family YMCA** (3901 Landis St., ☎ 619/283–2251) and the **Downtown YMCA** (500 W. Broadway Ave., ☎ 619/232–7451) are both centrally located. The **Magdalena Ecke YMCA** (200 Saxony Rd., Encinitas, ☎ 619/942–9622) is convenient for visitors to the North County.

Tennis

Most of the more than 1,300 courts spread around the county are in private clubs, but there are a few public facilities. **Morley Field** (☎ 619/295–9278), in Balboa Park, has 25 courts, 19 of which are lighted. Nonmembers can make reservations after paying a nominal fee for the use of the courts; if you're lucky, a court may be available when you come in to pay the fee. The **La Jolla Recreation Center** (☎ 619/552–1658) offers 9 free public courts near downtown La Jolla, 5 of them lighted. There are 12 lighted courts at **Robb Field** (☎ 619/531–1563) in Ocean Beach, with a small day-use fee.

The list of hotel complexes with tennis facilities includes the **Bahia Resort Hotel** (☎ 619/488–0551); **Hilton San Diego** (☎ 619/276–4010); the **Hotel Del Coronado** (☎ 619/435–6611); the **Kona Kai Beach and Tennis Resort** (☎ 619/222–1191); the **LaCosta Resort and Spa** (☎ 619/438–9111); and the **Rancho Bernardo Inn and Country Club** (☎ 619/487–1611). Intense tennis instruction is available at **Rancho Bernardo Inn Tennis College** (☎ 619/675–8474) in Rancho Bernardo.

Volleyball

Ocean Beach, South Mission Beach, Del Mar, and Moonlight Beach are the most popular congregating points for beach-volleyball enthusiasts. A warning: The competition can be fierce. Some of the best players in the world can show up on any given day.

Waterskiing

Mission Bay is one of the most popular waterskiing areas in southern California. It is best to get out early when the water is smooth and the crowds are thin. Boats and equipment can be rented from **Seaforth Boat Rentals** (1641 Quivira Rd., near Mission Bay, ☎ 619/223–1681). The private **San Diego and Mission Bay Boat and Ski Club** (2606 N. Mission Bay Dr., ☎ 619/276–0830) operates a slalom course and ski jump in Mission Bay's Hidden Anchorage. Permission from the club or the Mission Bay Harbor Patrol (☎ 619/291–3900) must be obtained to use the course and jump.

Windsurfing

Also known as sailboarding, windsurfing is a sport best practiced on smooth waters, such as Mission Bay or the Snug Harbor Marina at the intersection of I–5 and Tamarack Avenue in Carlsbad. It's a tricky sport to learn, but it can be a lot of fun for novices as well as experts. Rentals and instruction are available at the **Bahia Resort Hotel** (998 W. Mission Bay Dr., ☎ 619/488–0551); the **Catamaran Resort Hotel** (3999 Mission Blvd., ☎ 619/488–1081); **Mission Bay Sportcenter** (1010 Santa Clara Pl., ☎ 619/488–1004); the **San Diego Sailing Center** (1010 Santa Clara Pl., ☎ 619/488–0651); and **Windsport** (844 W. Mission Bay Dr., ☎ 619/488–4642), all in the Mission Bay area. The

Snug Harbor Marina (4215 Harrison St., Carlsbad, ☎ 619/434–3089) also offers rentals and instruction. More experienced windsurfers will enjoy taking a board out on the ocean. Wave jumping is especially popular at the Tourmaline Surfing Park in La Jolla and in the Del Mar area.

SPECTATOR SPORTS

Ever since the Clippers left for Los Angeles, San Diego hasn't had a professional basketball franchise. But it does have just about every other type of sporting team and event, including a few that are exclusive to the area. For information on tickets to any event, contact **Teleseat** (☎ 619/452–7328). **San Diego Jack Murphy Stadium** is at the intersection of I–8 and I–805.

Baseball

The **San Diego Padres** (☎ 619/283–4494) slug it out for bragging rights in the National League West from April through September. Matches with such rivals as the hated Los Angeles Dodgers and San Francisco Giants are usually the highlights of the home season at San Diego Jack Murphy Stadium.

Tickets range from $5 to $11 and are usually readily available, unless the Padres are in the thick of the pennant race.

Basketball

There's no pro team, but the **San Diego State University Aztecs** (☎ 619/283–7378) are gaining national prominence. The Aztecs, competing in the Western Athletic Conference with such powers as Utah State and Brigham Young University, play at the Peterson Gym at the San Diego State campus (☎ 619/594–6947) December–March. Tickets are a bargain at $5 for adults, $3 for children.

The **University of San Diego** (☎ 619/260–4600), vying for points in the West Coast Athletic Conference with such schools as Pepperdine, the University of San Francisco, and the University of California at Santa Barbara, competes with the top teams in the country.

Dog Racing

In Tijuana, anorexic-looking greyhounds chase the electric bunny around the Agua Caliente track nightly, except Tuesday. *See* Spectator Sports *in* Chapter 11, Tijuana, Rosarito Beach, and Ensenada, for details.

Football

After almost a decade of less-than-stellar seasons, the **San Diego Chargers** (☎ 619/280–2111) have enjoyed a spectacular resurgence. The Chargers were one of the original AFL franchises, originally based in Los Angeles. They fill San Diego Jack Murphy Stadium August through December. Games with AFC West rivals Los Angeles Raiders and Denver Broncos are always particularly intense.

The San Diego State University Aztecs compete in the exciting Western Athletic Conference. The biggest game of the year is always a showdown with Brigham Young University. The winner of the WAC plays in the **Holiday Bowl** (☎ 619/283–5808), always known as one of the most exhilarating bowl games, and renowned for its exciting finishes. The big bowl game is played near the end of December in San

Diego Jack Murphy Stadium, which is where the Aztecs play home games.

Golf

The La Costa Resort and Spa (☎ 619/438–9111) hosts the prestigious **Tournament of Champions** in January, featuring the winners of the previous year's tournaments. The **Buick Invitational** brings the pros to the Torrey Pines Municipal Golf Course in February (☎ 619/452–3226). In spring, **Ladies Professional Golf Association** is held at the Stoneridge Country Club (☎ 619/487–2117).

Horse Racing

Begun in the 1930s by Bing Crosby, Pat O'Brien, and their Hollywood cronies, the annual summer meeting of the **Del Mar Thoroughbred Club** (☎ 619/755–1141) on the Del Mar Fairgrounds—"Where the Turf Meets the Surf"—attracts hordes of Beautiful People, along with the best horses and jockeys in the country. The meeting begins in July and continues through early September, every day except Tuesday. But that isn't the end of horse-racing action in Del Mar. The Del Mar Fairgrounds also serves as a satellite-wagering facility (☎ 619/755–1167) with TV coverage of betting on races from tracks throughout California. Take I–5 north to the Via de la Valle Road exit.

Ice Hockey

The **San Diego Gulls** (☎ 619/688–1800), competing in and dominating the International Hockey League, bring an exciting game of hockey to this area. Games are played October–April at the San Diego Sports Arena (☎ 619/224–4171), with ticket prices ranging from $6 to $15.50.

Jai Alai

You can place bets on this vigorous sport, often called the world's fastest game, in Tijuana's Fronton Palacio. *See* Spectator Sports *in* Chapter 11, Tijuana, Rosarito Beach, and Ensenada.

Over-the-Line

As much a giant beach party as a sport, this game is a form of beach softball played with three-person teams. Every July, the world championships are held on Fiesta Island, with two weekends of wild beer drinking and partying. Some good athletes take part in the games, too. Admission is free, but parking is impossible and traffic around Mission Bay can become unbearable. Call the Old Mission Beach Athletic Club (☎ 619/688–0817) for more information.

Soccer

The most successful professional franchise in town is the **San Diego Sockers** (☎ 619/224–4625) indoor soccer team. The team has dominated the game, winning championships in the defunct North American Soccer League and the Major Indoor Soccer League, as well as in the current Continental Indoor Soccer League. Games are raucous, since San Diegans love to support their Sockers. The season runs October–May at the San Diego Sports Arena (☎ 619/224–4171). Take the Rosecrans exit from I–5 west to Sports Arena Boulevard and turn right.

7 Dining

By Kathryn
Shevelow

Updated by
Albert M.
Columbo

IN SPITE OF ITS RANKING as the second-largest city in California, San Diego was, until recently, a rather slow-paced, provincial place. The fine weather and splendid beaches that contribute so much to the city's beauty also fostered an open-air, daytime-oriented culture that did little to encourage a sophisticated nightlife. San Diegans seemed to prefer suburban quietude to urban activity; after dark, downtown was given over to sailors, bars, and sex shops.

The restaurant scene was dominated by fast food, overcooked fish, and upper-class stodge. "Good food," with few exceptions, was the quasi-Continental fare served at the kind of indeterminate Chamber of Commerce restaurant humorist Calvin Trillin calls "La Maison de la Casa House." If the one bright light was always the abundance of authentic Mexican restaurants, even these did not often venture far beyond the standard fare of tacos, beans, and burritos.

But all that has begun to change in the past few years. Redevelopment of the downtown area has created a substantial nightlife scene, with a proliferation of clubs and good restaurants—especially on 4th and 5th avenues—that is nothing short of astonishing. Other areas have shared in the new sense of energy. It wasn't long ago that the streets of sleepy La Jolla turned in for the night at sunset (especially in the winter) and the uptown area (Hillcrest, Mission Hills, Normal Heights) was a semi-urban landscape of dreary streets punctuated by an occasional bar. Now night crawlers can party hearty in both sections of town after dark.

All this bodes well for residents and visitors who like to eat. True, for all the efforts it may make in that direction, San Diego is not Los Angeles or San Francisco, and perhaps will never be: There has not yet developed among San Diegans the kind of exacting culinary standards one finds in the demanding and vociferous residents of a truly great food city. Still, one can eat very well these days in San Diego.

Adding to the current proliferation of good restaurants specializing in California cuisine and European (especially Italian) cooking, various immigrant groups have recently arrived in San Diego, bringing their culinary traditions with them. The city now boasts a rich selection of Latin American, Middle Eastern, and Asian cuisines. The many Vietnamese restaurants throughout the city are especially noteworthy. Influenced by Chinese and French cooking styles, Vietnamese food retains its own character: Typically it is inexpensive, fresh, healthy, and very tasty. Particularly recommended are the noodle soups called "pho," the beef grilled in grape leaves, and the many dishes served to be wrapped at the table in lettuce and rice paper. Excellent Vietnamese restaurants, along with their equally good Chinese, Korean, and Japanese counterparts, can be found along Convoy Street and Linda Vista Road in Kearny Mesa; **Pho Hoa** (6921 Linda Vista Rd., ☎ 619/492–9108) and **Vietnam Seafood Restaurant** (6931 Linda Vista Rd., ☎ 619/292–8889) are just two of many.

San Diego is an informal city. The advised attire at most of the restaurants listed below is casual. Only one of the restaurants listed below requires men to wear ties.

Restaurants are grouped first by location, then by type of cuisine.

CATEGORY	COST*
$$$$	over $50
$$$	$30–$50
$$	$20–$30
$	under $20

per person, without tax (7.75%), service, or drinks

Downtown

American

$$$ ★ **Rainwater's.** This tony restaurant is as well known around town for the size of its portions as for the high quality of its cuisine. The menu includes a number of meat and fish dishes, but this is really the place to come if you crave a perfectly done, thick and tender steak. All the entrées are accompanied by such tasty side dishes as shoestring potatoes, onion rings, and creamed corn. The food is pricey, but the satisfaction level is high. ✕ *1202 Kettner Blvd. (2nd floor),* ☎ *619/233–5757. Reservations advised. AE, DC, MC, V. No lunch weekends.*

$$ **California Café.** On the top level of Horton Plaza, this stylish dining room with lots of windows and potted palms serves stylish California cuisine to match. The imaginative menu, which changes daily, may include smoked duck ravioli with basil and goat cheese, soba noodle salad with lemon wasabi dressing and wild mushrooms, or New Mexican chili fettuccine with shrimp and smoked corn. The crusty Italian bread is baked daily on the premises. ✕ *Upper Level, Horton Plaza,* ☎ *619/238–5440. Reservations advised. AE, D, DC, MC, V.*

$ **Croce's.** A tribute to the late singer-songwriter Jim Croce run by his widow, Ingrid, the popular Croce's used to be known more for its nightly jazz and pleasant, clublike ambience than for its cuisine. But with a new chef in the kitchen, Croce's now complements its high-quality music with high-quality food. The menu offers good salads and a range of appealing entrées; try the swordfish in grape leaves or the chicken cakes. Even those who are not jazz aficionados will find this restaurant a good bet for late-night dining, since Croce's kitchen doesn't close until midnight. ✕ *802 5th Ave.,* ☎ *619/233–4355. Reservations accepted. AE, D, DC, MC, V.*

$ **Dakota Grill & Spirits.** Housed in a historic building restored to a posh grandeur, Dakota's ambience is nothing short of elegant. Diners indulge themselves on a sensational American mixed-grill cuisine. House favorites are shrimp Tasso (shrimp sautéed with Cajun ham, sweet peas, and ancho-chile cream; basil-garlic linguine with steamed mussels; and Cowboy Steak (marinated skirt steak with smoked tomato salsa). Don't miss the homemade desserts like key lime pie or chocolate pecan torte covered in caramel sauce. ✕ *901 5th Ave. at E St.,* ☎ *619/234–5554. Reservations advised. AE, D, DC, MC, V. No lunch weekends.*

Cajun and Creole

$–$$ ★ **Bayou Bar and Grill.** The ceiling fans revolving lazily over this attractive room, with dark-green wainscoting and light-pink walls, help create a New Orleans atmosphere for the spicy Cajun and Creole specialties served here. You may start with a bowl of superb seafood gumbo and then move on to the sausage, red beans, and rice, the duck esplanade,

92

San Diego Dining

or any of the fresh Louisiana Gulf seafood dishes. A tempting selection of rich Louisiana desserts includes bread pudding, praline cheesecake, and Creole pecan pie. ✕ *329 Market St.,* ☎ *619/696–8747. Dinner reservations suggested. AE, D, DC, MC, V. No lunch Mon. or Tues.*

Chinese

$–$$ **Panda Inn.** Even if you're allergic to shopping, the Panda Inn is rea-
★ son enough to come to Horton Plaza. Arguably the best Chinese restaurant in town, this dining room at the top of the plaza serves subtly seasoned and attractively presented Mandarin and Szechuan dishes in an elegant setting that feels far removed from the rush of commerce below. The fresh seafood dishes are noteworthy, as are the Peking duck, spicy Szechuan bean curd, and twice-cooked pork. Indeed, it's hard to find anything on this menu that's not outstanding. ✕ *506 Horton Plaza,* ☎ *619/233–7800. Reservations advised. AE, D, DC, MC, V.*

Continental

$$$ **Dobson's.** At lunchtime, local politicos and media types rub elbows at
★ the long, polished bar of this highly regarded restaurant; the show biz contingent arrives in the evening in stretch limos. Although the small two-tier building is suggestive of an earlier era—the lower level looks like a men's club and the upper level sports a wrought-iron balcony, elegant woodwork, and gilt cornices—there's nothing outdated about the cuisine. Among the range of carefully prepared entrées, which change daily, may be roasted quail with fig sauce or chicken risotto. The tasty house salad is laced with fennel and goat cheese, and Dobson's signature dish, a superb mussel bisque, comes topped with a crown of puff pastry. The wine list is excellent. ✕ *56 Broadway Circle,* ☎ *619/231–6771. Reservations advised. AE, DC, MC, V. No lunch Sat.; closed Sun.*

Greek

$ **Athens Market.** This cheerful eatery, decorated with Aegaean island scenes, bustles with downtown office workers and members of San Diego's small but active Greek community. As in many Greek restaurants, the appetizers here—such as *taramousalata* (fish roe dip) and stuffed grape leaves—can be superior to the somewhat heavy traditional beef and lamb entrées. Greek music, folk dancing, and belly dancers add to the festive atmosphere on weekend evenings. The adjacent Victorian-style coffeehouse, under the same ownership, keeps late hours for night owls in search of a caffeine fix. ✕ *109 W. F St.,* ☎ *619/234–1955. Reservations suggested. AE, D, DC, MC, V.*

Italian

$$–$$$ **Bella Luna.** A recent, welcome addition to the "Italianization" of 5th Avenue, this small, stylish restaurant, whose owner hails from the island of Capri, more than holds its own against its longer-established neighbors. Paintings of "beautiful moons" in many shapes and sizes adorn the walls, and the service is gracious and attentive. The menu features dishes from all over Italy: Try the stuffed mozzarella appetizer or the calamari in tomato sauce. Pastas are particularly recommended, especially the linguine *alle vongole verace* (with clams in their shells), the fettuccine with salmon, and the black squid-ink linguine served with a spicy seafood sauce; if you still have room for an entrée, consider the rack of lamb. ✕ *748 5th Ave.,* ☎ *619/239–3222. Reservations advised. AE, MC, V.*

No matter where you go, travel is easier when you know the code.^{SM}

dial 1 800 CALL ATT®

Dial 1 800 CALL ATT and you'll always get through from any phone with any card* and you'll always get AT&T's best deal.** It's the one number to remember when calling away from home.

*Other long distance company calling cards excluded.
**Additional discounts available.

AT&T
Your True Choice

$$–$$$ **Trattoria La Strada.** La Strada specializes in Tuscan cuisine prepared
★ so well that your taste buds will be convinced they've died and gone
to Italy. Try the *antipasto di mare,* with tender shrimp and shellfish,
or the salad La Strada, with wild mushrooms, walnuts, and delectable
shaved Parmesan. The pastas, particularly the *pappardelle all'anitra*
(wide noodles with a duck sauce), are excellent. The noise level can be
high in the two high-ceilinged dining rooms; if you don't feel like rais-
ing your voice, you can always check out the fashions worn by the stylish
young diners. ✕ *702 5th Ave.,* ☎ *619/239–3400. Reservations advised.
AE, D, DC, MC, V. No lunch weekends.*

$$ **Fio's.** Glitzy young singles mingle with staid business-suit types in this
lively, popular place, one of the earliest of the trendy Italian restau-
rants now proliferating in the Gaslamp Quarter. Contemporary vari-
ations on traditional Italian cuisine are served in a high-ceilinged,
brick-and-wood dining room overlooking the 5th Avenue street scene.
The menu includes a range of imaginative pizzas baked in the wood-
fired oven and classic Italian dishes. ✕ *801 5th Ave.,* ☎ *619/234–3467.
Reservations advised. AE, D, DC, MC, V. No lunch weekends.*

$$ **Panevino.** This brick-walled Italian café is often crowded with diners
who prefer its casual bistro atmosphere to the more trendy tone of neigh-
boring restaurants. But the menu here is as au courant as any other in
San Diego. Particularly recommended are the imaginative selection of
pizzas and pastas: The spinach ravioli is always a good bet. You could
easily make a meal of one of the excellent stuffed foccaccias and a salad
or a plate of grilled vegetables, although a range of tasty and sometimes ambitious entrées is also offered; if it's available, try the quail
cooked in balsamic vinegar. Panevino is one of the few good downtown restaurants outside of Horton Plaza that's open for lunch on weekends. ✕ *722 5th Ave.,* ☎ *619/595–7959. Reservations advised. AE,
D, DC, MC, V.*

Seafood

$$$ **Anthony's Star of the Sea Room.** The Anthony's chain of local seafood
restaurants, one of the oldest in San Diego, has long been serving up
adequately prepared seafood dishes to tourists and residents alike.
The flagship of the Anthony's fleet, the Star of the Sea Room, is much
more formal and expensive than the others. The menu offers an enor-
mous selection of fresh fish from around the world, and if the recipes
are less exciting than those at other seafood restaurants, the magnifi-
cent harbor views go far in the way of compensation. Many of the dishes
are prepared at the table. ✕ *1360 N. Harbor Dr.,* ☎ *619/232–7408.
Reservations strongly advised. Jacket and tie. AE, D, DC, MC, V. No
lunch.*

$–$$$ **The Fish Market.** This bustling, informal restaurant offers diners a
choice from a large variety of extremely fresh fish, mesquite grilled and
served with lemon and tartar sauce. Also good are shellfish dishes, such
as steamed clams or mussels. Most of what is served here has lived in
the water, but even dedicated fish-avoiders may think it worth their
while to trade selection for the stunning view. Enormous plate-glass
windows look directly out onto the harbor, and if you're lucky enough
to get a windowside table, you can practically taste the salt spray. This
is one of the rare places where families with young children can feel
comfortable without sacrificing their taste buds. A more formal and
expensive upstairs restaurant, The Top of the Market, offers a good
Sunday brunch. ✕ *750 N. Harbor Dr.,* ☎ *619/232–3474 for the Fish
Market or 619/234–4867 for the Top of the Market; also in Del Mar,
at 640 Via de la Valle,* ☎ *619/755–2277. Reservations accepted up-*

stairs and for 8 or more downstairs, and at Del Mar. AE, D, DC, MC, V.

Coronado

Home of beautiful beaches, an elegant old resort hotel, and one of the country's major naval stations, Coronado unfortunately does not abound in good restaurants. And those that are not bad tend to be over-priced. If you wish to eat in Coronado, here are some of your best bets, listed in descending order from very expensive ($$$$) to moderate ($$): **Marius,** in the Le Meridien Hotel (☎ 619/435–3000); **Peohe's** (1201 1st St., ☎ 619/437–4474); **Chez Loma** (1132 Loma Ave., ☎ 619/435–0661); **Primavera Ristorante** (932 Orange Ave., ☎ 619/435–0454); and the **Crown Room** and the **Prince of Wales Room** in the Hotel Del Coronado (☎ 619/435–6611).

Uptown

American

$ Hamburger Mary's. Kin of the gay franchise, this outdoor restaurant is as popular for its casual atmosphere as for its burgers. Enjoy the Hawaiian-style Diamond Back Burger, the hearty Billy Burger, the savory veggie burger, or the delicious prime rib. Also enjoy the great domestic and imported beers like Warthog, Heineken, and Corona. ✕ *308 University Ave., Hillcrest,* ☎ *619/491–0040. No reservations. AE, MC, V.*

$ Hob Nob Hill. The type of place where regulars arrive on the same day of the week at the same time and order the same meal they've been having for the past 20 years, this comforting restaurant is still under the same ownership and management as it was when it started in 1944; with its dark wood booths and patterned carpets, Hob Nob Hill seems suspended in the 1950s. But you don't need to be a nostalgia buff to appreciate the bargain-priced American home cooking—dishes such as pot roast, fried chicken, and corned beef like your mother never really made. Reservations are particularly suggested on Sunday, when everyone comes for the copious breakfasts. ✕ *2271 1st Ave.,* ☎ *619/239–8176. Reservations accepted. AE, D, MC, V.*

California

$$ California Cuisine. Across the street from the Uptown District, this minimalist chic dining room—gray carpet, stark white walls, and black-and-white photographs of urban landscapes—offers a suitably innovative menu. Daily selections may include grilled fresh venison served with wild mushrooms and mashed potatoes; the tasty warm chicken salad entrée is a regular feature. You can count on whatever you order to be carefully prepared and elegantly presented. Service is knowledgeable and attentive, the wine list is good, and the desserts are seriously tempting. Heat lamps make the back patio a romantic year-round option. ✕ *1027 University Ave.,* ☎ *619/543–0790. Reservations advised. AE, D, DC, MC, V. No lunch weekends; closed Mon.*

$–$$ Canes California Bistro. A light-filled neighborhood bistro, whose walls are decked, appropriately enough, with canes of all kinds, Canes attracts a diverse group of diners, from senior citizens to families to Uptown trendies. They come for food that is similarly diverse—everything from meat loaf and mashed potatoes to hamburgers with sun-dried tomato *aioli* (garlic mayonnaise) to pastas with roasted garlic and gorgonzola—and consistently good. The weekend buffet brunch features excellent breakfast breads, French beef stew, and yellow corn pancakes with sour cream and golden caviar. ✘ *Vermont St. (at University Ave. in the Uptown District),* ☎ *619/299–3551. Reservations advised. AE, D, DC, MC, V.*

Greek

$–$$ **Calliope's Greek Cuisine.** One of the best Greek restaurants in town, Calliope moves beyond the standard Hellenic fare to offer tasty variations on traditional dishes. Included on the menu, along with a good moussaka and lamb souvlaki, are fettuccine Aegean, topped with shrimp, fresh fish, and mushrooms in a tomato wine sauce, and artichokes Athenian, served over linguine in a tomato-herb sauce. Fans of Greek wines will see not only the usual retsinas but also a selection of harder-to-find regional bottles. The white-walled dining room is light and airy. ✘ *3958 5th Ave.,* ☎ *619/291–5588. Reservations advised. AE, D, DC, MC, V.*

Italian

$ **Pizza Nova.** Voted "Best Pizza Restaurant" by *San Diego* magazine and *San Diego Home and Garden,* Pizza Nova serves up 22 delicious varieties, including roasted garlic chicken, shrimp pesto, and Mexican lime. Just as appetizing are the 14 mouthwatering pasta entrées; chicken tequila fettuccine is one of the most popular. ✘ *3955 5th Ave., Suite 101, The Village Hillcrest,* ☎ *619/296–6682. Reservations accepted. AE, D, DC, MC, V.*

$ **Sally D's.** A step above the old family tradition, this friendly establishment is a favorite among locals who return for great Italian food cooked up by Sally. Try Shrimp D's Pizza, baked mostoccolia and veal, or eggplant parmigiana. ✘ *1288 University Ave., Hillcrest Colonnade,* ☎ *619/291–1288. Reservations accepted. AE, D, MC, V.*

Mexican

$ **El Indio Shop.** El Indio has been serving some of the city's best Mexican fast food since 1940. The menu is extensive; try the large burritos, the *tacquitos* (fried rolled tacos) with guacamole, or the giant quesadillas. You can eat at one of the indoor tables or on the patio across the street; El Indio is also perfect for beach-bound takeout. ✘ *3695 India St.,* ☎ *619/299–0333; 115 W. Olive Dr., San Ysidro,* ☎ *619/690–1122. D, MC, V. San Ysidro shop closed Sun.*

Thai

$–$$ **Thai Chada.** Don't be put off by appearances. Although it's housed in
★ a corner building that looks like a hamburger joint, this is one of the best Thai restaurants in town; the large windows and comfortable booths provide a low-key setting for consistently excellent food. Try any of the noodle dishes, especially the *pad thai,* rice noodles fried with fresh shrimp, egg, bean sprouts, scallions, and ground peanuts; the Tom Ka Kai chicken soup, with coconut milk, lemon grass, lime juice, and scallions; or the roast duck curry. A sister restaurant, Thai Chada 2, has recently opened in Pacific Beach. ✘ *142 University Ave.,* ☎ *619/297–9548; Thai Chada 2, 1749 Garnet Ave.,* ☎ *619/270–1888. Reservations advised. AE, D, DC, MC, V. Sat. lunch at Thai Chada 2 only; both restaurants no lunch on Sun.*

$ **Thai Saffron.** In recent years, San Diego has seen an upsurge in the growth of take-out restaurants offering tasty, health-conscious food. Saffron is one of the earliest and best of the eateries that specialize in chicken spit-roasted over a wood fire, accompanied by an appealing selection of side dishes. The chicken is wonderfully moist and comes with a choice of sauces: Try the peanut or chili. Among the accompaniments, the Cambodian salad is particularly fresh and crunchy. There's limited outdoor seating, but this is an ideal place to pick up lunch or dinner to take to Mission Bay or the beach. ✗ 3731B India St., ☎ 619/574–0177. No reservations. MC, V.

Old Town

Latin American

$–$$ Berta's Latin American Restaurant. A San Diego rarity—and particularly surprising in a section of town where the food often leans toward the safe and touristy—Berta's features a wide selection of Latin American regional dishes and a nice list of Latin American wines. While the wines are largely Chilean, the food, which manages to be wonderfully tasty and health-conscious at the same time, ranges all over the map. Try the Brazilian seafood *vatapa*, shrimp, scallops, and fish served in a sauce flavored with ginger, coconut, and chilis, or the Peruvian *pollo a la huancaina*, chicken with chilis and a feta cheese sauce. Service is friendly and helpful. The simple dining room is small, but there's also a patio. ✗ 3928 Twiggs St., ☎ 619/295–2343. Reservations advised weekends. AE, MC, V.

Mexican

$ Old Town Mexican Café. Singles congregate at the bar and families crowd into the wooden booths of this boisterous San Diego favorite, decked out with plants and colorful piñatas; an enclosed patio takes the overflow from both groups. You'll find all the Mexican standards here, as well as specialties such as *carnitas*, chunks of roast pork served with fresh tortillas and condiments. The enchiladas with spicy ranchero or green chili sauce are nice variations on an old theme. You can watch the corn tortillas being handmade on the premises and pick up a dozen to take home with you. ✗ 2489 San Diego Ave., ☎ 619/297–4330. Reservations accepted for 10 or more. AE, D, MC, V.

Seafood

$$–$$$ Cafe Pacifica. Like its sister restaurant, Pacifica Grill and Rotisserie, Cafe Pacifica offers a menu that changes daily and features an impressive array of imaginative appetizers, salads, pastas, and entrées; it also does a crème brûlée worth blowing any diet for. The emphasis here is on seafood, however, and this restaurant serves some of the best in town. You can't go wrong with any of the fresh fish preparations grilled over mesquite and served with an herb-butter sauce, a Mexican-inspired salsa, or a fruit chutney. Other good bets include the tasty pan-fried catfish; yummy, greaseless fish tacos; and superb crab cakes. ✗ 2414 San Diego Ave., ☎ 619/291–6666. Reservations advised. AE, D, DC, MC, V.

Beaches

Belgian

$$–$$$ Belgian Lion. The lace curtains at the windows of a rather forbidding white building, partially enclosed by a high wall, are the only hints of the cozy dining room within, where hearty Belgian dishes have been served to discerning diners for years. Among the signature dishes is the cassoulet, a wonderful rich stew of white beans, lamb, pork, sausage, and duck that makes you feel protected from the elements (even in San Diego, where there aren't many elements to be protected from). Lighter meals include sea scallops with braised Belgian endive or steamed salmon with leeks. An impressive wine list was carefully designed to complement the food. ✕ *2265 Bacon St., Ocean Beach,* ☎ *619/223–2700.* <u>*Reservations strongly advised.*</u> *AE, D, DC, MC, V. No lunch. Closed Sun.–Wed.*

Italian

$ **Tosca's.** This popular Pacific Beach eatery is in some way typical of pizza restaurants everywhere, with its fluorescent lighting and red-checkered vinyl tablecloths. But you are, after all, in California, which means you can opt for wheat or semolina crusts for your individually sized pizzas or calzones; choose toppings or fillings from an array of exotic ingredients, including artichokes, pesto, and feta cheese; and wash it all down with a microbrew from Sierra Nevada (on tap, yet). The young servers are cheerful and helpful. ✕ *3780 Ingraham St.,* ☎ *619/274–2408. AE, D, DC, MC, V.*

Mexican

$–$$ **Palenque.** A welcome alternative to the standard Sonoran-style café,
★ this family-run restaurant in Pacific Beach serves a wonderful selection of regional Mexican dishes. Recommendations include the chicken with mole, served in the regular chocolate-based or green chili version, and the mouthwatering *camarones en chipotle*, large shrimp cooked in a chili and tequila cream sauce (an old family recipe of the proprietor). Piñatas and paper birds dangle from the thatched ceiling, and seating is in comfortable round-backed leather chairs; a small deck in front is nice for warm-weather dining. Palenque is a bit hard to spot from the street and service is often slow, but the food is worth your vigilance and patience. ✕ *1653 Garnet Ave., Pacific Beach,* ☎ *619/272–7816. Reservations advised. AE, D, DC, MC, V.*

Thai

$–$$ **Karinya Thai.** This popular restaurant in Pacific Beach serves excellent Thai cuisine in a relaxed but pretty setting; in one room, diners recline on colorful floor cushions at low tables. It's hard to go wrong with any of the dishes on the extensive menu. You could concoct a meal from appetizers alone: The stuffed chicken wings and spicy fish cakes are particularly recommended. Among the entrées, the scallops in three sauces, beef strips with broccoli, and pad thai noodles are all worth a try. ✕ *4475 Mission Blvd.,* ☎ *619/270–5050. Reservations suggested. No lunch Sat.–Mon. MC, V.*

La Jolla

American

$ **Choices.** Off the beaten path and rather low on atmosphere—it's in the Sports and Health Center at the north of the Scripps Clinic complex—this small cafeteria offers indoor and outdoor tables with an ocean view, and very tasty, low-fat, low-cholesterol food. There's an excellent all-you-can-eat salad bar and a daily selection of healthy sandwiches and entrées. Choices is open for breakfast and lunch during the week but closes at 7 PM Monday–Thursday; it shuts down at 3 PM on Friday but reopens at 6 PM for dinner and folk music. ✕ *10820 N. Torrey Pines Rd.,* ☎ *619/554–3663. No reservations. AE, MC, V. Closed weekends.*

$ **Hard Rock Cafe.** If you've been to Hard Rock Cafes in other cities, you'll know what to expect here. This high-energy shrine to rock-and-roll and American food cranks its music up to ear-shattering decibels and hangs rock memorabilia on every available inch of wall space. This is not a place to come for intimate—or audible—conversation, but the burgers are fine and you can bring home a T-shirt to commemorate the occasion. You don't have to be accompanied by a teenager, although it helps. ✗ *909 Prospect St.,* ☎ *619/454–5101. No reservations. AE, DC, MC, V.*

$ **Pannikin Brockton Villa.** Connected with the local chain of trendy coffeehouses, this informal restaurant in a restored beach house overlooks La Jolla Cove and the ocean. Come here for good coffee, decent muffins and pastries, and stunning views. You'll have to fight the crowds on sunny weekends. The Pannikin opens for breakfast; call ahead for dinner hours (summer only). ✗ *1235 Coast Blvd.,* ☎ *619/454–7393. No reservations. AE, MC, V.*

Continental

$$$ **Top O' the Cove.** Although the reliable but rather stolid menu of this La Jolla institution has been surpassed by glitzier newcomers, year after year San Diego diners give high marks for romance to this cozy, intimate spot with a beautiful ocean view. The filet mignon and roasted rack of lamb are reliable choices; calorie-counters may opt for the boneless chicken breast sautéed with shrimp and shellfish or sliced duck breast with Armagnac walnut sauce. The service is attentive but not overbearing, and the award-winning wine list is enormous. ✗ *1216 Prospect St.,* ☎ *619/454–7779. Reservations advised. AE, DC, MC, V.*

$$–$$$ **Triangles.** In an attractive, if slightly stiff, setting—clubby dark wood booths in a contemporary high-rise bank building—this bar and grill in the Golden Triangle area strives for variety. The menu, which changes daily, may include sautéed sweetbreads, potato knishes, ravioli stuffed with porcini mushrooms, or shrimp cassoulet. Along with rich dishes, you'll also find many lighter and vegetarian preparations—nice for the health-conscious diner or the overstuffed vacationer. A small patio, surrounded by lush landscaping, is pleasant at lunch. ✗ *4370 La Jolla Village Dr., in the Northern Trust Bldg.,* ☎ *619/453–6650. Reservations advised. AE, MC, V. No lunch Sat.; closed Sun.*

Deli

$ **SamSon's.** As close as you'll come to a real Jewish deli in San Diego, SamSon's has dill pickles set out on the tables; the menu and portions are enormous. If you're having trouble deciding, go for one of the daily soup-and-sandwich specials, especially the whitefish when it's available. And you can't go wrong with a lox plate for breakfast (SamSon's opens at 7 AM) or a corned beef sandwich for lunch. The two ample dining rooms are decorated in corny show-biz style, with movie stills covering the walls. ✗ *8861 Villa La Jolla Dr.,* ☎ *619/455–1462. Reservations accepted. AE, D, DC, MC, V.*

Indian

$$ **Star of India.** Rather higher priced than most other local Indian restaurants, the Star of India offers the best Indian food in town in a soothing setting of bamboo and quiet pastels. Particularly recommended are the chicken *tikka masala,* prepared tandoori style in a cream and tomato curry, and *saag gosht,* lamb in a spinach curry. Seafood dishes are generally the least successful. The excellent nan bread, baked in the tandoor oven, comes either plain or stuffed with a variety of fillings. An all-you-can-eat buffet lunch, available daily, is a good way to satisfy your curiosity about a variety of different dishes. ✗ *1000 Prospect St.,* ☎ *619/459–3355; 423 F St.,* ☎ *554–9891. Reservations advised, especially weekends. AE, D, DC, MC, V.*

Italian

$$ **Ristorante Piatti.** On weekends, this trattoria-style restaurant is filled to overflowing with a lively mix of trendy singles and local families, who keep returning for the excellent country-style Italian food. A wood-burning oven turns out excellent breads and pizzas, and imaginative pastas include the *pappardelle fantasia* (wide saffron noodles with shrimp, fresh tomatoes, and arugula) and a wonderfully garlicky spaghetti *alle vongole* (served with clams in the shell). Among the *secondi* are good versions of roast chicken and Italian sausage with polenta. A fountain splashes softly on the tree-shaded patio, where heat lamps allow diners to sit out even on chilly evenings. ✕ *2182 Av. de la Playa,* ☎ *619/454–1589. Reservations strongly advised. AE, MC, V.*

Pacific Rim

$$$ **Cafe Japengo.** In one of the most stylish dining rooms in town, framed by elegant marbled walls, accented with leafy bamboo trees, and dotted with unusual black-iron sculptures, Cafe Japengo serves excellent Pacific Rim cuisine. The inspiration for this eclectic and imaginative menu is largely Asian, with many North and South American touches. There's a selection of grilled, wood-roasted, and wok-fried entrées for dinner; try the 10-ingredient fried rice, the shrimp and scallops with dragon noodles, or the grilled swordfish with wild mushrooms. The curry fried calamari and the Japengo potstickers appetizers are guaranteed to stimulate your taste buds. You can also order fine sushi from your table or from a seat at the sushi bar. Although it is located in the very trendy, postmodern Aventine center, Cafe Japengo largely escapes the frenzied, noisy singles scene characteristic of the other restaurants in the complex. Unfortunately, the quality of the service doesn't match that of the food. ✕ *8960 University Center La.,* ☎ *619/450–3355. Reservations advised. AE, D, DC, MC, V. No lunch weekends.*

Seafood

$$$ **George's at the Cove.** At most restaurants you get either good food or ★ good views; at George's, you don't have to choose. The elegant main dining room, with a wall-length window overlooking La Jolla Cove, is renowned for its daily fresh seafood specials; the menu also offers several good chicken and meat dishes. The delectable three-mushroom soup, accented with sherry and rosemary, and the salmon-and-shrimp sausage make fine starters. The charbroiled apple-smoked salmon entrée is highly recommended, as are any of the shellfish pastas. Desserts are uniformly excellent. For more informal dining, try the Cafe ($$) on the second floor. The outdoor Terrace ($$), on the top floor, affords a sweeping view of the coast; wonderful for breakfast, lunch, or brunch on a fine day, the Terrace (like the Cafe) does not take reservations, so you may have a wait. ✕ *1250 Prospect St.,* ☎ *619/454–4244. Reservations advised for main dining room. AE, D, DC, MC, V.*

8 Lodging

THERE ARE ACCOMMODATIONS in San Diego to satisfy every taste, ranging from grand luxury high-rises to funky beach cottages. Because new hotels are continually under construction, the city has a surplus of rooms—which means lower prices for those who shop around. The older properties in Hotel Circle frequently offer special rates and free tickets to local attractions, while many luxury hotels promote lower-priced weekend packages to fill rooms after the week's convention and business customers have departed. When you make reservations, find out about any specials, and book well in advance, especially during the busy summer season.

By Sharon K. Gillenwater and Edie Jarolim

San Diego is very spread out, so the first thing to consider when selecting lodgings here is location. The various neighborhoods are rather diverse: You can choose to stay in the middle of a bustling metropolitan center or to kick back in a serene beach getaway. If you select one of the many hotels with a waterfront location and extensive outdoor sports facilities, you need never leave the premises. If you plan to do a lot of sightseeing, however, you may take into account a hotel's proximity to the attractions you most want to visit. In general, price need not be a major factor in your decision: Even the most expensive areas offer some reasonably priced—albeit rather modest—rooms.

If you are planning an extended stay or need lodgings for four or more people, consider an apartment rental. **Oakwood Apartments** (3866 or 3883 Ingraham St., 92109; ☎ 619/490–2100 booking for both) offers comfortable, furnished apartments in the Mission Bay area with maid service and linens; there's a minimum 30-day stay. At **San Diego Vacation Rentals** (1565 Hotel Circle S, Suite 390, 92108, ☎ 619/296–1000 or 800/222–8281), you can rent a coastal home or condo at competitive weekly and monthly rates.

Those wishing to find bed-and-breakfast accommodations in town can contact the **Bed & Breakfast Guild of San Diego** (☎ 619/523–1300), which currently lists 11 high-quality member inns, or **Bed & Breakfast Directory for San Diego** (Box 3292, 92136, ☎ 619/297–3130 or 800/619–ROOM), which covers San Diego County.

To reserve a room in any property in this chapter, you can contact Fodor's new toll-free lodging reservations hot line (☎ 1–800–FODORS–1 or 1–800–363–6771; 0800–89–1030 in Great Britain; 0014/800–12–8271 in Australia; 1800–55–9101 in Ireland).

CATEGORY	COST*
$$$$	over $165
$$$	$110–$165
$$	$70–$110
$	under $70

*for a double room in high (summer) season, excluding 10.5% San Diego room tax

Coronado

Staying in Coronado is a unique experience: This quiet, out-of-the-way place feels as though it exists in an earlier, more gracious era. The peninsula, home to many wealthy retirees and naval personnel from the North Island Naval Air station, is connected to the mainland by the Silver Strand isthmus, but most tourists come here via the Coronado Bay Bridge or the ferry that leaves from San Diego's Embarcadero. With boutiques and restaurants lining Orange Avenue, the main street, and its fine beaches, Coronado is great for a getaway, but if you plan to see many of San Diego's attractions, you'll probably spend a lot of time commuting across the bridge or riding the ferry.

$$$$ **Le Meridien.** Flamingos greet you at the entrance of this resort, offer-
★   ing 16 acres of lushly landscaped grounds. This is a modern, $90 million complex, but it doesn't shout "I'm new and expensive." Instead, the low-slung, Cape Cod–style buildings perfectly capture Coronado's understated old-money ambience. The large rooms and suites are done in a cheerful, California–country French fashion, with colorful Impressionist prints; all rooms have separate showers and tubs and come with plush robes and Limoge bath accessories. (Watch out for what looks like a gift basket on the vanity, though—it's an extension of the minibar.) The spa facilities are top-notch, as is the award-winning Marius Restaurant, which serves innovative French Provençale cuisine. *2000 2nd St., 92118, ☎ 619/435–3000 or 800/543–4300, FAX 619/435–3032. 300 rooms (including 7 suites and a 28-unit villa complex). 2 restaurants, 3 pools, massage, sauna, spa, steam room, 6 tennis courts, aerobics, exercise room, marina. AE, D, DC, MC, V.*

$$$$ **Loews Coronado Bay Resort.** You can park your boat at the 80-slip marina of this resort, set on a 15-acre private peninsula on the Silver Strand. Didn't bring it along this time? Never mind. You can rent one here. Rooms are somewhat formally but tastefully decorated, with pale yellows, pinks, and greens, and flowered bedspreads; all have furnished balconies with views of water—either bay, ocean, or marina. The Commodore Kids Club offers a nice variety of programs for children ages 4–12, and there's nightly entertainment in the hotel lounge. *4000 Coronado Bay Rd., 92118, ☎ 619/424–4000, FAX 619/424–4400 or 800/235–6397. 438 rooms, 25 suites. 3 restaurants, deli, 3 pools, 2 spas, 5 tennis courts, fitness center, marina, windsurfing, boating, jet skiing, bicycles. AE, D, DC, MC, V.*

$$$–$$$$ **Hotel Del Coronado.** Built in 1888, "the Del" is a historic and social landmark (*see* Tour 2 *in* Chapter 2, Exploring San Diego). The rooms and suites in the original ornate Victorian building are charmingly quirky. Some have sleeping areas that seem smaller than the baths, while others are downright palatial; two are even said to come with a resident ghost. The public areas are grand, if perhaps a bit dark for modern tastes; a lower-level shopping arcade lined with historic photographs is fascinating, but tear yourself away to stroll around the hotel's lovely manicured grounds. More standardized accommodations are available in the newer high-rise. Service can be a bit chaotic; there's often a long line at the front desk. *1500 Orange Ave., 92118, ☎ 619/435–6611 (hotel), 619/522–8000 or 800/HOTEL–DEL (reservations), FAX 619/522–8262. 691 rooms. 3 restaurants, deli, pool, sauna, steam room, 8 tennis courts, croquet, bicycles, beach. AE, D, DC, MC, V.*

$$–$$$ **Glorietta Bay Inn.** The main building of this property—located across the street from the Hotel Del, adjacent to the Coronado harbor, and near many restaurants and shops—was built in 1908 for sugar baron John D. Spreckels, who once owned most of downtown San Diego. Rooms here and in the newer motel-style buildings are attractively furnished, with flowered bedspreads and green rugs; all have refrigerators. Tours of the island's historical buildings depart from the inn's lobby three mornings a week (cost: $5). *1630 Glorietta Blvd., 92118, ☎ 619/435–3101 or 800/283–9383, FAX 619/435–6182. 98 rooms. Pool, bicycles. AE, D, DC, MC, V.*

Downtown

Downtown San Diego is still reaping the benefits of a redevelopment effort that began in the early 1980s and attracted many new hotels to the area. There is much to see within walking distance of downtown accommodations—Seaport Village, the Embarcadero, the historic Gaslamp Quarter, a variety of theaters and night spots, and the spectacular Horton Plaza shopping center. The zoo and Balboa Park are also nearby. In addition, a number of good restaurants have opened in this part of town in the past few years. For nonstop shopping, nightlife, and entertainment, downtown can't be beat. Visitors should be aware, however, that the area is still rather transitional; many streets are rather deserted at night, and street hustlers and homeless people mingle with the crowds of tourists and office workers during the daytime.

$$$$ **Hyatt Regency San Diego.** Opened in late 1992 adjacent to Seaport Vil-
★ lage, this high-rise successfully combines Old World opulence with California airiness and space. Palm trees pose next to ornate tapestry couches in the high-ceiling, light-filled lobby, and all of the masculine, British Regency–style guest rooms have views of the water. Although its proximity to the convention center attracts a large business trade (who can take advantage of an excellent Business Plan), this hotel also offers well-heeled leisure travelers a superb location and facilities. Sally's Restaurant serves fine innovative cuisine in a chic setting, and many who are not staying at the hotel come up to the 49th-floor lounge for the dazzling, 360 degree sunset views. ▥ *One Market Place,* ☎ *619/232–1234 or 800/233–1234,* ℻ *619/233–6464. 875 rooms (including 55 suites and Regency Club rooms). 2 restaurants, lobby lounge, piano bar, pool, 4 tennis courts, health club, boating. AE, D, DC, MC, V.*

$$$–$$$$ **Horton Grand Hotel.** A delightful Victorian confection opened in 1986 in the heart of the historic Gaslamp District, the Horton Grand comprises two 1880s hotels moved brick by brick from nearby locations. It features delightfully retro rooms, individually furnished with period antiques, ceiling fans, and gas-burning fireplaces. The choicest rooms are those overlooking a garden courtyard, which twinkles with miniature lights each night. There's high tea in the afternoon and jazz in the evening. The place is a charmer, but service can be a bit erratic. ▥ *311 Island Ave., 92101,* ☎ *619/544–1886, 800/542–1886, or 800/HERITAGE,* ℻ *619/239–3823. 132 rooms. Restaurant, lounge. AE, D, DC, MC, V.*

$$$–$$$$ **Westgate Hotel.** A nondescript modern high-rise hides what must be the most opulent hotel in town: The lobby, modeled after the anteroom at Versailles, has hand-cut Baccarat chandeliers; rooms are individually furnished with antiques, Italian marble counters, and bath fixtures with 14-karat-gold overlays. Afternoon high tea is served in the lobby to the accompaniment of harp music. If this is a bit formal for some tastes, breathtaking views of the harbor and the city from the ninth floor up will bring you back to the modern world. Horton Plaza is nearby and the Tijuana trolley stops right outside the door. ▥ *1055 2nd Ave., 92101,* ☎ *619/238–1818, 800/221–3802, or 800/522–1564 in CA,* ℻ *619/557–3737. 223 rooms. 3 restaurants, lounge, beauty salon, barbershop, exercise room. AE, D, DC, MC, V.*

$$$ **Doubletree Hotel at Horton Plaza.** Although it is fronted by a startling lighted blue obelisk, this 1987 high-rise is all understated marble, brass, and glass inside. The rooms are similarly elegant and low-key, with muted sea-green and coral color schemes. The lobby lounge at

San Diego Lodging

this business-oriented hotel is packed every night with local financiers and weary shoppers from the adjacent Horton Plaza; a piano player tinkles the ivories on weekends. ☎ *910 Broadway Circle, 92101,* ☎ *619/239–2200 or 800/528–0444,* FAX *619/239–0509. 450 rooms, 14 suites. Restaurant, lobby lounge, sports bar, pool, sauna, spa, 2 tennis courts, health club. AE, D, DC, MC, V.*

$$$ **Embassy Suites San Diego Bay.** It's a short walk to the convention center, the Embarcadero, and Seaport Village from one of downtown's most popular hotels. The front door of each spacious suite opens out onto the hotel's 12-story atrium. The contemporary-style decor is pleasant, and the views from rooms facing the harbor are spectacular. Business travelers will find it easy to set up shop here, and families can make good use of the in-room refrigerators, microwaves, and separate sleeping areas. A cooked-to-order breakfast and afternoon cocktails are complimentary, as are airport transfers. ☎ *601 Pacific Hwy., 92101,* ☎ *619/239–2400 or 800/362–2779,* FAX *619/239–1520. 337 suites. Restaurant, sports bar, pool, sauna, exercise room. AE, D, DC, MC, V.*

$$$ **Holiday Inn on the Bay.** On the Embarcadero and overlooking San Diego Bay, this high-rise hotel is convenient for vacationers as well as business travelers. Rooms are unsurprising but very spacious and comfortable, and views from the balconies are hard to beat. ☎ *1355 N. Harbor Dr., 92101,* ☎ *619/232–3861 or 800/465–4329,* FAX *619/232–4914. 600 rooms, 17 suites. Restaurant, bar, pool, laundry, airport and Amtrak shuttle. AE, D, DC, MC, V.*

$$$ **The Pan Pacific Hotel.** The excellent office and conference facilities at this striking pink hotel, built in 1991, draw business travelers, but the Pan Pacific is also fine for vacationers who want to be near all downtown shopping and restaurants; many of the upper-floor accommodations offer panoramic views of the city. The green prismlike sculpture that hangs from the 100-foot central atrium is a bit overwhelming, and the rather bland, beige-dominated standard rooms are not overly large, but this hotel has a very good health club and such extras as a complimentary airport shuttle. ☎ *400 W. Broadway, 92101,* ☎ *619/239–4500 or 800/626–3988,* FAX *619/239–3274. 436 rooms. 2 restaurants, bar, pool, spa, health club, business services. AE, D, DC, MC, V.*

$$$ **U.S. Grant Hotel.** Built in 1910 and reopened in 1985, this San Diego
★ classic is just across the street from Horton Plaza. Crystal chandeliers and polished marble floors in the lobby and Queen Anne–style mahogany furnishings in the rooms hark back to a more gracious era when such dignitaries as Charles Lindbergh and Franklin D. Roosevelt stayed here. These days, high-power business types still gather at the hotel's clubby Grant Grill. The Grand Heritage group, which bought this hotel in 1994, has gone to great pains to be historically accurate in its refurbishing. ☎ *326 Broadway, 92101,* ☎ *619/232–3121, 800/237–5029, or 800/HERITAGE,* FAX *619/232–3626. 220 rooms, including 60 suites. Restaurant, piano bar, exercise room. AE, D, DC, MC, V.*

$$–$$$ **Balboa Park Inn.** Directly across the street from Balboa Park, this B&B is housed in four Spanish Colonial–style 1915 residences connected by courtyards. Prices are reasonable for the romantic one- and two-bedroom suites. Each has a different flavor, including contemporary versions of Italian, French, Spanish, or early Californian; some have fireplaces, wet bars, whirlpool tubs, patios, and kitchens. Continental breakfast and a newspaper are delivered to guests every morning.

▦ *3402 Park Blvd., 92103,* ☎ *619/298–0823 or 800/938–8181,* ℻ *619/294–8070. 26 suites. Bar. AE, D, DC, MC, V.*

$$ **Harbor Hill Guest House.** This B&B, within walking distance of the harbor and Balboa Park, offers comfortable rooms in a three-story home, with a private entryway and full kitchen on each level. There's a pretty back garden and sun porch, and a carriage house connected to the main house provides a romantic getaway. Not fancy or antiques-filled, this is a cheerful, friendly place that's excellent for families as well as for couples or singles. Continental breakfast is included. ▦ *2330 Albatross St., 92101,* ☎ *619/233–0638. 6 rooms with bath. MC, V.*

$–$$ **Gaslamp Plaza Suites.** Built in 1913 as San Diego's first "skyscraper,"
★ this 11-story structure in the Gaslamp district is only a block from Horton Plaza. It's listed on the National Register of Historic Places; elegant public areas boast lovely old marble, brass, and mosaic. Accommodations—either petite- or one-bedroom suites—are done in shades of burgundy and pink in attractive European style, with contemporary dark wood furniture. Guests can enjoy the view and a complimentary Continental breakfast on the rooftop terrace. Many of the rooms rent as time shares; book ahead if you're visiting in high season. ▦ *520 E St., 92101,* ☎ *619/232–9500 or 800/874–8770,* ℻ *619/238–9945. 60 suites. Restaurant, airport and Amtrak shuttle. AE, MC, D, DC, V.*

$–$$ **Rodeway Inn.** Situated on one of the better streets downtown, this property is clean, comfortable, and nicely decorated. Continental breakfast is included in the room rate. ▦ *833 Ash St., 92101,* ☎ *619/239–2285, 800/228–2000, or 800/522–1528 in CA,* ℻ *619/235–6951. 45 rooms. Sauna. AE, D, DC, MC, V.*

$ **La Pensione.** This downtown budget hotel offers daily, weekly, and
★ monthly rates, and it's pleasant enough for one to want an extended stay. Rooms are modern, clean, and well designed, with good working areas and kitchenettes. The hotel is convenient to the restaurants of the city's version of Little Italy, and the café downstairs is a lovely place to linger over a cappuccino or provolone and proscuitto sandwich. ▦ *1700 India St., 92101,* ☎ *619/236–8000 or 800/232–HOTEL,* ℻ *619/236–8088. 81 rooms. Kitchenettes, laundry. AE, MC, V.*

$ **Super 8 Bayview.** There's nothing fancy about this motel, but the location is less noisy than those of other low-cost establishments. The accommodations are nondescript but clean, and there are rooms for nonsmokers, and some with refrigerators. Continental breakfast is included in the room rate. ▦ *1835 Columbia St., 92101,* ☎ *619/544–0164 or 800/537–9902,* ℻ *619/237–9940. 101 rooms. Laundry, airport and Amtrak shuttle, free parking. AE, DC, MC, V.*

Harbor Island/Shelter Island/Point Loma

Two man-made peninsulas between downtown and the lovely community of Point Loma, Harbor Island and Shelter Island are both bordered by grassy parks, tree-lined paths, lavish hotels, and good restaurants. Harbor Island is closest to the downtown area and less than five minutes from the airport, while narrower Shelter Island is nearer to Point Loma. Both locations command breathtaking views of the bay and the downtown skyline. Not all the lodgings listed here are on the islands themselves, but all are in their vicinity.

$$$$ **Sheraton Harbor Island Resort.** Converted in 1992 into a single complex connected by a shuttle bus, former neighbors Sheraton Grand (now called the West Tower) and Sheraton Harbor Island East (the East Tower) have been undergoing massive refurbishing ever since. The East Tower, upgraded and expanded in a $32 million renovation completed in 1994, has the better sports facilities. The smaller, more intimate West Tower, which reopened in March 1995 after $17 million worth of work, offers larger rooms, with a separate area suitable for business entertaining. Rooms throughout are California-style spiffy, and views from the upper floors of both sections are superb, but because the West Tower is closest to the water, it affords fine outlooks from the lower floors, too. ☎ *1380 Harbor Island Dr., 92101,* ☎ *619/291–2900 or 800/325–3535,* FAX *619/692–2337. 1,048 rooms. 3 restaurants, 2 bars, deli, 3 pools, massage, sauna, spa, 4 tennis courts, health club, jogging, boating, airport shuttle. AE, D, DC, MC, V.*

$$$ **Bay Club Hotel & Marina.** Rooms in this appealing low-rise Shelter Island property are large, light, and attractively furnished with rattan tables and chairs and Polynesian tapestries; all have refrigerators and offer views of either the bay or the marina from outside terraces. A buffet breakfast and limo service to the airport or Amtrak are included in the room rate. ☎ *2131 Shelter Island Dr., 92106,* ☎ *619/224–8888 or 800/672–0800, 800/833–6565 in CA,* FAX *619/225–1604. 105 rooms. Restaurant, pool, spa, exercise room, bicycles, free parking. AE, D, DC, MC, V.*

$$$ **Travelodge Hotel–Harbor Island.** One of the chain's more upscale properties, this Travelodge offers visitors the views and amenities of more expensive hotels, plus such perks as in-room coffeemakers and complimentary parking, airport shuttle, and local phone calls. Those staying on the two executive floors also get free Continental breakfast as well as afternoon hors d'oeuvres and champagne. The attractive public areas and guest rooms are light and airy. The Waterfront Cafe & Club overlooks the marina; sometimes singer Florence Henderson pulls her boat into a slip and joins in the karaoke evenings here. ☎ *1960 Harbor Island Dr., 92101,* ☎ *619/291–6700 or 800/578–7878,* FAX *619/293–0694. 207 rooms. Restaurant, bar, pool, exercise room, jogging, car rental. AE, D, DC, MC, V*

$$–$$$ **Humphrey's Half Moon Inn.** This sprawling South Seas–style resort has many grassy open areas with palm trees and tiki torches. The rooms are attractive, with rattan furnishings and nautical-style lamps; some have harbor or marina views. Locals throng to Humphrey's, the on-premises seafood restaurant, and to the jazz lounge; the hotel also hosts outdoor jazz concerts June–October. ☎ *2303 Shelter Island Dr., 92106,* ☎ *619/224–3411 or 800/542–7400 (weekdays 8–5), 800/345–9995 (reservations),* FAX *619/224–3478. 182 rooms.Restaurant, bar, pool, putting green, spa, croquet, Ping-Pong, boating, bicycles, airport and Amtrak shuttle. AE, D, DC, MC, V.*

$$–$$$ **Kona Kai Plaza Las Glorias Resort and Marina.** This 11-acre property was gutted in 1994 and rebuilt from the ground up. It hadn't yet opened when we visited, but the Kona Kai's prime location—with San Diego Bay on one side, a marina on the other—and its expansive new recreational facilities make it well worth checking out. Accommodations include two-level town houses along with standard rooms and suites. ☎ *1551 Shelter Island Dr., 92106,* ☎ *619/222–1191, 800/566–2524 or 800/342–AMIGO,* FAX *619/222–9738. 207 units. Restaurant, 2 pools, sauna, spa, 2 tennis courts, jogging, volleyball, beach, airport and Amtrak shuttle, free parking. AE, D, DC, MC, V.*

$$ **Best Western Posada Inn.** One of the more upscale members of the Best Western chain, the Posada Inn is not on Harbor Island but is located

on one of the neighboring thoroughfares adjacent to Point Loma. Many of the rooms, which are clean, comfortable, and nicely furnished, have wonderful views of the harbor. A number of excellent seafood restaurants are within walking distance. ⚏ *5005 N. Harbor Dr., 92106, ☎ 619/224–3254 or 800/528–1234, FAX 619/224–2186. 112 rooms. Restaurant, bar, pool, spa, exercise room, airport shuttle. AE, D, DC, MC, V.*

$$ **Best Western Shelter Island Marina Inn.** This waterfront inn, with an airy, skylit lobby, is a good choice if you have a boat to dock; guest slips are available in the adjacent marina. Both harbor- and marina-view rooms are available. Standard accommodations are fairly small; if you're traveling with family or more than one friend, the two-bedroom suite with an eat-in kitchen is a good deal. ⚏ *2051 Shelter Island Dr., 92106, ☎ 619/222–0561 or 800/922–2336, FAX 619/222–9760. 68 rooms, 29 suites. Restaurant, bar, pool, spa, free parking. AE, D, DC, MC, V.*

$ **Outrigger Motel.** A good bet for those traveling as a family, this motel, adjacent to the two resort peninsulas, is less expensive than its offshore counterparts and offers large rooms with eat-in kitchens. Across the street from the Outrigger are fishing docks and the famous Point Loma Seafoods Market and Restaurant. It's a short, scenic walk along the bay from here to Harbor Island. Rooms have gotten a bit shabby in recent years, but the price is still right. ⚏ *1370 Scott St., 92106, ☎ 619/223–7105. 37 rooms with kitchens. Pool, laundry. AE, D, DC, MC, V.*

$ **TraveLodge Point Loma.** For far less money, you'll get the same view here as at the higher-priced hotels. Of course, there are fewer amenities and the neighborhood (near the navy base) isn't as serene, but the rooms, all with coffeemakers, are adequate and clean. ⚏ *5102 N. Harbor Dr., 92106, ☎ 619/223–8171 or 800/525–9055, FAX 619/222–7330. 45 rooms. Pool. AE, D, DC, MC, V.* ·

Hotel Circle/Mission Valley/Old Town

Lining both sides of the stretch of I–8 that lies between Old Town and Mission Valley are a number of moderately priced accommodations that constitute the so-called Hotel Circle. A car is an absolute necessity here, since the only nearby road is the busiest freeway in San Diego. Although not particularly scenic or serene, this location is convenient to Balboa Park, the zoo, downtown, the beaches, the shops of Mission Valley, and Old Town. Mission Valley hotels, near movie theaters and restaurants as well as shops, are more upscale than those of Hotel Circle but generally less expensive than comparable properties at the beaches. Old Town itself has a few picturesque lodgings and is developing a crop of modestly priced chain hotels along nearby I–5; when you're making reservations, request a room that doesn't face the freeway.

$$$–$$$$ **Red Lion Hotel.** Across from Fashion Valley Mall and adjacent to the Brickyard Hazard Center, which hosts a seven-plex cinema, four major restaurants, a food pavilion, and more than 20 shops, the Red Lion is also convenient to I–8. Public areas are light-filled and comfortable, well suited to this hotel's large business clientele. Rooms are spacious and decorated in attractive contemporary pastels, with light wood furniture. ⚏ *7450 Hazard Center Dr., 92108, ☎ 619/297–5466 or 800/547–8010, FAX 619/297–5499. 300 rooms. Restaurant, 2 pools, hot tub, nightclub, airport shuttle, free parking. AE, D, DC, MC, V.*

$$$ **Best Western Hacienda Hotel Old Town.** This pretty white hotel, with balconies and Spanish tile roofs, is in a quiet part of Old Town, away from the freeway and the main retail bustle. The layout of this former shopping complex is a bit confusing, and accommodations are not really large enough to earn the "suite" label the hotel gives them, but they're decorated in tasteful Southwestern style and equipped with microwaves, coffeemakers, minifridges, clock radios, and VCRs. ⛶ *4041 Harney St., 92110,* ☎ *619/298–4707 or 800/888–1991,* ⛶ *619/298– 4771. 150 suites. Restaurant, pool, free parking. AE, D, DC, MC, V.*

$$$ **San Diego Marriott Mission Valley.** This high-rise sits in the middle of
★   the San Diego River valley, where the dry riverbed has been graded and transformed over the years into a commercial zone with sleek office towers and sprawling shopping malls. It has lots of facilities for business travelers but also caters to vacationers, with comfortable rooms, a friendly staff, a piano lounge, and free transportation to the malls. ⛶ *8757 Rio San Diego Dr., 92108,* ☎ *619/692–3800 or 800/228– 9290,* ⛶ *619/692–0769. 52 rooms. Restaurant, bar, pool, sauna, tennis court, exercise room, free parking. AE, D, DC, MC, V.*

$$–$$$ **Heritage Park Bed & Breakfast Inn.** One of the beautifully restored mansions in Old Town's Heritage Park, this romantic 1889 Queen Anne has eight quaint guest rooms and a suite decorated with period antiques. Breakfast and afternoon refreshments are included in the room rate. ⛶ *2470 Heritage Park Row, 92110,* ☎ *619/295–7088 or 800/995– 2470. 6 rooms with bath, 2 rooms with shared bath, 1 2-bedroom suite. AE, MC, V.*

$$–$$$ **Ramada Inn Old Town.** The most established of the new hotels and motels springing up along I–5 at Old Town, the hacienda-style Ramada has Spanish Colonial–style fountains, courtyards, and painted tiles, and Southwest-style decor in the rooms. Breakfast, cocktail reception, and transfers to the airport, bus, and Amtrak are all complimentary. ⛶ *2435 Jefferson St., 92110,* ☎ *619/260–8500 or 800/272–6232,* ⛶ *619/297– 2078. 152 rooms. Restaurant, pool, airport and Amtrak shuttle. AE, D, DC, MC, V.*

$$–$$$ **San Diego Mission Valley Hilton.** Directly fronting I–8, this property has soundproofed rooms decorated in contemporary southwestern style. When you're indoors, the attractive modern accommodations, along with the stylish public areas and lush greenery in the back, make you forget this business-oriented hotel's proximity to the freeway. Children stay free, and small pets are accepted ($25). ⛶ *901 Camino del Rio S, 92108,* ☎ *619/543–9000, 800/733–2332, or 800/HILTONS,* ⛶ *619/543–9358. 350 rooms. Restaurant, bar, sports bar, pool, spa, fitness center, airport shuttle, free parking. AE, D, DC, MC, V.*

$$ **Hanalei Hotel.** As its name suggests, the theme of this friendly Hotel
★   Circle property is Hawaiian: Palm trees, waterfalls, koi ponds, and tiki torches abound here. A two-story complex offers poolside rooms, and a high-rise building surrounds a lovely Hawaiian-style garden. The rooms were refurbished in 1993–94 with tropical prints in rich colors; some have tile floors, and others have wall-to-wall carpeting. Guests have access to an adjacent golf course, and free transport is provided to local malls and Old Town. ⛶ *2270 Hotel Circle N, 92108,* ☎ *619/297– 1101 or 800/882–0858,* ⛶ *619/297–6049. 412 rooms. 2 restaurants, bar, pool, spa, free parking. AE, D, DC, MC, V.*

$ **Days Inn Hotel Circle.** Rooms in this large complex are generally par for the chain-motel course but have the perk of minifridges; some units also have stoves. ⛶ *543 Hotel Circle S, 92108,* ☎ *619/297–8800 or 800/227–4743 (weekdays 8–4:30), 800/325–2525 (central reservations),* ⛶ *619/298–6029. 280 rooms. Restaurant, pool, beauty salon, spa, laundry. AE, D, DC, MC, V.*

$ Padre Trail Inn. This standard, family-style motel is located slightly southwest of Mission Valley. Old Town, shopping, and dining are all within walking distance. ☎ *4200 Taylor St., 92110,* ☎ *619/297–3291 or 800/255–9988,* FAX *619/692–2080. 100 rooms. Restaurant, bar, pool. AE, D, DC, MC, V.*

La Jolla

Million-dollar homes line the beaches and hillsides of La Jolla, one of the world's most beautiful, prestigious communities. The village—the heart of La Jolla—is chockablock with expensive boutiques, galleries, and restaurants. Don't despair, however, if you're not old money or even nouveau riche; this popular vacation spot has sufficient lodging choices for every pocket, even those on a budget.

$$$$ Sheraton Grande Torrey Pines. The view of the Pacific from this low-
★ rise, high-class property atop the Torrey Pines cliffs is superb. The hotel blends into the clifftop, looking rather insignificant until you step inside the luxurious lobby and gaze out at the sea and the 18th hole of the lush green Torrey Pines golf course. Amenities include complimentary butler service—just pick up the phone in the morning and a carafe of Starbucks coffee and a newspaper will be delivered to your room, gratis. The oversize accommodations, tastefully decorated in muted tones, are simple but elegant; all offer balconies or terraces. In addition to easy access to one of the best public golf courses in town, guests also have privileges at the excellent health club–sports center next door ($7.50). A special sports concierge can help organize your outdoor activities. ☎ *10950 N. Torrey Pines Rd., 92037,* ☎ *619/558–1500 or 800/325–3535,* FAX *619/450–4584. 400 rooms, including 17 suites. Restaurant, bar, in-room safes, pool, 3 tennis courts, exercise room, bicycles. AE, D, DC, MC, V.*

$$$–$$$$ La Valencia. A La Jolla landmark, this pink Art Deco confection drew
★ film stars down from Hollywood in the 1930s and '40s for its lovely setting and views of La Jolla Cove (*see* Tour 7 *in* Chapter 2, Exploring San Diego). The clientele is a bit older and more staid these days, but the hotel is still in prime condition. Many of the individually decorated rooms have a genteel European look, with antique pieces and plush, richly colored rugs. The restaurants are excellent, the Whaling Bar is a popular gathering spot, and the hotel is ideally located near the shops and restaurants of La Jolla village and what is arguably the prettiest beach in San Diego. Prices are quite reasonable if you're willing to look out on the village, but on a clear, sunny day, the ocean views may be worth every extra penny. ☎ *1132 Prospect St., 92037,* ☎ *619/454–0771 or 800/451–0772,* FAX *619/456–3921. 100 rooms. 3 restaurants, bars, pool, exercise room, library. AE, MC, V.*

$$$–$$$$ Sea Lodge. This low-lying compound, on the excellent La Jolla Shores beach, has a definite Spanish flavor to it, with its palm trees, fountains, red-tile roofs, and Mexican tile work. The attractive rooms feature rattan furniture, nautical-design bedspreads, and terra-cotta lattice-board walls; all have hair dryers, coffeemakers, refrigerators, and irons as well as wooden balconies that overlook lush landscaping and the sea. Early reservations are a must; families will find plenty of room and distractions for both kids and parents. ☎ *8110 Camino del Oro, 92037,* ☎ *619/459–8271 or 800/237–5211,* FAX *619/456–9346. 128 rooms, 19 with kitchenettes. Restaurant, bar, pool, hot tub, sauna, 2 tennis courts, golf course, Ping-Pong, beach. AE, D, DC, MC, V.*

$$$ Colonial Inn. A tastefully restored Victorian-era building, this is the oldest hotel in La Jolla, offering turn-of-the-century elegance in its public spaces; in keeping with the period, rooms are a bit formal and staid.

Ocean views cost more than village views. On one of La Jolla's main thoroughfares but not in the thick of its busiest people traffic, the Colonial Inn is near boutiques, restaurants, and the cove. ☎ *910 Prospect St., 92037, ☎ 619/454–2181, 800/832–5525, or 800/826–1278 in CA, FAX 619/454–5679. 75 rooms. Restaurant, bar, pool. AE, DC, MC, V.*

$$$ Hyatt Regency La Jolla. Designed by Michael Graves (who counts New York's Whitney Museum addition among his unfinished projects), the Hyatt is the cornerstone of the Aventine complex in La Jolla's Golden Triangle, about 10 minutes from the beach and the village. The postmodern mix of design elements of the striking lobby is carried out into the spacious, comfortable rooms, where warm cherry-wood furnishings contrast with austere gray closets (their stainless-steel handles make them look rather like large wall safes). The hotel's four trendy restaurants include the excellent Cafe Japengo (*see* Chapter 7, Dining); you can work off some of the calories at one of the best health clubs in the city. Rates are lower on the weekends at this business-oriented hotel. ☎ *3777 La Jolla Village Dr., 92122, ☎ 619/552–1234 or 800/233–1234, FAX 619/552–6066. 400 rooms and suites. 4 restaurants, bar, pool, spa, 2 tennis courts, health club, jogging, basketball. AE, D, DC, MC, V.*

$$$ Scripps Inn. You'd be wise to make reservations well in advance for this small, quiet inn tucked away on Coast Boulevard; its popularity with repeat visitors ensures that it is booked year-round. Available kitchen facilities and lower weekly and monthly rates (not available in the summer season) make it particularly attractive to long-term guests. All the rooms are individually decorated and offer ocean views; two have fireplaces. A lovely Continental breakfast is served in the lobby each morning. ☎ *555 Coast Blvd. S, ☎ 619/454–3391, FAX 619/459–6758. 13 rooms. Kitchenettes. AE, D, MC, V.*

$$–$$$ Bed & Breakfast Inn at La Jolla. Built in 1913 by Irving Gill, this B&B is located in a quiet section of La Jolla just down the street from the Museum of Contemporary Art. The individually decorated rooms cover a wide range of sizes and styles—some are done in Laura Ashley prints, others feature wicker or rattan furnishings—but all are pretty and well tended and come with fresh fruit, sherry, and terry robes. The lovely gardens in the back were planned by Kate Sessions, who was instrumental in landscaping Balboa Park. ☎ *7753 Draper Ave., 92037, ☎ 619/456–2066. 16 rooms, 15 with private bath. Refrigerators, library. MC, V.*

$$–$$$ Best Western Inn by the Sea. In a quiet section of La Jolla Village, within five blocks of the beach, the five-story Inn by the Sea has all the modern amenities at reasonable rates for La Jolla. Rooms are done in cheerful pastel tones and have private balconies with views of either the sea or the village. Continental breakfast, newspaper, and local phone calls are on the house. ☎ *7830 Fay Ave., 92037, ☎ 619/459–4461 or 800/462–9732, FAX 619/456–2578. 132 rooms. Pool, exercise room, free parking. AE, D, DC, MC, V.*

$$–$$$ La Jolla Cove Motel. Offering studios and suites, some with spacious oceanfront balconies, this motel overlooks the famous La Jolla Cove beach. If it doesn't have the charm of some of the older properties of this exclusive area, this motel gives its guests the same first-class views at much lower rates. A complimentary Continental breakfast is included in the room rate. The free underground lot is also a bonus in a section of town where a parking spot is a prime commodity. ☎ *1155 S. Coast Blvd., 92037, ☎ 619/459–2621 or 800/248–2683. 117 rooms. Kitchenettes, pool, spa, putting green, coin laundry. AE, D, MC, V.*

$$–$$$ **Prospect Park Inn.** This European-style inn rents a wide variety of ap-
★ pealing rooms, many with sweeping ocean views from their balconies.
Located in a prime spot in La Jolla village, it's near some of the best
shops and restaurants in town and one block away from the beach.
Continental breakfast is included in the very reasonable room rate, and
parking is free. There is no smoking on the premises. ⌧ *1110 Prospect
St., 92037,* ☎ *619/454–0133 or 800/433–1609,* FAX *619/454–2056.
23 rooms. Bar, kitchenettes. AE, D, DC, MC, V.*

$$ **La Jolla Palms Inn.** In the southern section of La Jolla, near some ex-
cellent beaches, this modest motel is also near a wide variety of shops
and restaurants. Many of the rooms are remarkably large, with huge
closets; some have kitchenettes, and three suites offer separate eat-in
kitchens. The rooms are nothing to write home about, but this is an
excellent value for families who want to stay in this tony area and still
have a few dollars left over for shopping. Complimentary Continen-
tal breakfast is offered. New owners are planning substantial renova-
tions and room upgrades. ⌧ *6705 La Jolla Blvd., 92037,*
☎ *619/454–7101 or 800/451–0358,* FAX *619/454–6957. 58 rooms.
Pool, spa, billiards, laundry. AE, D, DC, MC, V.*

$$ **Summer House Inn.** Don't expect an idyllic hideaway: Summer House
Inn stands at the intersection of two of the busiest roads in La Jolla.
Still, this pleasant, modern high-rise is five minutes from the village, a
few blocks from the beach, convenient to freeway entrances, and reasonably priced. Rooms are done in a pleasant contemporary style; those
on the north side, away from Torrey Pines Road, are quietest, while
those on the highest floors have the best views (and are, accordingly,
more expensive). Locals come to Elario's restaurant, on the top floor,
for its excellent live jazz. ⌧ *7955 La Jolla Shores Dr., 92037,*
☎ *619/459–0261 or 800/666–0261,* FAX *619/459–7649. 90 rooms.
Restaurant, kitchenettes, pool, beauty salon, massage, spa. AE, D, DC,
MC, V.*

$$ **Torrey Pines Inn.** Located on a bluff between La Jolla and Del Mar,
★ this hotel commands a view of miles and miles of coastline. It's adja-
cent to the public Torrey Pines Golf Course, one of the best in the county,
and very close to scenic Torrey Pines State Beach and nature reserve;
the village of La Jolla is a 10-minute drive away. Most of the rooms
have been renovated with dark wood furnishings and Asian fabrics.
This off-the-beaten-path inn is a very good value, especially for golfers.
⌧ *11480 N. Torrey Pines Rd., 92037,* ☎ *619/453–4420, 800/995–
4507 (hotel central), or 800/777–1700 for central reservations,* FAX
*619/453–0691. 74 rooms. Restaurant, 2 bars, coffee shop, pool. AE,
D, DC, MC, V.*

Mission Bay and Beaches

Staying near the water is a priority for most people who visit San Diego.
Mission and Pacific beaches have the highest concentration of small
hotels and motels. Both these areas have a casual atmosphere and a
busy coastal thoroughfare offering endless shopping, dining, and
nightlife possibilities. Mission Bay Park, with its beaches, bike trails,
boat-launching ramps, golf course, and grassy parks, is also a hotel haven.
You can't go wrong with any of these locations, as long as the frenzy
of hundreds at play doesn't bother you.

$$$–$$$$ **Catamaran Resort Hotel.** If you check in at the right time, parrots will
★ herald your arrival at this appealing hotel, set between Mission Bay
and Pacific Beach; the two resident birds are often poised on a perch
in the lushly landscaped lobby, replete with a koi fish pond. The
grounds are similarly tropical, and tiki torches light the way for guests

staying at one of the six two-story buildings or the 14-story high-rise (the view from the upper floors of the latter is spectacular). The popular Cannibal Bar hosts Top 40s and rock-and-roll groups, while a classical or jazz pianist tickles the ivories at the Moray Bar; Catamaran guests can also take advantage of the entertainment facilities at the sister Bahia Hotel. Children 18 or under stay free. ⌕ *3999 Mission Blvd., 92109, ☎ 619/488–1081, 800/288–0770, or 800/233–8172 in Canada,* FAX *619/490–3328 (reservations), 619/488–1619 (front desk). 312 rooms. Restaurant, bar, coffee shop, piano bar, pool, spa, exercise room, nightclub. AE, D, DC, MC, V.*

$$$–$$$$ **Crystal Pier Motel.** You can drive your car onto the Crystal Pier and park in front of one of this classic motel's blue-and-white cottages, equipped with kitchenettes and patios overlooking the sea. You'll be lulled to sleep by the gentle lapping of waves against wooden pilings; the cries of sea gulls provide a pleasant wake-up call. A landmark since the 1930s, this place is no longer the bargain it once was, nor does it have the amenities of the other properties in its price category; you're paying for character and a unique proximity to the ocean. But it retains a loyal following nevertheless; call four to six weeks in advance for reservations. Weekly and monthly rates are available in winter. The more people you come with, the more reasonable this place is: The cottages sleep up to four but cost the same no matter what the occupancy. ⌕ *4500 Ocean Blvd., ☎ 619/483–6983 or 800/748–5894,* FAX *619/483–6811. 26 cottages. Kitchenettes. 3-night minimum stay June 15–Sept. 15., 2-night minimum rest of yr. D, MC, V.*

$$$–$$$$ **San Diego Princess Resort.** This 44-acre resort is so beautifully landscaped that it's been the setting for a number of movies, and it offers a wide range of recreational activities, as well as access to a marina. A major renovation in 1993–94 brightened up rooms with colorful new fabrics and plush carpeting; unfortunately, the walls between them remain motel thin. All rooms have private patios and coffeemakers, and a number have kitchens. Of the resort's various eateries, the Barefoot Bar and Grill is the most fun; guests and visitors come here to kick off their shoes and boogie in a sand-filled, strobe-lit setting. ⌕ *1404 W. Vacation Rd., 92109, ☎ 619/274–4630 or 800/344–2626,* FAX *619/581–5929. 462 cottages. 3 restaurants, 2 bars, 5 pools, sauna, 6 tennis courts, 18-hole putting golf course, croquet, health club, jogging, volleyball, boating, bicycles. AE, D, DC, MC, V.*

$$$ **Bahia Resort Hotel.** This huge complex, on a 14-acre peninsula in Mission Bay Park, offers tastefully furnished studios and suites with kitchens; many have wood-beamed ceilings and attractive tropical decor. The hotel's *Bahia Belle* cruises Mission Bay at sunset, and guests can return for yuks at the on-premises Comedy Isle club. Rates are reasonable for a place so well located—within walking distance of the ocean—and offering so many amenities, including use of the facilities at the Catamaran Hotel. ⌕ *998 W. Mission Bay Dr., 92109, ☎ 619/488–0551, 800/288–0770, or 800/233–8172 in Canada,* FAX *619/490–3328 (reservations), 619/488–7055. 321 rooms. Restaurant, bar, piano bar, pool, spa, 2 tennis courts, bicycles, rollerblading, comedy club. AE, D, DC, MC, V.*

$$$ **Hyatt Islandia.** Located in Mission Bay Park, one of San Diego's most appealing seashore areas, the Islandia has rooms in several low-level, lanai-style units, as well as marina suites and rooms in a high-rise building. Many of the tastefully modern accommodations overlook the hotel's gardens and fish pond; others have dramatic views of the bay area. This hotel is famous for its lavish Sunday champagne brunch. In winter, whale-watching expeditions depart from the Islandia's marina. ⌕ *1441 Quivira Rd., 92109, ☎ 619/224–1234 or 800/233–1234,*

FAX *619/224–0348. 422 rooms. 2 restaurants, pool, spa, exercise room, marina, boating. AE, D, DC, MC, V.*

$$$ **San Diego Hilton Beach and Tennis Resort.** Spread out on the picturesque grounds of this deluxe resort, low-level bungalows are surrounded by trees, Japanese bridges, and ponds; a high-rise building offers accommodations with lovely views of Mission Bay Park. The Kids Club Program offers complimentary day care for children over age 5 (daily during the summer, on weekends the rest of the year), and the sports facilities on the property are excellent. Tickets (and discounts) for various area attractions can be picked up at the concierge desk and charged to your room. The property underwent a $25 million renovation in 1994–95, with rooms redone in a contemporary version of Spanish-colonial style. ☎ *1775 E. Mission Bay Dr., 92109,* ☎ *619/276–4010 or 800/445–8667,* FAX *619/275–7991. 357 rooms. Restaurant, bar, coffee shop, pool, putting greens, 5 tennis courts, exercise room, boating, marina, bicycles, playground, car rental. AE, D, DC, MC, V.*

$$–$$$ **Dana Inn & Marina.** This hotel, which has an adjoining marina, is a bargain in the Mission Bay area. If accommodations are not as grand as those in the nearby hotels, they're more than adequate. There are many on-premises sports facilities, and the Dana Inn is within walking distance of Sea World, the beach, and a pleasant park. ☎ *1710 W. Mission Bay Dr., 92109,* ☎ *619/222–6440, 800/DANA–INN, or 800/345–9995 (central reservations),* FAX *619/222–5916. 196 rooms. Restaurant, pool, spa, 2 tennis courts, Ping-Pong, shuffleboard, boating. AE, D, DC, MC, V.*

$$ **Pacific Shores Inn.** One of the better motels in the Mission Bay area, this property is only a half-block from the beach and has nicely decorated rooms. Kitchen units with multiple beds for families are available at reasonable rates; your pet (under 20 lbs.) can stay, too, for an extra $25. Continental breakfast is included in the room rate. ☎ *4802 Mission Blvd., 92109,* ☎ *619/483–6300 or 800/367–6467,* FAX *619/483–9276. 55 rooms. Pool, laundry. AE, D, DC, MC, V.*

$$ **Surfer Motor Lodge.** This high-rise is right on the beach and directly behind a shopping center with many restaurants and boutiques. Rooms are plain, but those on the upper floors have excellent views. ☎ *711 Pacific Beach Dr., 92109,* ☎ *619/483–7070 or 800/787–3373,* FAX *619/274–1670. 52 rooms. Restaurant, bar, pool, bicycles. AE, DC, MC, V.*

$–$$ **Ocean Manor Apartment Hotel.** Some folks have been returning for
★ 20 years to this well-priced Ocean Beach hotel, which rents units by the day (three-day minimum for those with kitchens), week, or month in winter; you'll need to reserve months in advance. Guests at this charming place have included everyone from retired generals to Svetlana Stalin. Located on Sunset Cliffs, Ocean Manor offers lovely views; the beach below has long since washed away, but other beaches are within walking distance and Point Loma is a 10-minute drive away. The comfortable studios and one- and two-bedroom suites are furnished plainly in the style of the 1950s—which is when the amiable owners took over the place. There is no maid service, but fresh towels are always provided. A limited number of garages are available for $1 a night. ☎ *1370 Sunset Cliffs Blvd., 92107,* ☎ *619/222–7901 or 619/224–1379 (guest calls). 22 units. Pool, Ping-Pong, shuffleboard. MC, V.*

$ **Mission Bay Motel.** Located a half-block from the beach, this motel offers centrally located, modest units, some with kitchenettes. Great restaurants and nightlife are within walking distance, but you may find the area a bit noisy. ☎ *4221 Mission Blvd., 92109,* ☎ *619/483–6440. 50 rooms. Pool. MC, V.*

Hostels

Banana Bungalow San Diego (707 Reed Ave., Mission Beach 92109, ☎ 619/273–3060 or 800/5–HOSTEL).

HI–Elliot Hostel (3790 Udall St., San Diego 92107, ☎ 619/223–4778).

HI–Hostel on Broadway (500 W. Broadway, San Diego 92101, ☎ 619/525–1531).

Jim's San Diego (1425 C St., San Diego, 92101, ☎ 619/235–0234, FAX 619/399–4216).

YWCA of San Diego (1012 C St., San Diego 92101, ☎ 619/239–0355).

9 The Arts and Nightlife

THE ARTS

By Marael
Johnson

Updated by
Albert M.
Columbo

TOP NATIONAL touring companies perform regularly at the Civic Theatre, Golden Hall, Symphony Hall, and East County Performing Arts Center. San Diego State University, the University of California at San Diego, private universities, and community colleges present a wide variety of performing arts programs, from appearances by well-known artists to student recitals. The daily *San Diego Union* lists current attractions and complete movie schedules. The *Reader,* a free weekly that comes out each Thursday, devotes an entire section to upcoming cultural events as well as current theater and film reviews. *San Diego* magazine publishes a monthly "What's Doing" column that lists arts events throughout the county and reviews of current films, plays, and concerts.

It is best to book tickets well in advance, preferably at the same time you make hotel reservations. There are various outlets for last-minute tickets, though you risk either paying top rates or getting less-than-choice seats—or both.

Half-price tickets to most theater, music, and dance events can be bought on the day of performance at the **TIMES ARTS TIX Ticket Center** (Horton Plaza, ☎ 619/238–3810). Only cash is accepted. Advance full-price tickets may also be purchased through ARTS TIX.

Visa and MasterCard holders may buy tickets for many scheduled performances through **Ticketmaster** (☎ 619/220–8497). Service charges vary according to the event, and most tickets are nonrefundable.

Theater

Blackfriars Theatre (121 Broadway, Suite 203, ☎ 619/232–4088), formerly the Bowery, is acclaimed by critics and theater goers for its premieres of high-quality works by both famous playwrights and soon-to-be-discovered artists.

Coronado Playhouse (1775 Strand Way, Coronado, ☎ 619/435–4856), a cabaret-type theater near the Hotel del Coronado, stages regular dramatic and musical performances. Dinner packages are offered on Friday and Saturday.

Diversionary Theatre (4545 Park Blvd., University Heights, ☎ 619/574–1060) is a gay and lesbian theater that stages comedies and dramas on gay themes for the whole community.

Gaslamp Quarter Theatre at the Hahn Cosmopolitan Theatre (444 4th Ave., ☎ 619/234–9583). The resident theater company stages comedies, dramas, mysteries, and musicals in the 250-seat Hahn Cosmopolitan Theatre, located in the Gaslamp Quarter.

La Jolla Playhouse (Mandell Weiss Center for the Performing Arts, University of California at San Diego, ☎ 619/550–1010). From May to November, look for exciting and innovative presentations, under the artistic direction of Michael Greif. Many Broadway productions, such as *A Walk in the Woods, Big River,* and works by Neil Simon, have previewed here before heading for the East Coast.

La Jolla Stage Company (750 Nautilus St., La Jolla, ☎ 619/459–7773) presents lavish productions of Broadway favorites and popular comedies year-round in Parker Auditorium at La Jolla High School.

Lawrence Welk Resort Theatre (8860 Lawrence Welk Dr., Escondido, ☎ 619/749–3448 or 800/932–9355). About a 45-minute drive from downtown, this famed dinner theater puts on polished Broadway-style productions with a professional cast.

Old Globe Theatre (Simon Edison Centre for the Performing Arts, Balboa Park, ☎ 619/239–2255) is the oldest professional theater in California, performing classics, contemporary dramas, experimental works, and putting on the famous summer Shakespeare Festival at the Old Globe and its sister theaters, the Cassius Carter Centre Stage and the Lowell Davies Festival Theatre.

RUSE Marquis Public Theater (3717 India St., ☎ 619/295–5654) presents contemporary, experimental, and original plays on the main stage and in the smaller gallery.

San Diego Comic Opera (Casa del Prado Theatre, Balboa Park, ☎ 619/231–5714) has four different productions of Gilbert and Sullivan and similar works from October through July.

San Diego Repertory Theater (79 Horton Plaza, ☎ 619/235–8025), San Diego's first resident acting company, performs contemporary works year-round on the 550-seat Lyceum stage and in a 225-seat theater that can be rearranged to suit the stage set.

Sledgehammer Theatre (1620 6th Ave., ☎ 619/544–1484) is one of the cutting-edge theaters in San Diego; it stages avant-garde pieces in St. Cecilia's church.

Starlight Musicals (Starlight Bowl, Balboa Park, ☎ 619/544–7827; but phone disconnected off-season) is a local summertime favorite; this series of popular musicals is presented in an outdoor amphitheater from mid-June through early September.

Sushi Performance and Visual Art (633 9th Ave., ☎ 619/235–8466), a nationally acclaimed group, provides an opportunity for well-known performance artists to do their thing.

UCSD Theatre (Warren Theatre and Mandell Weiss Theatre, University of California at San Diego campus, La Jolla, ☎ 619/534–6467). The students of the University of California at San Diego's theater department take the stage in the theaters used by La Jolla Playhouse in the summer months and present first-rate productions from September to May.

Concerts

Copley Symphony Hall (1245 7th Ave., ☎ 619/699–4200). The San Diego Symphony Orchestra is the only California symphony that has its own concert hall. The performance season runs October–May, with a series of outdoor pop concerts held near Seaport Village during the summer.

Open-Air Theatre (San Diego State University, ☎ 619/594–6884). Top-name rock, reggae, and popular artists pack in the crowds for summer concerts under the stars.

Organ Pavilion (Balboa Park, ☎ 619/226–0819). Robert Plimpton performs on the giant 1914 pipe organ at 2 PM on most Sunday afternoons and on most Monday evenings in summer. All concerts are free.

Sherwood Auditorium (700 Prospect St., La Jolla, ☎ 619/454–2594). Many classical and jazz events are held in the 550-seat auditorium in the San Diego Museum of Contemporary Art. August–May, La Jolla

Chamber Music Society presents internationally acclaimed chamber ensembles, orchestras, and soloists. San Diego Chamber Orchestra, a 35-member ensemble, performs once a month, October–April.

Sports Arena (2500 Sports Arena Blvd., ☎ 619/224–4176). Big-name rock concerts play to more than 14,000 fans, using an end-stage configuration, so all seats face in one direction.

Spreckels Theatre (121 Broadway, ☎ 619/235–9500). This beautiful downtown theater, built more than 80 years ago and designated a landmark in 1972, hosts a wide range of musical events—everything from Mostly Mozart to small rock concerts. Ballets and theatrical productions are also held here. Its good acoustics, as well as its historical interest, make this an appealing place to come for a show of any kind.

Opera

Civic Theatre (202 C St., ☎ 619/236–6510). The San Diego Opera draws international artists and has developed an impeccable reputation. The season of five operas runs January–April in the 3,000-seat, state-of-the-art auditorium. English translations of works sung in their original languages are projected on a large screen above the stage.

Dance

California Ballet (☎ 619/560–5676). Four high-quality contemporary and traditional works, from story ballets to Balanchine, are performed September–May. The *Nutcracker* is staged annually at the Civic Theatre; other ballets take place at Poway Center for the Performing Arts (15500 Espola Rd., Poway, ☎ 619/748–0505), the Lyceum, and Nautilus Bowl at Sea World.

Issacs McCaleb & Dancers (☎ 619/296–9523). Interpretative dance presentations, incorporating live music, are staged at major theaters and concert halls around San Diego County.

Film

First-run international films are screened at the **Cove** (7730 Girard Ave., La Jolla, ☎ 619/459–5404), **Guild** (3827 5th Ave., ☎ 619/295–2000), and **Park** (3812 Park Blvd., ☎ 619/294–9264) theaters.

Hillcrest Cinemas (3965 5th Ave., ☎ 619/299–2100). Owned and operated by Landmark, the owners of the Guild, Park, Cove, and Ken, this posh new multiplex shuns mainstream Hollywood blockbusters in favor of art and foreign films. You can even get espresso at the snack bar.

Ken Cinema (4061 Adams Ave., ☎ 619/283–5909). The roster of art/revival films changes almost every night, and many programs are double bills.

Sherwood Auditorium (*see* Concerts, *above*) regularly hosts foreign and classic film series and special cinema events, including the wildly popular Festival of Animation (January–March).

NIGHTLIFE

By Dan Janeck
Updated by
Alberto
Columbo

The unbeatable variety of sun-and-surf recreational activities is the prime reason tourists come to San Diego, but most visitors are surprised and delighted by the new momentum the city gains after dark. The highly mercurial nightlife scene is constantly growing—the flavor of the month may be Top 40 or contemporary, reggae, pop-jazz, or strictly rock-and-roll. Live pop and fusion jazz have become especially popular—some say they are the ideal music for San Diego's typically laid-back lifestyle—and they can easily be found at a dozen or so venues throughout the county. Music at local rock clubs and nightclubs ranges from danceable contemporary Top 40 to original rock and new wave by San Diego's finest up-and-coming groups. Discotheques and bars in the Gaslamp Quarter and at Pacific and Mission beaches tend to be the most crowded spots in the county on the weekends, but don't let that discourage you from visiting these quintessential San Diego hangouts. Authentic country-western music is also an option for those willing to go a bit farther afield. And should your tastes run to softer music, there are plenty of piano bars in which to unfrazzle and unwind. Check the free weekly *Reader* for band information or *San Diego* magazine's "Restaurant & Nightlife Guide" for the full range of nightlife possibilities.

California law prohibits the sale of alcoholic beverages after 2 AM. Bars and nightclubs usually stop serving at about 1:40 AM. You must be 21 to purchase and consume alcohol, and most places will insist on current identification. Be aware that California also has some of the most stringent drunk-driving laws in the United States; roadblocks are not an uncommon sight.

Bars and Nightclubs

Cannibal Bar. At this tropical-theme bar and nightclub in the Catamaran Resort Hotel, you'll hear oldies, contemporary jazz, blues, and swing. *3999 Mission Blvd., Pacific Beach,* ☎ *619/488–1081.* ⊘ *Wed.–Sun. 7 AM–2 PM. Entertainment 9 PM–1:30 AM. AE, D, DC, MC, V.*

Characters. Out-of-towners and university students gather at this bar in the La Jolla Marriott to relax and watch their favorite sports on 10 televisions and two big screens. *4240 La Jolla Village Dr., La Jolla,* ☎ *619/587–1414.* ⊘ *Daily 4 PM–1:30 AM. AE, DC, MC, V.*

Club Fifth Avenue. One of the Gaslamp Quarter's newer nightspots, this place is fast becoming one of the more popular destinations for San Diego's young professionals. There's a dress code (no jeans, T-shirts, or tennis shoes) on Friday and Saturday nights. Entertainment varies nightly, and there is a nominal cover charge. *835 5th Ave., downtown,* ☎ *619/238–7191.* ⊘ *Wed.–Sun. 8 PM–2 AM. AE, D, DC, MC, V.*

Club 66. Located under the restaurant Dakota's, this impressive club with stainless-steel decor and gas-station memorabilia is modeled after Route 66. You'll have fun dancing, rockin' with the band, or just taking it all in. Admission is free to Dakota's patrons. *901 5th Ave., downtown,* ☎ *619/234–4166.* ⊘ *Wed.–Sat. 8 PM–2 AM. AE, D, DC, MC, V.*

The Daily Planet. You can't miss this glorified neighborhood bar, painted in neon purple, yellow, and green. The crowd is fun-loving and unpretentious. On weekends at around 9 PM, the pool tables make way for a great DJ or a local band. *1200 Garnet Ave., Pacific Beach,* ☎ *619/272–6066.* ⊘ *Mon.–Thurs. 11 AM–2 AM, weekends 9 AM–2 AM. MC, V.*

E Street Alley. Off the street down a short alley, this club is a marvel for the senses. The Blue Room is a plush lounge of blue-velvet-covered walls, artwork, big velvet seats romantically paired in mood lighting and a handsome bar with live jazz on Thursday and blues the rest of the week. Club E is a smartly designed spacious dance club with a DJ spinning Top 40 tunes. Chino's is an exquisite restaurant featuring an American cuisine with a Southeast Asian flare open 11:30 AM–2:30 PM and 5:30 PM–11 PM. *914 4th Ave. (on E St. between 4th and 5th), downtown,* ☎ *619/231–9200,* ☉ *Tues.–Thurs. 10 PM–2 AM, Fri. and Sat. 8 PM–2 AM. AE, D, DC, MC, V.*

Hard Rock Cafe. Part of the international chain, this is a great place to party amid an impressive collection of rock-and-roll memorabilia. *909 Prospect St., La Jolla,* ☎ *619/454–5101.* ☉ *Mon.–Thurs. 11:30 AM–11 PM, weekends 11:30 AM–midnight. AE, DC, MC, V.*

Islands Lounge. Tropical decor and Hawaiian music give this lounge in the Hanalei Hotel its unique character and attract a steady stream of regulars. *2270 Hotel Circle N, Mission Valley,* ☎ *619/297–1101.* ☉ *In summer, Mon.–Thurs. 4 PM–11 PM, weekends 10 AM–1:30 AM. In winter, Mon.–Thurs. 5 PM–10 PM, Fri.–Sat. 5 PM–11 PM, and Sun. 10–10. AE, D, DC, MC, V.*

Karl Strauss' Old Columbia Brewery & Grill. The first microbrewery in San Diego draws a downtown crowd to its excellent beers—try the Gaslamp Gold—accompanied by beer-battered fish-and-chips, hefty onion rings, and huge burgers. *1157 Columbia St., downtown,* ☎ *619/234–2739.* ☉ *Sun.–Thurs. 11:30 AM–midnight, Fri. and Sat. till 1 AM. MC, V.*

Megalopolis. This funky little club isn't nearly as large or as flashy as the name may suggest, but an eclectic roster of blues, rock, and folk bands is reason enough to visit. *4321 Fairmount Ave., Kensington,* ☎ *619/584–7900.* ☉ *Tues.–Sat. 8 PM–2 AM. No credit cards.*

Old Bonita Store & Bonita Beach Club. This South Bay hangout with a DJ who spins retro house music attracts singles 25–35. *4014 Bonita Rd., Bonita,* ☎ *619/479–3537.* ☉ *Sun.–Thurs. 8:30 PM–midnight, Fri. and Sat. 8:30 PM–1:30 AM. AE, D, MC, V.*

Pacific Beach Bar and Grill. Just steps away from the beach, this popular nightspot has a huge outdoor patio so you can enjoy star-filled skies as you party with locals and visitors alike. There is plenty to see and do, from billiards and satellite sports to an interactive trivia game. *860 Garnet Ave., Pacific Beach,* ☎ *619/272–4745.* ☉ *Daily 11 AM–2 AM. AE, D, MC, V.*

Patrick's II. This downtown pub with definite Irish tendencies is a prime place to hear live New Orleans–style jazz, blues, and rock. *428 F St., downtown,* ☎ *619/233–3077.* ☉ *Entertainment nightly 9 PM–2 AM. No credit cards.*

Princess of Wales. This midtown British pub–style watering hole is the place for Anglophiles in general and groupies of the royals in particular: Hundreds of photos of Princess Di are plastered on the walls. You can order from the extensive menu of British food and 15 imported British beers. *1665 India St., downtown,* ☎ *619/238–1266.* ☉ *Daily 11 AM–1 AM. AE, V.*

Jazz Clubs

Croce's. The intimate jazz cave of restaurateur Ingrid Croce (singer-songwriter Jim Croce's widow) features superb acoustic-jazz musicians and an interesting menu. Next door, Croce's Top Hat puts on live R&B nightly 9 PM–2 AM. *802 5th Ave., Gaslamp Quarter,* ☎ *619/233–4355.* ☉ *Nightly 7:30 PM–2 AM. AE, D, DC, MC, V.*

Elario's. This club, on the top floor of the Summer House Inn, has a sumptuous ocean view and an incomparable lineup of internationally acclaimed jazz musicians every month. *7955 La Jolla Shores Dr., La Jolla,* ☎ *619/459–0541.* ☉ *Nightly shows at 8:20, 9:45, and 11. AE, DC, MC, V.*

The Green Circle. This modern jazz dance club showcases live bands on Wednesday and Thursday nights. The mostly under-30 crowd grooves to music that varies from acid jazz to blues and soul. *827 F St., Gaslamp Quarter,* ☎ *619/232–8080.* ☉ *Tues.–Sun. 7:30 PM–2 AM. MC, V.*

Humphrey's. This is the premier promoter of the city's best jazz, folk, and light-rock summer concert series held out on the grass. The rest of the year the music moves indoors for some first-rate jazz Sunday and Monday. *2241 Shelter Island Dr.,* ☎ *619/523–1010 for taped concert information.* ☉ *Entertainment 8 PM–midnight. AE, D, DC, MC, V.*

Pal Joey's. This humble neighborhood bar has a loyal clientele that enjoys dancing Friday and Saturday nights to the band's authentic jazz and blues with a lot of soul. *5147 Waring Rd., Allied Gardens, near San Diego State University,* ☎ *619/286–7873.* ☉ *Daily 10 AM–2AM, weekend entertainment 9 PM–1:30 AM. MC, V.*

Rock Clubs

Belly Up Tavern. Located in converted Quonset huts, this eclectic live-concert venue hosts critically acclaimed artists who play everything from reggae, rock, new wave, Motown, and folk to—well, you name it. Always a fun choice, the Belly Up attracts people of all ages. Sunday nights are usually free and feature local R&B artists. *143 S. Cedros Ave., Solana Beach,* ☎ *619/481–9022.* ☉ *Daily 11 AM–1:30 AM. Entertainment 9:30 PM–1:30 AM. MC, V.*

Bodie's. This Gaslamp Quarter bar hosts the best rock and blues bands in San Diego, as well as up-and-coming bands from out of town. *528 F St.,* ☎ *619/236–8988.* ☉ *Daily 6 AM–2 AM. No credit cards.*

Casbah. This small club showcases rock, reggae, funk, and every other kind of band—except Top 40—every night of the week. *2501 Kettner Blvd., near the airport,* ☎ *619/232–4355.* ☉ *Live bands nightly at 9:30. No credit cards.*

Iguanas. Though south of the border in Tijuana, Iguanas is considered a local club for the 18–21 crowd who can't get into San Diego's clubs. Tickets to the concerts by top-name bands that play here are available through Ticketron (☎ 619/278–TIXS); there's also DJ dance music on other nights. A bus shuttles patrons back and forth from the border to the club; the sober and queasy will not want to be on it on the return run. *Pueblo Amigo Shopping Ct., Tijuana,* ☎ *011–52–66/82–4967.* ☉ *Nightly 8 PM–2 AM, with concerts beginning at 10. MC, V.*

Spirit. This original-music club emphasizes the top local alternative and experimental-rock groups. *1130 Buenos Ave., Bay Park, near Mission Bay,* ☎ *619/276–3993.* ☉ *Nightly 8 PM–1 AM. No credit cards.*

Winston's Beach Club. Local bands, reggae groups, and, occasionally, '60s rock bands play this bowling alley turned rock club. The crowd here can get rowdy. *1921 Bacon St., Ocean Beach,* ☎ *619/222–6822.* ☉ *Live bands nightly 9 PM–2 AM. MC, V.*

Country-Western Clubs

Big Stone Lodge. The rustic dance hall, formerly a Pony Express station in the last century, now showcases the two-steppin' tunes of the house band, consisting of the owners. If you don't know country-western dances, don't fret; free lessons are given on some nights. *12237 Old Pomerado Rd., Poway,* ☏ *619/748–1135.* ⊘ *Entertainment Tues.–Thurs. 8 PM–12:30 AM, Fri. and Sat. 9 PM–1:30 AM, Sun. 5:30 PM–9:30 PM. DC, MC, V.*

The Country Club. Here you'll find live country bands on Wednesday, Friday, and Saturday; there are jam sessions on Sunday. *1121 3rd Ave., Chula Vista,* ☏ *619/426–2977.* ⊘ *Live music nightly 8 PM–2 AM. No credit cards.*

In Cahootz. A great sound system, a large dance floor, and occasional big-name performers make this lively spot a choice destination for cowgirls and -boys and city slickers alike. Free dance lessons every day except Wednesday and happy hour seven days a week are among the many incentives this bar provides for you to stop by. *5373 Mission Center Rd., Mission Valley,* ☏ *619/291–8635.* ⊘ *Weeknights 5 PM–2 AM, weekends 5:30 PM–2 AM. AE, D, MC, V.*

Leo's Little Bit O' Country. This is one of the largest country-western dance floors in the county. Leo's is another fun place to come for free dance lessons. *680 W. San Marcos Blvd., San Marcos,* ☏ *619/744–4120.* ⊘ *Tues.–Sat. 5 PM–1 AM, Sun. 4 PM–midnight. Entertainment Tues.–Sat. 8:30 PM–1 AM, Sun. 6:30 PM–midnight. MC, V.*

Magnolia Mulvaney's. This is a mainstay for East County residents, who come to listen to country music. *8861 N. Magnolia Ave., Santee,* ☏ *619/448–8550.* ⊘ *Wed. and Thurs. 6:30 PM–11 PM, Fri. and Sat. 6:30 PM–1:30 AM, Sun. 5 PM–11 PM. Entertainment nightly. AE, MC, V.*

Wrangler's Roost. This is a country-western haunt that appeals to both the longtime cowboy customer and the first-timer. There are free dance lessons Tuesday–Saturday nights. *6608 Mission Gorge Rd.,* ☏ *619/280–6263.* ⊘ *Daily 2 PM–2 AM. MC, V. Entertainment Wed.–Sat. 9 PM–2 AM.*

Zoo Country. Enjoy live music Friday through Sunday or a DJ seven nights a week at the new hangout for line-dancin', two-steppin' cowpersons. Free dance lessons are offered Friday, Saturday, and Sunday. *1340 Broadway, El Cajon,* ☏ *619/442–9900.* ⊘ *Tues.–Sun. 5:30 PM–11 PM. AE, D, MC, V.*

Comedy Clubs

Comedy Isle. Located in the Bahia Resort Hotel, this club offers the latest in local and national talent. *998 W. Mission Bay Dr., Mission Bay,* ☏ *619/488–6872.* ⊘ *Shows Wed., Thurs., and Sun. 8:30 PM, Fri. and Sat. 8:30 and 10:30 PM. Reservations accepted. AE, DC, MC, V.*

The Comedy Store. In the same tradition as the Comedy Store in West Hollywood, San Diego's version hosts some of the best national touring and local talent. *916 Pearl St., La Jolla,* ☏ *619/454–9176.* ⊘ *Shows Tues.–Thurs. at 8 PM, Fri. and Sat. at 8 and 10:30 PM, Sun. at 8:30 PM. AE, MC, V.*

Discos

Club Emerald City. Alternative dance music and an uninhibited clientele keep this beach-town spot unpredictable—which is just fine with everyone. *945 Garnet Ave., Pacific Beach,* ☎ *619/483–9920.* ☉ *Tues.–Sun. 8:30 PM–2 AM. No credit cards.*

Club Tremors. Adjacent to Pacific Beach Bar and Grill, the party continues in this impressive disco with nonstop dance music and friendly people. It's a definite hot spot for those on the (21–35) singles scene. *860 Garnet Ave., Pacific Beach,* ☎ *619/272–7278.* ☉ *Tues.–Sun. 8:30 PM–2 AM. AE, D, MC, V.*

Johnny M's. Get down to '70s and '80s dance music at this huge disco. A blues room is open Wednesday, Friday, and Saturday from 10 PM to 1:30 AM, and the DJ plays from 8 PM until 1:30 AM. *801 4th St., Gaslamp Quarter,* ☎ *619/233–1131.* ☉ *Tues.–Sat. 8 PM–2 AM; restaurant open daily 11 AM–midnight. AE, D, MC, V.*

Olé Madrid. Slick back your hair and enjoy the loud, continuous beat at this Euro-style disco for the very chic. *755 5th Ave., Gaslamp Quarter,* ☎ *619/557–0146.* ☉ *Weekdays 11:30 AM–2 AM, weekends 5 PM–2 AM. AE, MC, V.*

For Singles

Dick's Last Resort. On weekends, fun-loving party people and anyone else looking to meet the opposite sex line up to get into this enormous barnlike restaurant and bar. Dick's has live Dixieland music and one of the most extensive beer lists in San Diego. Don't be offended by the surly waitstaff—their "attitudes" are part of the gimmick. *345 4th Ave., downtown,* ☎ *619/231–9100.* ☉ *Daily 11 AM–2 AM. AE, MC, V.*

El Torito. Notable happy hours and the central location attract yuppies and students to this Mission Valley Mexican restaurant. *445 Camino del Rio S,* ☎ *619/296–6154.* ☉ *Daily 11 AM–2 AM. AE, D, DC, MC, V.*

The U. S. Grant Hotel. This place is the classiest spot in town for meeting fellow travelers while relaxing with a scotch or martini at the mahogany bar. The best local Latin, jazz, and blues bands alternate appearances during the week. It's definitely for the over-30 business set. *326 Broadway, downtown,* ☎ *619/232–3121.* ☉ *Daily 11:30 AM–1:30 AM. AE, D, DC, MC, V.*

Piano Bars/Mellow

Hotel del Coronado. The fairy-tale hostelry that has hosted royalty and former presidents features beautiful piano music in its Crown Room and Palm Court, with dance-oriented standards in the Ocean Terrace Lounge. *1500 Orange Ave., Coronado,* ☎ *619/435–6611.* ☉ *Daily 10:30 AM–1:30 AM. AE, D, DC, MC, V.*

Top O' the Cove. Show tunes and standards from the '40s to the '80s are the typical piano fare at this magnificent Continental restaurant in La Jolla. *1216 Prospect St.,* ☎ *619/454–7779.* ☉ *Entertainment Wed.–Sun. 8 PM–11 PM. AE, DC, MC, V.*

Westgate Hotel. One of the most elegant settings in San Diego offers piano music in the Plaza Bar. *1055 2nd Ave., downtown,* ☎ *619/238–1818.* ☉ *Daily 11 AM–2 AM. Entertainment Mon.–Sat. 8:30 PM–closing. AE, D, DC, MC, V.*

Gay Bars and Discos

Bourbon Street. This classy piano bar with relaxing surroundings and a courtyard out back resembles those seen in New Orleans. There's live entertainment nightly. *4612 Park Blvd., University Heights,* ☎ *619/291–0173.* ⊘ *Weekdays 12 PM–2 AM, Sat. 11 AM–2 AM, Sun. 9 AM–2 AM. D, MC, V.*

The Brass Rail. Established in the early sixties, this is the oldest gay bar in San Diego. Monday and Tuesday nights feature a drag show; the rest of the week is left for dancing. *3796 5th Ave., Hillcrest,* ☎ *619/298–2233.* ⊘ *Daily 10 AM–1:30 AM. No credit cards.*

The Flame. A San Diego landmark, this friendly dance club caters to lesbians most of the week. On Tuesday, the DJ spins for the very popular Boys' Night, and on Friday there's a drag show. *3780 Park Blvd., Hillcrest,* ☎ *619/295–4163.* ⊘ *Daily 5 PM–2AM. No credit cards.*

Flicks. A video bar with music and comedy to look at if you're not too busy looking at everyone else. Drink specials and video formats vary each night. *1017 University Ave, Hillcrest,* ☎ *619/297–2056.* ⊘ *Daily 2 PM–2 AM. No credit cards.*

Kickers. At this country music club cowboys are rounded up to do the latest country line-dance. Don't know how to line-dance? Free lessons are given weekdays from 7 to 8:30 PM. Hungry after all that dancing? Hamburger Mary's on the premises serves until 11 PM on weekends. *308 University Ave. Hillcrest,* ☎ *619/491–0400.* ⊘ *Mon.–Sat 7 PM–2 AM, Sun. 4 PM–2 AM. No credit cards.*

Rich's San Diego. Muscular go-go boys dance to house music for a lively crowd at this popular dance club. Thursday night's Club Hedonism features groove house and tribal rhythms. *1051 University Ave., Hillcrest,* ☎ *619/497–4588.* ⊘ *Thurs.–Sat. 9 PM–2 AM, Sun. 7 PM–2 AM. No credit cards.*

West Coast Production Company. This three-story discotheque is really three clubs in one: two dance floors and a rooftop video bar overlooking the downtown skyline. Wednesday night is the ever-popular Thrash Disco celebration, which draws the masses from near and far. *2028 Hancock St., Middletown,* ☎ *619/295–3724.* ⊘ *Wed., Fri., Sat. 9 PM–2 AM. MC, V.*

Wolf's. A levi/leather bar that's open late every night, Wolf's occasionally presents special exhibits and demonstrations. *3404 30th St., North Park,* ☎ *619/291–3730.* ⊘ *Daily 6 PM–4 AM. No credit cards.*

10 Excursions from San Diego

By Kevin Brass

Updated by
Albert M.
Columbo

SAN DIEGO COUNTY is larger than nearly a dozen U.S. states, with a population of more than 2 million—the second-largest county in California. It sprawls from the Pacific Ocean, through dense urban neighborhoods, to outlying suburban communities that seem to sprout overnight on canyons and cliffs. The Cleveland National Forest and Anza Borrego Desert mark the county's eastern boundaries, and the busiest international border in the United States—some 60 million people a year legally cross between Baja California and San Diego—its southern line. To the north, the marines at Camp Pendleton practice land, sea, and air maneuvers in southern California's largest coastal greenbelt, the demarcation zone between the congestion of Orange and Los Angeles counties and the mellower expansiveness of San Diego.

This chapter explores some of the day or longer trips you could schedule to areas outside the city of San Diego—to the North County, to inland and mountain communities, and to the desert.

THE SAN DIEGO NORTH COAST

To say the north-coast area of San Diego County is different from the city of San Diego is a vast understatement. From the northern tip of La Jolla to Oceanside, a half-dozen small communities each developed separately from urban San Diego—and from one another. The rich and famous were drawn early on to Del Mar, for example, because of its wide beaches and Thoroughbred horse-racing facility. Just a couple of miles away, agriculture, not paparazzi, played a major role in the development of Solana Beach and Encinitas. Up the coast, Carlsbad still reveals elements of roots directly tied to the old Mexican rancheros and the entrepreneurial instinct of John Frazier, who told people the area's water could cure common ailments. In the late 19th century, not far from the current site of the posh La Costa Hotel and Spa, Frazier attempted to turn the area into a massive replica of a German mineral springs resort.

Today, the north coast is a booming population center. An explosion of development throughout the 1980s turned the area into a northern extension of San Diego. The freeways started to take on the typically cluttered characteristics of most southern California freeways.

Beyond the freeways, though, the communities have maintained their charm. Some of the finest restaurants, beaches, and attractions in San Diego County can be found in the area, a true slice of southern California heritage. From the plush estates and rolling hills of Rancho Santa Fe and the beachfront restaurants of Cardiff to Mission San Luis Rey, a well-preserved remnant of California's first European settlers in Oceanside, the north coast is a distinctly different place.

Exploring

Numbers in the margin correspond to points of interest on the San Diego North Coast map.

Any journey around the north-coast area naturally starts at the beach, and this one begins at **Torrey Pines State Beach,** just south of Del Mar. At the south end of the wide beach, perched on top of the cliffs, is the
① Torrey Pines State Reserve, one of only two places (the other place is Santa Rosa Island off the coast of northern California) where the Tor-

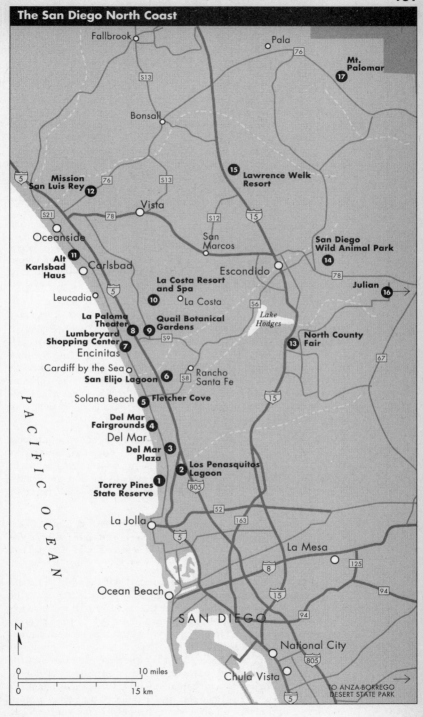

rey pine tree grows naturally (*see* Tour 7 *in* Chapter 2, Exploring San Diego, for details). ☎ *619/755–2063.* ☛ *$4 per car.* ☉ *Daily 9–sunset.*

② To the east of the state beach is **Los Penasquitos Lagoon,** one of the many natural estuaries that flow inland between Del Mar and Oceanside. Following Old Highway 101, the road leads into the small village of **Del Mar,** best known for its chic shopping strip, celebrity visitors, and wide beaches. Years of spats between developers and residents have resulted in the **Del Mar Plaza,** hidden by boulder walls and **③** clever landscaping at the corner of Old Highway 101 and 15th Street. The upper level has a large deck and a view out to the ocean, and the restaurants and shops are excellent barometers of the latest in southern California style. A left turn at 15th Street leads to Seagrove Park, a small stretch of grass overlooking the ocean, where concerts are performed on summer evenings. A right turn on Coast Boulevard provides access to Del Mar's beautiful beaches, particularly popular with Frisbee and volleyball players.

Less than a half mile north, Coast Boulevard merges with Old Highway 101. Across the road are the **Del Mar Fairgrounds,** home to more **④** than 100 different events a year, ranging from a cat show to an auto race. *Via de la Valle Rd. exit west from I–5,* ☎ *619/259–1355 for recorded events line.*

The fairgrounds also host the annual summer meeting of the **Del Mar Thoroughbred Club** (aka "Where the Turf Meets the Surf"). The track brings the top horses and jockeys to Del Mar, along with a cross section of the rich and famous, eager to bet on the ponies. Crooner Bing Crosby and his Hollywood buddies, Pat O'Brien, Gary Cooper, and Oliver Hardy, among others, organized the track in the '30s, primarily because Crosby thought it would be fun to have a track near his Rancho Santa Fe home. Del Mar soon developed into a regular stop for the stars of stage and screen.

During the off-season, horse players can still gamble at the fairgrounds, thanks to a satellite wagering facility. Races from other California tracks are televised, and people can bet as if the races were being run right there. Times vary, depending on which tracks in the state are operating. ☎ *619/755–1167. Racing season: July–Sept., Wed.–Mon. Post time 2 PM.*

Next to the fairgrounds, on Jimmy Durante Boulevard, is a small exotic bird-training facility, **Freeflight,** which is open to the public. Visitors are allowed to handle the birds—a guaranteed child pleaser. *2132 Jimmy Durante Blvd.,* ☎ *619/481–3148.* ☛ *$1.* ☉ *Daily 10–4.*

Following Via de la Valle Road east from I–5 will take you to the exclusive community of **Rancho Santa Fe,** one of the richest areas in the United States. Groves of huge, drooping eucalyptus trees, first imported to the area by a railroad company in search of trees to grow for railroad ties, cover the hills and valleys, hiding the posh estates. The little village of Rancho has some elegant and quaint—and overpriced—shops and restaurants. But it is no accident that there is little else to see or do in Rancho; the residents guard their privacy religiously. Even the challenging Rancho Santa Fe Golf Course, the original site of the Bing Crosby Pro-Am and considered one of the best courses in southern California, is still open only to members of the Rancho Santa Fe community.

Back along the coast, along Old Highway 101 north of Del Mar, is the quiet little oceanside community of **Solana Beach.** A highlight of Solana Beach is **Fletcher Cove,** located at the west end of Lomas Santa Fe Drive. Early Solana settlers used dynamite to blast the cove out of the overhanging cliffs. Called Pill Box by the locals because of a bunkerlike lifeguard station that overlooks it, the Fletcher Cove beach is easy to reach and features a large parking lot replete with a small basketball court, a favorite of local pickup-game players.

To the north, separating Solana Beach from Cardiff, is the **San Elijo Lagoon,** home to many migrating birds. Trails wind around the entire area.

As you continue along Old Highway 101, past the cluster of hillside homes that make up Cardiff and beyond the campgrounds of the San Elijo State Beach, the palm trees of Sea Cliff Roadside Park (Swami's to the locals) and the golden domes of the Self-Realization Fellowship mark the entrance to downtown **Encinitas.** The Self-Realization Fellowship was built at the turn of the century and is a retreat and place of worship for the followers of a Native American religious sect. Its beautiful gardens are open to the public.

A recent landmark of Encinitas (which was incorporated as a city in 1986, including the communities of Cardiff, Leucadia, and Olivenhain) is the **Lumberyard Shopping Center,** a collection of small stores and restaurants that anchors the downtown shopping area. There is a huge selection of shopping centers inland at the intersection of Encinitas Boulevard and El Camino Real.

An older landmark of Encinitas is the **La Paloma Theater** (471 1st St., near the corner of Encinitas Blvd., ☎ 619/436–7469), at the north end of town. Built in the 1920s as a stop for traveling vaudeville troupes, it has served as a concert hall, movie theater, and meeting place for the area ever since. Plays are still being rehearsed and performed here.

Encinitas is best known as the Flower Capital of the World, and although the flower industry is not as prevalent as it once was, the city is still home to Paul Ecke Poinsettias, the largest producer of the popular Christmas blossom. A sampling of the area's dedication to horticulture can be found at the **Quail Botanical Gardens,** home to thousands of different varieties of plants, especially drought-tolerant species. Horticultural lectures are given here, and there are often plant sales. *230 Quail Gardens Dr. (take Encinitas Blvd. east from I–5 and turn left on Quail Gardens Dr.),* ☎ *619/436–3036. Parking: $1.* ⊙ *Daily 8–5; closed 1st Mon. of every month.*

Old Highway 101 continues north through **Leucadia** (named after a famous Greek promontory), a small community best known for its small art galleries and stores. At the north end of Leucadia, La Costa Avenue meets Old Highway 101. Following La Costa Avenue east, past the Batiquitos Lagoon, you'll come to **La Costa Resort and Spa** (*see* Lodging, *below*), once famous for its high-profile guests and reputed mafia ties and now noted for its excellent golf and tennis facilities.

La Costa is technically part of the city of **Carlsbad,** which is centered farther north, west of the Tamarack Avenue and Elm Avenue exits of I–5. In Carlsbad, Old Highway 101 is called Carlsbad Boulevard. Large rancheros owned by wealthy Mexicans were the first settlements inland; the coastal area was developed by an entrepreneur, John Frazier, who lured people to the area with talk of the healing powers of mineral water bubbling from a coastal well. The water was found to have the same properties as water from the German mineral wells of Karlsbad—hence the name of the new community. Remnants from the era, including the original well, are found at the **Alt Karlsbad Haus,** a small museum–gift shop carrying northern European wares. *2802A Carlsbad Blvd.,* ☎ *619/729–6912.* ☉ *Mon.–Sat. 10–5, Sun. noon–5.*

North of Carlsbad is **Oceanside,** home of Camp Pendleton, the country's largest marine base, as well as a beautiful natural harbor teeming with activity. **Oceanside Harbor** (☎ 619/966–4570) is the north-coast center for fishing, sailing, and all ocean-water sports. Salty fisherman types tend to congregate at Oceanside Pier.

Another highlight of a visit to Oceanside is the **California Surf Museum,** which charts the history of surfing from balsa-wood boards up through the present Fiberglas state-of-the-art. Exhibits change regularly. *308 N. Pacific St.,* ☎ *619/721–6876.* ☛ *Free; donations appreciated.* ☉ *Thurs.–Mon. noon–4, expanded hrs in summer.*

Oceanside is also home to **Mission San Luis Rey,** built by Franciscan friars in 1798 to help educate and convert local Native Americans. One of the best-preserved missions in the area, San Luis Rey was the 18th and largest of the California missions. Retreats are still held here, but a picnic area, gift shop, and museum are also on the grounds today. Self-guided tours are available. *4050 Mission Ave. (take Mission Ave. east from I–5),* ☎ *619/757–3651.* ☛ *$3 adults, $1 children.* ☉ *Mon.–Sat. 10–4:30, Sun. noon–4:30.*

Dining

Given the north coast's reputation as a suburban area, there is a surprisingly large selection of top-quality restaurants here. In fact, San Diegans often take the drive north to enjoy the variety of cuisines offered in the North County. *See* the chart *in* Chapter 7, Dining, for price categories.

Cardiff

$$ **The Chart House.** The beach and the sunset above the Pacific are the chief attractions of this surfside dining spot. Entrées include fresh fish, seafood, and beef dishes; there's also a good salad bar. ✕ *2588 Hwy. 101,* ☎ *619/436–4044. Reservations advised. AE, D, DC, MC, V. No lunch; Sun. brunch.*

Del Mar

$$$ **Tourlas.** The restaurant at Del Mar's posh L'Auberge resort has undergone a sea change, with a new name and chef and a shift in cooking style from French to contemporary California. The menu is small but impressive: Such appetizers as corn meal–covered crab cakes might be followed by rack of lamb on couscous or halibut coated in pine nuts. The setting is lovely, and the service is attentive. ✕ *1540 Camino del Mar,* ☎ *619/259–1515. Reservations advised. AE, D, DC, MC, V.*

$$ **Cilantro's.** For a taste of gourmet Mexican and southwestern-style food—creative dishes full of subtle spices—Cilantro's in Del Mar offers a wide variety of unusual creations, including shark fajitas and spit-roasted chicken with a mild chili sauce. The inexpensive tapas menu, with such delicacies as crab tostadas and three-cheese quesadillas, is a little easier on the wallet. ✕ *3702 Via de la Valle,* ☎ *619/259–8777. Reservations advised. AE, MC, V.*

$$ **Epazote.** The sister restaurant to Cilantro's, located in the Del Mar Plaza, Epazote serves a similar menu of Cal-Mex cuisine with a southwestern touch. The fresh fish specials, which change daily, are particularly

recommended, as are the salads, the selection of imaginative tacos, and the killer margaritas. There's a great ocean view from the patio. ✕ *1555 Camino del Mar, Suite 322,* ☎ *619/259–9966. Reservations advised. AE, MC, V.*

$$ **Il Fornaio.** Located within the Del Mar Plaza, this talk-of-the-town ristorante features northern Italian cuisine, such as fresh seafood, homemade pastas, and crispy pizzas. The outdoor piazza affords a splendid ocean view. ✕ *1555 Camino del Mar, Suite 301,* ☎ *619/755–8876. Reservations advised. AE, DC, MC, V.*

$$ **Pacifica Del Mar.** Yet another fine Del Mar Plaza restaurant boasting a stunning view, Pacifica Del Mar is related to the downtown and Old Town Pacifica restaurants and, like them, emphasizes an imaginative California cuisine of fresh ingredients prepared with southwestern, Cajun, Italian, and Pacific Rim touches. Start with the scrumptious smoked corn, chicken, and black-bean chowder, and then go on to the grilled prawn salad, blackened catfish, or one of the free-range chicken dishes. Desserts are tasty, and the wine list is excellent. ✕ *1555 Camino del Mar, Suite 321,* ☎ *619/792–0476. Reservations advised. AE, D, DC, MC, V.*

$ **Johnny Rockets.** This '50s-style malt-and-burger joint, on the Del Mar Plaza's lower level, dishes up juicy burgers, thick malts, and fries to die for. Booth and counter seating come complete with nickel-a-tune jukeboxes. ✕ *1555 Camino del Mar, Suite 102,* ☎ *619/755–1954. MC, V.*

Encinitas

$ **Rico's Taco Shop.** Short on frills but long on great food, this Mexican fast-food café is a local favorite. Come here for excellent chicken taquitos, carne asada burritos, and the best fish burritos and tacos in town. The owners are friendly and health conscious, too: No lard is used in the recipes. Rico's is open daily for breakfast, lunch, and dinner. ✕ *165-L S. El Camino Real, in the Target Shopping Center,* ☎ *619/944–7689. No credit cards.*

$ **Vigilucci's.** A welcome addition to the culinary revitalization of First Street in Encinitas, this Italian trattoria has a cozy, bistrolike atmosphere, knowledgeable Italian waiters, and a stylish menu. The pastas are particularly good: Try the *spaghetti al funghetto,* with a fresh mushroom sauce, or the *tagliatelle alla bolognese,* with ground duck, chicken, and veal in a tomato sauce. The locally made bread is excellent, but the wine list needs upgrading. ✕ *505 1st St. (Hwy. 101),* ☎ *619/942–7332. Reservations advised. AE, D, DC, MC, V. No lunch weekends.*

Rancho Santa Fe

$$$ **Mille Fleurs.** This gem of a French auberge brightens a tiny village sur-
★ rounded by country estates. Within a mile of Chino's, the county's most famous vegetable farm, where the chef shops daily, this is a most romantic hideaway, with tempting cuisine to enhance the mood. ✕ *6009 Paseo Delicias,* ☎ *619/756–3085. Reservations strongly advised. AE, D, DC, MC, V. No lunch weekends.*

Solana Beach

$ **California Pizza Kitchen.** Bright, noisy, and cheerful, this popular restaurant in Solana Beach's attractive new Boardwalk shopping center produces a selection of designer pizzas from its wood-fired oven, ranging from the conventional to the outlandish. If Caribbean-shrimp, tuna-melt, or moo-shu-chicken pizzas are too exotic for you, try the duck sausage (particularly recommended), the mixed grill vegetarian, or the five-cheese and tomato pizzas. Pastas are good, too, as are the enormous salads. Delivery is available. ✗ *437 S. Hwy. 101,* ☎ *619/793–0999. No reservations. AE, D, DC, MC, V.*

$ **Chung King Loh.** One of the better Chinese restaurants along the coast, Chung King Loh offers an excellent variety of Mandarin and Szechuan dishes. Take-out and delivery services are available. ✗ *552 Stevens Ave.,* ☎ *619/481–0184. Reservations advised. AE, D, DC, MC, V. No lunch Sun.*

$ **Fidel's.** Rich in North County tradition, both Fidel's restaurants serve a wide variety of well-prepared Mexican dishes in a low-key, pleasant atmosphere. The original restaurant in Solana Beach, a two-story building with an outdoor patio area, is particularly nice and draws a lively crowd. ✗ *607 Valley Ave.,* ☎ *619/755–5292; 3003 Carlsbad Blvd., Carlsbad,* ☎ *619/729–0903. Reservations accepted for 8 or more only. MC, V.*

Lodging

See the chart *in* Chapter 8, Lodging, for price categories. Many hotels offer discount rates from October to May.

Carlsbad

$$$$ **La Costa Hotel and Spa.** Don't expect glitz and glamour at this famous resort; it's surprisingly low-key, with low-slung buildings and vaguely southwestern–style rooms decorated in neutral tones. The sports facilities, especially golf and tennis, are excellent, and La Costa includes such other amenities as supervised children's activities and a movie theater. A variety of nutrition and stress-reduction classes are available. ⌖ *2100 Costa del Mar Rd., Carlsbad 92009,* ☎ *619/438–9111 or 800/854–5000,* FAX *619/438–9007. 480 rooms. 5 restaurants, pool, beauty salon, massage, spa, golf, 23 tennis courts, exercise room, theater. AE, D, DC, MC, V.*

$$$–$$$$ **Carlsbad Inn Beach Resort.** The palm trees seem a bit out of place on the manicured lawn of this sprawling European-style inn, with its gabled roofs and stone supports, but this is Carlsbad after all, where *alte* Germany meets southern California. The public areas and rooms are decorated in appealing Old World style; all the accommodations have VCRs, many offer kitchenettes, and some have fireplaces and private spas. ⌖ *3075 Carlsbad Blvd., 92008,* ☎ *619/434–7020 or 800/235–3939,* FAX *619/729–4853. 60 rooms. Pool, sauna, health club. AE, D, DC, MC, V.*

$$ **Best Western Beach View Lodge.** Reservations are essential at this reasonably priced hotel near the beach. A Mediterranean-style low-rise building hosts a variety of attractively decorated rooms with light-wood or whitewashed furnishings; all have refrigerators, and kitchens, private balconies, and fireplaces are also available. Families tend to settle in for a week or more. Complimentary Continental breakfast is included in the rates. ⌖ *3180 Carlsbad Blvd., 92008,* ☎ *619/729–1151, 800/535–5588 or 800/BEACHVU in CA,* FAX *619/729–1151. 41 rooms. In-room safes, pool, sauna. AE, D, DC, MC, V.*

Del Mar

$$$–$$$$ **L'Auberge Del Mar Resort and Spa.** Across the street from the Del Mar Plaza and one block from the ocean, L'Auberge is modeled on the Tudor-style Hotel Del Mar, playground for Hollywood's elite in the early 1900s. The inn is filled with dark-wood antiques, fireplaces, and lavish floral arrangements. Spacious rooms and suites are tastefully if not memorably decorated, with beige dominating the color scheme. The grounds are attractively landscaped, with stone paths leading to gazebos and

pools; the spa specializes in European herbal... ✆ 1540 Camino del Mar, Del Mar 92014... 800/553–1336, FAX 619/755–4940. 123 room... 2 pools, beauty salon, spa, 2 tennis courts, ex... MC, V.

$$ **Stratford Inn.** The inn offers a pleasant atmosphere just... ter of town and three blocks from the ocean. Rooms are large, with ample closet space and dressing areas; some have ocean views. Suites with kitchenettes are available. Continental breakfast is complimentary. ✆ 710 Camino del Mar, 92014, ☎ 619/755–1501 or 800/446–7229, FAX 619/755–4704. 98 rooms. 2 pools. AE, D, DC, MC, V.

Encinitas

$$ **Moonlight Beach Hotel.** This folksy, laid-back motel is the closest to the beach at Encinitas. Rooms are basic but spacious and clean; all have kitchenettes. Weekly rates are available. ✆ 233 2nd St., 92024, ☎ 619/753–0623 or 800/323–1259. 24 rooms. AE, MC, V.

$$ **Radisson Inn Encinitas.** This attractively designed low rise blends nicely into an Encinitas hillside just east of Old Highway 101. Rooms have plush, richly colored rugs and comfy upholstered chairs; some have kitchenettes and/or ocean views. Continental breakfast is complimentary. ✆ 85 Encinitas Blvd., 92024, ☎ 619/942–7455 or 800/333–3333, FAX 619/632–9481. 91 rooms. Restaurant, bar. AE, D, DC, MC, V.

$ **Budget Motels of America.** Shag carpeting and kitschy murals decorate the rooms at this motel, but the place is clean, low-priced, and convenient to the beach and the freeway. No-smoking rooms are available, and Continental breakfast is included in the room rate. ✆ 133 Encinitas Blvd., 92024, ☎ 619/944–0260 or 800/795–6044, FAX 619/944–2803. 124 rooms. AE, MC, V.

Leucadia

$ **Pacific Surf.** This motel is clean, comfortable, and near all the shops and restaurants of Encinitas. All rooms have kitchens, and there are discounts for extended stays. ✆ 1076 Rte. 101N, 92024, ☎ 619/436–8763 or 800/795–1466. 30 rooms. Laundry. AE, D, DC, MC, V.

Oceanside

$ **Oceanside TraveLodge.** It's near the beach and centrally located. ✆ 1401 N. Hill St., 92054, ☎ 619/722–1244 or 800/255–3050, FAX 619/722–3228. 28 rooms. Laundry. AE, D, DC, MC, V.

Rancho Santa Fe

$$$$ **Rancho Valencia.** The sister hotel to La Jolla's La Valencia, this resort is so luxurious that several high-style magazines have chosen it for fashion backdrops and have named it the most romantic hideaway in the United States. The suites are in red-tile-roofed casitas with fireplaces and private terraces. Tennis is the other draw here, with 18 courts and a resident pro; rates include unlimited use of the courts. ✆ 5921 Valencia Circle, 92067, ☎ 619/756–1123 or 800/548–3664, FAX 619/756–0165. 43 suites. Restaurant, pool, 18 tennis courts, pool, sauna, croquet. AE, DC, MC, V.

North Coast Essentials

Arriving and Departing

BY CAR
Interstate 5, the main freeway artery connecting San Diego to Los Angeles, follows the coastline. To the west, running parallel to it, is Old

Highway 101, which never strays more than a quarter-mile from the ocean. Beginning north of La Jolla, where it is known as Torrey Pines Road, Old Highway 101 is a designated scenic route, providing access to the beauty of the coastline.

BY TRAIN
Amtrak (☎ 619/481–0114 in Del Mar, 619/722–4622 in Oceanside, or 800/872–7245) operates trains daily between Los Angeles, Orange County, and San Diego, with stops in Solana Beach and Oceanside. The last train leaves San Diego at approximately 9 PM each night; the last arrival is at approximately midnight.

BY BUS
The **San Diego Transit District** covers the city of San Diego up to Del Mar, where the **North County Transit District** (☎ 619/722–6283) takes over, blanketing the area with efficient, on-time bus service.

Greyhound (☎ 619/722–1587 in Oceanside, or 800/231–2222) has regular routes connecting San Diego to points north, with stops in Del Mar, Solana Beach, Encinitas, Escondido, Vista, and Oceanside.

BY TAXI
Several companies are based in the North County, including **Bernardo Cab Co.** (☎ 619/549–8445, or 619/592–9787 from Rancho Bernardo; ☉ 7 AM–7 PM) and **Bill's Cab Co.** (☎ 619/755–6737).

BY PLANE
Palomar Airport (☎ 619/431–4646), located in Carlsbad, 2 miles east of I–5 at 2198 Palomar Airport Road, is a general aviation airport run by the county of San Diego and open to the public. Commuter airlines sometimes have flights from Palomar to Orange County and Los Angeles.

Guided Tours
Civic Helicopters (2192 Palomar Airport Rd., ☎ 619/438–8424) offers whirlybird tours of the area. The tours run about $70 per person per half hour and go along the beaches to the Del Mar racetrack.

Important Addresses and Numbers
Carlsbad Convention and Visitors Bureau (Box 1246, Carlsbad 92008, ☎ 619/434–6093).

Del Mar Chamber of Commerce (1401 Camino del Mar, Suite 101, Del Mar 92014, ☎ 619/793–5292).

Oceanside Chamber of Commerce (928 North Hill St., Oceanside 92051, ☎ 619/722–1534).

INLAND NORTH COUNTY TO ESCONDIDO AND THE MOUNTAINS

Even though the coast is only a short drive away, the beach communities seem far removed from the mountain village of Julian or the quiet lakes of Escondido. Inland is the old California, where working farms and ranches are more common than the posh restaurants that mark the coastal landscape. The oak- and pine-covered mountains attracted prospectors seeking their fortune in gold long before tourists headed to the beaches. Home to wineries, old missions, freshwater lakes, and innumerable three-generation California families, the inland area of North County is the quiet, rural sister to the rest of San Diego County;

a visit to San Diego wouldn't be complete without at least a drive through this area.

Escondido (aka the Hidden Valley) is a thriving, rapidly expanding residential and commercial city of more than 80,000 people and the center of a wide variety of attractions and destination points. To the south, the three-story, enclosed North County Fair mall is something of a mecca for local shoppers, while animal lovers flock to the nearby Wild Animal Park, an extension of the San Diego Zoo, where animals roam free over the hills. To the north is an attraction of a completely different kind, Lawrence Welk Resort, a museum and resort complex that pays tribute to the late "Mr. Bubbles."

The mountains to the east of Escondido were once a remote outpost of the rugged West. Now they are a favorite spot for hikers, nature lovers, and apple-pie fanatics. Most of the last group head to Julian, an old mining town that is now famous for its annual apple festival. Nearby Cuyamaca Rancho State Park is full of excellent trails and well-preserved picnic and camping areas. To the north, perched in a park atop Mount Palomar, the Palomar Observatory is a haven for stargazers, and it has one of the most famous telescopes in the world.

Exploring

Numbers in the margin correspond to points of interest on the San Diego North Coast map.

❸ To shopping connoisseurs, **North County Fair** is a paradise, an 83-acre shopping complex with six major department stores and more than 175 specialty shops. *At the intersection of I–15 and Via Rancho Pkwy.,* ☎ *619/489–2332.*

❹ More than 2,500 animals roam the 1,800 acres of the **San Diego Wild Animal Park,** a zoo without cages. A 50-minute, 5-mile monorail trip is the best way to see the animals, but the park is also a pleasant area to walk around. There are daily bird and trained-animal shows (*see* Other Places of Interest *in* Chapter 2, Exploring San Diego, for more details). ☎ *619/480–0100. Take I–15 north to Via Rancho Pkwy. and follow signs.* ☛ *$18.95 adults, $17.05 senior citizens, $11.95 children 2–12; admission includes all shows and monorail tour. Parking: $3.* ☉ *Daily at 9; call ahead for closing hrs, which vary with season.*

About a mile east of the Wild Animal Park, on San Pasqual Valley Road, are a monument and museum commemorating the site of the **Battle of San Pasqual.** On December 6, 1846, a troop of Americans, including famous frontier scout Kit Carson, was defeated by a group of Californios (Spanish-Mexican residents of California). This was the Californios' most notable success during the war (21 Americans were killed), but the Americans, with support from Commodore Stockton in San Diego, did regain control of the region. *15808 San Pasqual Valley Rd., Escondido,* ☎ *619/220–5430.* ☛ *Free.* ☉ *Fri.–Sun. 10–5.*

Deer Park Vintage Cars and Wine (29013 Champagne Blvd., ☎ 619/749–1666), also in Escondido, is a branch of the award-winning Napa Valley Deer Park Winery. Outside are a few select models from a collection of more than 50 vintage convertibles. There is also a delicatessen for impromptu picnics. Other popular local wineries include **Bernardo Winery** (13330 Paseo del Verano N, Rancho Bernardo, ☎ 619/487–1866), **Menghini Winery** (1150 Julian Orchards Dr., Julian, ☎ 619/765–2072), and **Ferrara Winery** (1120 W. 15th Ave., Escondido, ☎ 619/745–7632).

⑮ Following I–15 north past central Escondido leads to the **Lawrence Welk Resort.** Complete with a dinner theater housing a museum of Welk memorabilia, the complex also includes a hotel and two golf courses. *8860 Lawrence Welk Dr.,* ☎ *619/749–3000.* ☛ *Free.* ☉ *Museum: daily 10–5, except during dinner theater performances.*

⑯ For more organic pleasures, the small mountain village of **Julian** provides an enchanting glimpse at life in the mountains; to get there from Escondido, take Route 78 east. Gold was discovered in the area in 1869; quartz was unearthed a year later. More than $15 million worth of gold was taken from local mines in the 1870s. Today, this charming mountain town retains many historic false-front buildings from its mining days. When gold and quartz became scarce, the locals turned to growing apples and pears, now the lifeblood of the little town. The pears are harvested in September, the apples in October. The annual Julian Apple Days, first staged in 1909, begin mid-September.

Hour-long tours of an authentic Julian gold mine are offered by the **Eagle Mining Company.** There are also a small rock shop and gold-mining museum on the premises. *C St., 5 blocks east from the center of town,* ☎ *619/765–0036.* ☛ *$7 adults, $3 children under 16, $1 children under 5.* ☉ *Tours given daily 10–3, weather permitting.*

Just a few minutes to the south of Julian are the 26,000 scenic acres of **Cuyamaca Rancho State Park** (☎ 619/765–0755). The park's hills feature several varieties of oak and pine trees, small streams, and meadows and provide a quiet escape for nature lovers. Primitive campsites are available. Camping is also permitted in the **Cleveland National Forest** (☎ 619/673–6180) to the south of I–8.

⑰ There are no apples or gold mines on **Mount Palomar**—just one of the world's largest reflecting telescopes. Touring the observatory is a fascinating way to spend an afternoon. The park surrounding the observatory is full of lovely picnic areas and hiking trails. Also, don't forget to stop at Mother's Kitchen, the only restaurant on the mountain, which features some excellent vegetarian dishes. *Take Rte. 76 east from I–15 and follow signs,* ☎ *619/742–2119.* ☛ *Free.* ☉ *Observatory for self-guided tours: daily 9–4. Closed Dec. 24–25.*

For those interested in the old missions that pepper the southern California landscape, **Mission San Antonio de Pala,** built in 1816, still serves the Native Americans of the Pala reservation. Displays in a small museum include artifacts from the original mission. *On Rte. 76 on the way to Mount Palomar,* ☎ *619/742–3317.* ☛ *$2 adults, $1 children under 13.* ☉ *Museum and gift shop: Tues.–Sun. 10–3.*

Dining

See the chart *in* Chapter 7, Dining, for price categories.

Escondido

$$ **150 Grand Cafe.** This recent addition to the Escondido dining scene brings fine cuisine to a city in need of it. An ambitious menu of California-style dishes prepared with a European flair is served in a lovely, comfortable dining room. Try the filet mignon in port wine accompanied by a spinach salad. ✕ *150 W. Grand Ave.,* ☎ *619/738–6868. Reservations advised. AE, DC, MC, V.*

$ **Hernandez' Hideaway.** Isolated on a small road off Valley Parkway near lovely Lake Hodges, this is a popular hangout for local Mexican-food lovers. The ample weekend brunch is particularly popular. ✕ *19320 Rancho Lake Dr.,* ☎ *619/746–1444. Reservations advised on weekends. Full bar. AE, DC, MC, V.* ☺ *3* PM *Tues.–Fri.; closed Mon.*

Fallbrook

$$ **Le Bistro.** Located in the quiet, rural community of Fallbrook, this well-respected restaurant has two dining rooms: The elegant one upstairs specializes in veal and shrimp dishes, and a more casual café downstairs offers patio as well as indoor dining. ✕ *119 N. Main St.,* ☎ *619/723–3559. Reservations advised. AE, D, DC, MC, V. Upstairs: no lunch, closed Mon.; downstairs: closed Sun.*

Rancho Bernardo

$$$ **El Bizcocho.** In the luxurious dining room of the Rancho Bernardo Inn,
★ El Bizcocho has a well-deserved reputation throughout San Diego County for consistently superb cuisine, with high-quality ingredients and careful preparations. You won't go wrong with anything on the Continental menu, but the roast duck, fresh seafood dishes, and rack of lamb are particularly recommended. A pianist plays nightly. The restaurant also serves an excellent Sunday brunch. ✕ *17550 Bernardo Oaks Dr.,* ☎ *619/487–1611. Reservations advised. Jacket required. AE, D, DC, MC, V.*

$ **Acapulco.** Part of a high-quality Mexican restaurant chain with outlets throughout the inland area, these restaurants are large and friendly and serve good margaritas. ✕ *16785 Bernardo Center Dr.,* ☎ *619/487–6701; 1020 W. San Marcos Blvd., San Marcos,* ☎ *619/471–2150; 1541 E. Valley Pkwy., Escondido,* ☎ *619/741–9922. Reservations strongly advised. AE, MC, V.*

San Marcos

$$ **Fish House Veracruz.** All but the most inveterate fish-haters will be pleased with this very popular restaurant, offering a casual family atmosphere, simple and tasty preparations, and very fresh fish. ✕ *360 Villa Veracruz,* ☎ *619/744–8000. No reservations. AE, D, MC, V. No lunch Sun.*

Vista

$$ **La Paloma.** A popular Mexican restaurant with ambitions, La Paloma was noted in *Gourmet* magazine for its lobster fajitas. The menu is extensive, including well-prepared versions of old favorites along with more unusual dishes such as paella and turkey carnitas. This place is well worth a trip to Vista. ✕ *116 Escondido Ave.,* ☎ *619/758–7140. Reservations advised. AE, D, DC, MC, V. No lunch weekends.*

Lodging

See the chart *in* Chapter 8, Lodging, for price categories.

Escondido

$$ **Lawrence Welk Resort.** About 15 minutes north of Escondido, this pleasant inn is far from everything except the theater, museum, and golf courses of the complex saluting Welk. The rooms have a Southwestern flavor, with bleached woods and mauve and turquoise furnishings. ▥ *8860 Lawrence Welk Dr., 92026,* ☎ *619/749–3000 or 800/932–9355,* ℻ *619/749–9537. 132 rooms. Restaurant, pool, spa, 2 golf courses, tennis courts, theater. AE, DC, MC, V.*

Fallbrook

$$ **Pala Mesa Resort Hotel.** The main attraction at this verdant, 205-acre property is the excellent golf course. The large, comfortable rooms were renovated in 1993 in California ranch style, with light maple armoires and mauve marble baths. ☎ *2001 Old Hwy. 395, 92028,* ☎ *619/728–5881 or 800/722–4700,* FAX *619/723–8292. 133 rooms. Restaurant, grill, snack bar, pool, spa, 4 tennis courts, golf course, health club. AE, DC, MC, V.*

Julian

$$ **Pine Hills Lodge.** This secluded mountain lodge, which dates back to 1912, has an on-site dinner theater (Friday and Saturday year-round). The rooms are clean but decorated in what the owner dubs early Salvation Army style. Some cabins have fireplaces. ☎ *2960 La Posada, 92036,* ☎ *619/765–1100. 12 cabins with private bath, 6 lodge rooms with shared bath. AE, D, DC, MC, V.*

$ **Julian Lodge.** This bed-and-breakfast near the center of town is a replica of a Julian hotel that was popular in the late 19th century. The rooms and public spaces are furnished with antiques; on chilly days, guests can warm themselves at the large stove in the lobby. Breakfast is buffet style. *Box 1930, 4th and C Sts., 92036,* ☎ *619/765–1420 or 800/542–1420. 23 rooms with private bath. AE, MC, V.*

Rancho Bernardo

$$$$ **Rancho Bernardo Inn.** You can be pampered and relaxed here while enjoying a game on the championship golf course or a sublime Sunday brunch at El Bizcocho (*see* Dining, *above*). The country-style rooms have large floral bouquets, plush easy chairs, and tiled baths. The health club offers three types of intense massages, and a children's camp is available in August, on holiday weekends, and during school breaks. ☎ *17550 Bernardo Oaks Dr., 92128,* ☎ *619/487–1611 or 800/854–1065,* FAX *619/673–0311. 287 rooms. 2 restaurants, 2 bars, 2 pools, 12 tennis courts, golf course, health club. AE, D, DC, MC, V.*

$$$ **Carmel Highland Doubletree Golf and Tennis Resort.** Country living is emphasized at this pale-pink compound bordering a 6,500-acre golf course. The packages for golf, tennis, or fitness regimes are quite reasonable. This is a good spot for a totally relaxing weekend. ☎ *14455 Penasquitos Dr., 92129,* ☎ *619/672–9100 or 800/622–9223,* FAX *619/672–9166. 172 rooms. 2 restaurants, bar, deli, 2 pools, golf course, 6 tennis courts, health club. AE, D, DC, MC, V.*

Inland North County Essentials

Arriving and Departing

BY CAR

Escondido sits at the intersection of Route 78, which heads west from Oceanside, and I–15, the inland freeway connecting San Diego to Riverside, 30 minutes to the north of Escondido. Del Dios Highway winds from Rancho Santa Fe through the hills past Lake Hodges to Escondido. Route 76, which connects with I–15 a few miles north of Escondido, veers east to Mount Palomar. Route 78 leads out of Escondido to Julian and Ramona. To reach the mountain areas from San Diego, take I–8 east to Route 79 north.

North County Transit District (☎ 619/743–6283) has routes criss-crossing the Escondido area.

Yellow Cab Company (☎ 619/745–7421) has a base in Escondido.

Important Addresses and Numbers
San Diego North County Convention & Visitors Bureau (720 N. Broadway, Escondido 92025, ☎ 619/745–4741).

Julian Chamber of Commerce (2129 Main St., Julian 92036, ☎ 619/765–1857).

THE DESERT

Every spring, the stark desert landscape east of the Cuyamaca Mountains explodes with color. It's the blooming of the wildflowers in the Anza-Borrego Desert State Park, less than a two-hour drive from central San Diego. The beauty of this annual spectacle, as well as the natural quiet and blazing climate, lures tourists and natives to the area. The area features a desert and not much more, but it is one of the favorite parks of those Californians who travel widely in their state. People seeking bright lights and glitter should look elsewhere. The excitement in this area stems from watching a coyote scamper across a barren ridge or a brightly colored bird resting on a nearby cactus or from a waitress delivering another cocktail to a poolside chaise longue. For hundreds of years, the only humans to linger in the area were Native Americans from the San Dieguito, Kamia, and Cahuilla tribes, but the extreme temperature eventually forced the tribes to leave, too. It wasn't until 1774, when Mexican explorer Captain Juan Bautista de Anza first blazed a trail through the area as a shortcut from Sonora to San Francisco, that modern civilization had its first glimpse of the oddly beautiful wasteland.

Today, more than 600,000 acres of desert are included in the Anza-Borrego Desert State Park, making it the largest state park in the contiguous 48 states. It is also one of the few parks in the country where people can camp anywhere. No campsite is necessary; just follow the trails and pitch a tent wherever you like.

Five hundred miles of road traverse the park, and visitors are required to stay on them so as not to disturb the ecological balance of the park. However, 28,000 acres have been set aside in the eastern part of the desert near Ocotillo Wells for off-road enthusiasts. General George S. Patton conducted field training in the Ocotillo area to prepare for the World War II invasion of North Africa, and the area hasn't been the same since.

The little town of Borrego Springs acts as an oasis in this natural playground. Not exactly like Palm Springs—it lacks the wild crowds and preponderance of insanely wealthy residents—Borrego is basically a small retirement community, with the average age of residents about 50. For visitors who are uninterested in communing with the desert without a shower and pool nearby, Borrego provides several pleasant hotels and restaurants.

We recommend visiting this desert between October and May to avoid the extreme summer temperatures. Winter temperatures are comfortable, but nights (and sometimes days) are cold, so bring a warm jacket.

Exploring

The **Anza-Borrego Desert State Park** is too vast even to consider exploring in its entirety. Most people stay in the hills surrounding Borrego Springs. An excellent underground **Visitor Information Center** (☎ 619/767–5311) and museum are reachable by taking the Palm Canyon Drive spur west from the traffic circle in the center of town. The rangers are helpful and always willing to suggest areas for camping or hiking. A short slide show about the desert is shown throughout the day. For a listing of the interpretive programs scheduled for the year, pick up a copy of the free park newspaper.

One of the most popular camping and hiking areas is **Palm Canyon,** just a few minutes west of the Visitor Information Center. A 1½-mile trail leads to a small oasis with a waterfall and palm trees. If you find palm trees lining city streets in San Diego and Los Angeles amusing, seeing this grove of native palms around a pool in a narrow desert valley may give you a new vision of the dignity of this tree. The Borrego Palm Canyon campground (on the desert floor, a mile or so below the palm oasis) is one of only two developed campgrounds with flush toilets and showers in the park. (The other is Tamarisk Grove Campground at the intersection of Route 78 and Yaqui Pass Road.)

Other points of interest include **Split Mountain** (take Split Mountain Road south from Route 78 at Ocotillo Wells), a narrow gorge with 600-foot perpendicular walls. You can drive the mile from the end of the paved road to the gorge in a passenger car if you are careful (don't get stuck in the sand). Don't attempt the drive in bad weather, when the gorge can quickly fill with a torrent of water; even if the sky is clear when you arrive, check ahead at the visitor center to find out if current road conditions allow for a safe trip.

On the way to Split Mountain (while you are still on the paved road), you'll pass a grove of the park's unusual **elephant trees** (10 feet tall, with swollen branches and small leaves). There is a self-guided nature trail; pick up a brochure at the parking lot.

You can get a good view of the Borrego Badlands from **Font's Point,** off Borrego–Salton Seaway (S22). The badlands are a maze of steep ravines that are almost devoid of vegetation and are best navigated by a four-wheel-drive vehicle.

In **Borrego Springs** itself, there is little to do besides lie or recreate in the sun. The challenging 18-hole Rams Hill Country Club course is open to the public (☎ 619/767–5000), as is the more modest course at the Borrego Roadrunner Club (☎ 619/767–5374). Borrego Resorts International Tennis (☎ 619/767–9748) has courts that are open to the public, as does La Casa del Zorro (☎ 619/767–5323). One of the best and most appreciated deals in town is the Borrego Springs High School pool (☎ 619/767–5337), at the intersection of Saddle and Cahuilla roads and open to the public during the summer.

Most people prefer to explore the desert in a motorized vehicle. While it is illegal to drive off the established trails in the state park, the **Ocotillo Wells State Vehicular Recreation Area** (☎ 619/767–5391), reached by following Route 78 east from Borrego, is a popular haven for off-road enthusiasts and those who drive vehicles that are not street legal. The sand dunes and rock formations are challenging as well as fun. Camping is permitted throughout the area, but water is not available. The only facilities are in the small town (really no more than a corner) of Ocotillo Wells.

To the east of Anza-Borrego is the Salton Sink, a basin that (although not as low as Death Valley) consists of more dry land below sea level than anywhere else in this hemisphere. The Salton Sea is the most recent of a series of lakes here, divided from the Gulf of California by the delta of the Colorado River. The current lake was created in 1905–07, when the Colorado flooded north through canals meant to irrigate the Imperial Valley. The water is extremely salty, even saltier than the Pacific Ocean, and it is primarily a draw for fishermen seeking corbina, croaker, and tilapia. Some boaters and swimmers also use the lake. The state runs a pleasant park, with sites for day camping, recreational vehicles, and primitive camping. *Take Rte. 78E to Rte. 111N,* ☏ *619/393–3059.*

Bird-watchers will love the **Salton Sea National Wildlife Refuge.** A hiking trail and observation tower make it easy to spot the dozens of varieties of migratory birds stopping at Salton Sea. *At the south end of Salton Sea, off Rte. 111,* ☏ *619/348–5278.*

Dining

Quality, not quantity, is the operable truism of dining in the Borrego area. Restaurants are scarce and hard to find, and many close on holidays during the summer, but the best are high quality. *See* the chart *in* Chapter 7, Dining, for price categories.

$ **Chinese Panda Restaurant.** The only business in a Quonset hut in Borrego Springs, this friendly Chinese restaurant serves tasty versions of Mandarin and Szechuan dishes. ✕ *818 Palm Canyon Dr.,* ☏ *619/767–3182. Reservations accepted. MC, V. Closed Mon. and Aug.*

$ **Mi Tenampa Cafe.** It may seem odd to find good Mexican seafood in the desert, but no stranger, perhaps, than this low-key restaurant's location—just off Christmas Circle. ✕ *747 Palm Canyon Dr., no* ☏. *No reservations. No credit cards. Closed Mon., Tues.*

Lodging

If camping isn't your thing, there are two very nice resorts near Borrego Springs that offer fine amenities minus the overdevelopment of Palm Springs. *See* the chart *in* Chapter 8, Lodging, for price categories. In the summer months, rates drop by as much as 50%.

$$–$$$$ **La Casa del Zorro.** This is a small, low-key resort complex in the heart of the desert. You need walk only a few hundred yards to be alone under the sky, and you may well see roadrunners crossing the highway. There are 17 different types of accommodations, set in comfortable one- to three-bedroom ranch-style houses complete with living rooms and kitchens; some three-bedroom suites have private pools, while other suites come with baby grand pianos. The elegant Continental restaurant puts on a good Sunday brunch. ⊡ *3845 Yaqui Pass Rd., 92004,* ☏ *619/767–5323 or 800/824–1884,* FAX *619/767–5963. 52 suites, 16 rooms, 19 casitas. Restaurant, 3 pools, 6 tennis courts, bicycles. AE, D, DC, MC, V.*

$$–$$$ **Palm Canyon Resort.** This is one of the largest properties in the area, with a hotel, an RV park, a restaurant, and recreational facilities. ⊡ *221 Palm Canyon Dr., 92004,* ☏ *619/767–5342 or 800/242–0044 in CA,* FAX *619/767–4073. 44 rooms. Restaurant, 2 pools, coin laundry. AE, D, DC, MC, V.*

Desert Essentials

Arriving and Departing

BY CAR
Take I–8 east to Route 79 north. Turn east on Route 78.

BY BUS
The Northeast Rural Bus System (NERBS, ☎ 619/765–0145) connects Julian, Borrego Springs, Oak Grove, Ocotillo Wells, Agua Caliente, Ramona, and many of the other small communities with El Cajon, 15 miles east of downtown San Diego, and the East County line of the San Diego trolley, with stops at Grossmont shopping center and North County Fair. Service is by reservation, and buses do not run on Sundays or on some holidays.

Important Addresses and Numbers
For general information about the Borrego and desert areas, contact the **Borrego Springs Chamber of Commerce** (622 Palm Canyon Dr., Box 66, Borrego Springs 92004, ☎ 619/767–5555). For details on the state park, phone or write the Visitor Center, **Anza-Borrego Desert State Park** (Box 299, Borrego Springs 92004, ☎ 619/767–5311). During the spring blooming season, a special wildflower hotline (☎ 619/767–4684) gives 24-hour recorded information on what is flowering at the time of your call and what is expected to bloom shortly. For campsite reservations, call MISTIX (☎ 800/444–7275).

11 Tijuana, Rosarito Beach, and Ensenada

By Maribeth
Mellin

Updated by
Edie Jarolim

SINCE YOU'VE COME as far as the southwesternmost city in the United States, take advantage of the opportunity and go *un poquito mas allá* (just a bit farther) and experience Mexico. Just 18 miles south of San Diego lies Baja California, a 1,000-mile-long stretch of beaches, desert, and hills that has long been a refuge for Californians with an urge to swim, surf, fish, and relax in a country unlike their own.

Tijuana, at the international border, is the most popular destination for day-trippers, who come for the souvenir shopping, sports events, and sophisticated Mexican dining. Laid-back Rosarito Beach, 18 miles south of Tijuana on the Pacific coast, attracts travelers in search of a more mellow Mexico. Ensenada, a major port, combines many elements of Tijuana and Rosarito but also retains its own character.

It is possible to visit Tijuana, Rosarito Beach, and Ensenada in a long, busy day. Begin by bypassing Tijuana and heading straight for the toll road to Rosarito Beach, about a 40-mile drive south. Once in Rosarito, stop at the gracious Rosarito Beach Hotel for breakfast, take a short walk on the beach in front of the hotel, and check out a few of the shops on Boulevard Juárez. Return to the toll road just south of the hotel and continue south for 45 miles to Ensenada. Take your time along this stretch of road, and exit at Salsipuedes and El Mirador to admire the view.

In Ensenada, park at the Plaza Marina on the waterfront and do your exploring on foot. Spend an hour or two wandering along Avenida López Mateos and its side streets, where you may find bargains on leather goods and jewelry in high-quality shops. Hussongs bar is an essential stop for rowdy types; culture-seekers should tour the Riviera del Pacifico, a former gambling palace built in the 1920s. Return to the waterfront for a quick run through the fish market and a snack of fish tacos, and try to be back on the road by early afternoon—and to save room for a lobster lunch at Puerto Nuevo, about 10 miles south of Rosarito.

If you finish lunch by mid-afternoon, you'll be able to reach Tijuana before nightfall. Once in the city, park in a lot by Calle 2A, the road that ties the highway to the border; walk up Calle 2A to Avenida Revolución, finish your souvenir shopping, and have dinner at a restaurant on the way back to your car. It's smart to wait until after 7 PM to cross the border, when rush-hour traffic has diminished.

A more leisurely tour would include an overnight stay in Rosarito Beach. By doing so, you can spend the morning in Tijuana seeing the sights and pricing possible purchases. Check into your hotel in Rosarito in the early afternoon, then visit the beach or the shops. Dine in Rosarito or Puerto Nuevo, get to bed early, and start off to Ensenada in the morning. Spend a half-day there, then head back to Tijuana, where you can pick up that last tacky souvenir from a salesman along the border traffic lines.

TIJUANA

As Mexico's fourth-largest city, Tijuana can no longer be called a border "town." The border crossing at Tijuana is the busiest in the United States. Residents of San Diego and Tijuana go back and forth regularly to work, shop, dine, and visit family and friends. The dollar is as

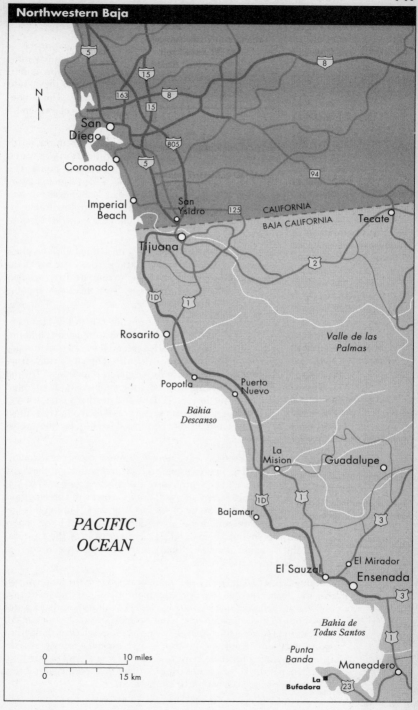

common as the peso, and Spanish and English blend into the border language of Spanglish, easing communication.

Before the turn of the century, when Tijuana became a recreational center for southern Californians, it was a ranch populated by a few hundred Mexicans. In the 1920s, Prohibition caused the city to boom: Americans seeking alcohol, gambling, and more fun than they could find back home flocked across the border, spending freely. Tijuana became the entry port for what some termed a "sinful, steamy playground," frequented by Hollywood stars and the idle rich.

When Prohibition was repealed, the flow of travelers from the north slowed to a trickle for a while, but Tijuana still captivated those in search of the sort of fun that was illegal or just frowned upon at home. The ever-growing number of servicemen in San Diego kept Tijuana's sordid reputation alive. Before the toll highway to Ensenada was finished in 1967, travelers going south drove straight through downtown Tijuana, stopping along Avenida Revolución and its side streets for supplies and souvenirs.

In the 1970s and '80s, Avenida Revolución, once lined with brothels and bars, underwent tremendous rehabilitation. Today the avenue is lined with shops and restaurants, all catering to tourists. Park benches and shade trees on brick paths winding away from the traffic encourage visitors to linger and watch the scenery.

The city's population has mushroomed—from 300,000 in 1970 to nearly 2 million today. Tijuana's instant neighborhoods of migrants and immigrants from throughout Latin America spread into canyons and dry riverbeds, over hillsides, and onto ocean cliffs. The city's infrastructure is incapable of keeping up with the surges in population: During the torrential rains in the winter of 1993, for example, floods and mud slides devastated entire sections of Tijuana and northern Baja, leaving thousands homeless. But the tourism sectors remained relatively intact even during the deluge, and visitors continued to shop for sombreros and serapes in the rain.

Tijuana's tourist attractions have remained much the same throughout the century. Betting on greyhounds is legal and popular at the Agua Caliente Racetrack, and the impressive El Palacio Frontón (Jai Alai Palace), where betting is also allowed, draws crowds of cheering fans to its fast-paced matches. Some of Mexico's greatest bullfighters appear at the oceanfront and downtown bullrings; some of Latin America's most popular musicians and dancers perform at the Cultural Center; and there are an extraordinary number of places in town that provide good food and drinks.

Shopping is one of Tijuana's other main draws. From the moment you cross the border, people will approach you or call out and insist that you look at their wares. If you drive, workers will run out from autobody shops to place bids on new paint or upholstery for your car. All along Avenida Revolución and its side streets, shops sell everything from tequila to Tiffany lamps; serious shoppers can spend a full day searching and bargaining for their items of choice. If you intend to buy food in Mexico, get the U.S. customs list of articles that are illegal to bring back, so your purchases won't be confiscated.

Exploring Tijuana

Numbers in the margin correspond to points of interest on the Tijuana map.

1 At the **San Ysidro Border Crossing,** a pedestrian walkway travels through the Viva Tijuana dining and shopping center and an adjacent lineup of stalls filled with the full spectrum of souvenirs and then goes **2** up Calle 2 into the center of town. **Mexitlán,** a museum-entertainment-shopping center, has scale models of the major architectural and cultural landmarks throughout Mexico, restaurants and shops featuring authentic cuisine and folk art, and frequent performances by folkloric dancers and musical groups. *Av. Ocampo between Calles 2 and 3,* ☎ *66/38–41–01* ☛ *Adults $3.25; children under 12 free.* ⊘ *Tues.–Fri. 10–6, weekends 12–8 (extended hrs in summer).*

Calle 2 intersects **Avenida Revolución,** lined with designer-clothing shops and restaurants, all catering to tourists. Many shopping arcades open onto Avenida Revolución; inside the front doors are mazes of small stands with low-priced pottery and other handicrafts.

3 **El Palacio Frontón (Jai Alai Palace)** is on Avenida Revolución between Calles 7a and 8a. The magnificent Moorish-style palace is an exciting place for watching and betting on fast-paced jai alai games (*see* Spectator Sports, *below*).

TIME OUT Among the many restaurants along Avenida Revolución, **La Especial** (Av. Revolución 718, ☎ 66/85–66–54) is a favorite for Mexican food that hasn't been fancied up for the tourists.

Between Boulevard Agua Caliente and the border is the **Río Tijuana** area, which runs parallel to the river. With its impressive Cultural Center and shopping complex, this section of town, along Avenida Paseo de los Héroes, is fast becoming Tijuana's Zona Rosa.

4 The **Cultural Center,** designed by the same architects who created Mexico City's famous Museum of Anthropology, introduces thousands of visitors to Mexican history. The Omnimax Theater features a cinematic tour of Mexico (which has become somewhat outdated); the bookstore has an excellent selection on Mexican history, culture, and arts in Spanish and English. Guest artists appear at the center regularly. The restaurant is a good place to relax and absorb all you've seen. It's about a 20-minute walk from Avenida Revolución to the Cultural Center, and you must cross some very busy thoroughfares: You're best off taking a taxi. *Paseo de los Héroes and Av. Independencia,* ☎ *66/84–11–11.* ☛ *Museum $1.60; museum and Omnimax Theater $5.50 for English-language shows, $2.30 for Spanish.* ☉ *Daily 11–7. English-language version of the film* El Pueblo del Sol *is presented daily at 2* PM.

5 Long, wide sidewalks lead from the Cultural Center to **Plaza Río Tijuana,** on Paseo de los Héroes, landscaped with shade trees and flowers. The enormous shopping complex houses good restaurants, department stores, and hundreds of shops. The plaza has become a central square of sorts, where holiday fiestas are held. Smaller shopping centers are opening all along the Paseo de los Héroes; Plaza Fiesta and Plaza de Zapatos are two of the finest.

6 The **Playas Tijuana** area, at the oceanfront, is slated next for development. For now, the area is a mix of modest and expensive residential neighborhoods, with a few restaurants and hotels. The long, isolated beaches are visited mostly by locals.

Shopping

The traditional shopping strip is Avenida Revolución, between Calles 1 and 8, lined with shops and arcades that display a wide range of crafts and curios. Bargaining is expected on the streets and in the arcades but not in the finer shops. **Sanborn's** (Av. Revolución at Calle 8, ☎ 66/88–14–62) carries beautiful crafts from throughout Mexico, excellent baked goods, and chocolates from Mexico City. The finest folk-art store in Tijuana, **Tolan** (Av. Revolución between Calles 7 and 8, ☎ 66/88–36–37) carries everything from antique carved wooden doors to tiny ceramic miniature village scenes. **La Piel** (Av. Revolución between Calle 4 and 5, ☎ 66/87–23–98), a recommended leather shop, offers dependable quality in jackets, backpacks, and luggage. **Ralph Lauren Polo Outlet** (Viva Tijuana Center, ☎ 66/88–76–98) is a licensed outlet for the designer's sportswear. **Sara's** (Av. Revolución at Calle 4, ☎ 66/88–29–32), one of the best department stores, features imported perfumes and fine clothing.

The Avenida Revolución shopping area spreads down Calle 1 to the pedestrian walkway leading from the border. The shops in **Plaza Revolución,** at the corner of Calle 1 and Avenida Revolución, stock good-quality crafts. Begin shopping at the stands along the border-crossing walkway, comparing prices as you travel toward Avenida Revolución. You may find that the best bargains are closer to the border, and you can pick up your piñatas and serapes on your way out of town.

Plaza Río Tijuana is described in Exploring Tijuana, *above,* as is **Mexitlán** on Avenida Ocampo, which stocks folk art from throughout

Mexico. **Pueblo Amigo** on Boulevard Paseo de los Héroes is a fanciful pseudo pueblo marketplace with boutiques. **Plaza Fiesta,** on Paseo de los Héroes across from Plaza Río Tijuana, has a collection of boutiques, jewelry stores, and stained-glass shops. Next door, the **Plaza de los Zapatos** sells designer shoes imported from throughout the world.

Spectator Sports

Bullfights

Bullfights, considered artistic spectacles, not sporting events, feature skilled matadors from throughout Mexico and Spain. They are held at **El Toreo de Tijuana** (Av. Agua Caliente, just outside downtown, ☎ 66/85–22–10) on Sunday at 4, May–September. In July and August, you can also see fights at the **Plaza de Toros Monumental** (Playas Tijuana area, Ensenada Hwy., ☎ 66/85–22–10) on Sunday at 4.

Greyhound Races

At the **Hipódromo de Agua Caliente,** still reminiscent of the glamorous years when Hollywood stars gambled here, horse racing was phased out in 1993, but greyhounds race nightly at 7:45 and at 2 on Saturday and Sunday. In the Foreign Book area, gamblers can bet on races taking place in California and shown at Caliente on TV monitors. *Blvd. Agua Caliente at Salinas,* ☎ *66/81–78–11 or 619/231–1919 in San Diego.*

Jai Alai

An ancient Basque sport, fast-paced jai alai is in some ways similar to handball but uses a long, curved basket strapped to the competitor's wrists. The Moorish-style **Palacio Frontón** is a good place to be introduced to this exciting game. *Av. Revolución and Calle 8,* ☎ *66/88–01–25 or 619/231–1919 in San Diego.* ☛ *$3–$5.*

Dining

There is no shortage of good eating in Tijuana, from *taquerías* (taco stands) to gourmet and Continental restaurants; Avenida Revolución resembles one long food court with places for every taste and budget. Street nightlife often becomes rowdy, with tourists demonstrating the effects of potent Mexican margaritas. Seafood is abundant; beef and pork are common, both grilled and marinated as *carne asada* and *carnitas* (marinated pork). Dress is casual, and reservations are not required unless otherwise noted. Some restaurants add a 15% service charge to the bill.

CATEGORY	COST*
$$$	$15–$20
$$	$8–$15
$	under $8

per person for a three-course meal, excluding drinks and service

$$$ **El Taurino.** Walk a few blocks west of Avenida Revolución and you're
★ in the true downtown Tijuana, where residents work, shop, and eat. One of their favorite spots is this cozy steak house. Request a menu in English and zero in on the beef selections, especially the New York steak, called *cabrería.* Shrimp and lobster are also good choices, and all come with soup or salad. ✕ *Calle 6 No. 7531,* ☎ *66/85–70–75. MC, V.*

$$$ **Pedrin's.** One of Tijuana's best seafood restaurants overlooks the Jai Alai Palace from a second-story garden room. Entrées come with deep-fried fish appetizers, fish chowder, salad, and a sweet after-dinner

drink. Recommended are *rajas shrimp*, with melted cheese and green chilies, and grilled lobster. ✕ *Av. Revolución 1115,* ☎ *66/85–40–52. AE, MC, V.*

$$ **La Fonda Roberto's.** This is by far the best restaurant in Tijuana for
★ traditional cuisine from the many culinary regions of Mexico. Try the meats with spicy achiote sauce and many varieties of mole. Portions are small, so order liberally and share. ✕ *Old Ensenada Hwy. (also called Calle 16 de Septiembre), near Blvd. Agua Caliente in the Siesta Motel,* ☎ *66/86–16–01. MC, V.*

$$ **La Leña.** The sparkling clean, white dining room in La Leña faces an
★ open kitchen where chefs grill unusual beef dishes, like *gaonera,* a tender fillet stuffed with cheese and guacamole, and you can see fresh tortillas being prepared. ✕ *Blvd. Agua Caliente 4560,* ☎ *66/86–47–52; Av. Revolución between Calles 4 and 5. AE, MC, V.*

$$ **La Taberna Española.** The mainstay of Plaza Fiesta's multiethnic cafés, this Spanish tapas bar attracts a youthful, sophisticated crowd. A sampling of *tapas* (appetizers) might include octopus in its own ink, a plate of spicy sausages, a wedge of Spanish tortilla with potatoes and eggs, and fava beans. Sit at the outdoor tables for a better view of the crowd waiting in line. ✕ *Plaza Fiesta, Paseo de los Héroes 10001,* ☎ *66/84–75–62. No credit cards.*

$$ **Tía Juana Tilly's.** Popular with both tourists and locals looking for revelry and generous portions of Mexican specialties, this is one of the few places where you can get *cochinita píbil,* a Yucatecán specialty made of roast pig, red onions, and bitter oranges. Part of the same chain is Tilly's Fifth Ave., catercorner to the original on Avenida Revolución. ✕ *Av. Revolución at Calle 7,* ☎ *66/85–60–24. AE, MC, V.*

$ **Carnitas Uruapan.** At this large, noisy restaurant, patrons mingle at long tables, toasting one another with chilled *cervezas* (beer). The main attraction is carnitas, sold by weight and served with homemade tortillas, salsa, cilantro, guacamole, and onions. ✕ *Blvd. Díaz Ordaz 550,* ☎ *66/81–61–81; Paseo de los Héroes at Av. Rodriguez, no* ☎. *No credit cards.*

Lodging

Tijuana's hotels are clustered downtown, along Avenida Revolución; near the country club on Boulevard Agua Caliente; and in the Río Tijuana area on Paseo de los Héroes. There are ample accommodations for all price levels. **Baja Information** (7860 Mission Center Ct., Suite 202, San Diego, CA 92108, ☎ 619/298–4105 or 619/299–8518; 800/225–2786 in the U.S.; 800/522–1516 in CA, AZ, and NV; FAX 619/294–7366) can reserve hotel rooms.

CATEGORY	COST*
$$$$	over $90
$$$	$60–$90
$$	$25–$60
$	under $25

All prices are for a standard double room, excluding service charge and sales tax (10%).

$$$$ **Gran Hotel.** The two mirrored towers of the hotel, which often hosts
★ parties for Tijuana's elite, are the city's most ostentatious landmarks. The rooms on the club floors are particularly extravagant, with separate seating areas, king-size beds, and astounding views of Tijuana's sprawl. ⌸ *Blvd. Agua Caliente 4558, 22420,* ☎ *66/81–70–00 or 800/472–6385,* FAX *66/81–70–16. 422 rooms with bath. Restaurant, pool, tennis courts, health club, nightclub, travel services. MC, V.*

$$ Corona Plaza. The interior of this building, which looks like a non-descript office tower, is surprisingly pleasant. Rooms, furnished in handsome bleached wood, overlook an atrium lobby and restaurant. For less noise and more air, ask for a second- or third-floor room near the pool. The bullring is within walking distance; other attractions are just a short taxi ride away. ☒ *Blvd. Agua Caliente 1426, 22450,* ☎ *66/81–81–83,* ℻ *66/81–81–85. Restaurant, pool. MC, V.*

$$ La Villa de Zaragoza. La Villa is a well-maintained, brown stucco motel with a good location—near the Jai Alai Palace and one block from Avenida Revolución. It has the nicest rooms downtown in this price range. ☒ *Av. Madero 1120, 22000,* ☎ *66/85–18–32. 42 rooms. Restaurant. MC, V.*

The Arts and Nightlife

Tijuana has toned down its Sin City image; much of the action now takes place at the **Jai Alai Palace** and the racetrack. Several hotels, especially the **Lucerna** and **Gran Hotel,** feature live entertainment. **Iguanas** (Blvd. Paseo de los Héroes, ☎ 66/82–49–67), at the Pueblo Amigo shopping center, is an 18-and-over club; appearances by new wave and rock artists draw as many patrons from San Diego as from Tijuana (*see* Rock Clubs *in* Chapter 9, The Arts and Nightlife).

Hard Rock Cafe (Av. Revolución 520 between Calles 1 and 2, ☎ 66/85–02–06) has the same menu and decor as other branches of the famous London club and is popular with both families and singles. **OH! Laser Club** (Paseo de los Héroes 56, ☎ 66/84–02–67) is one of the oldest discos in town, popular with the sophisticated set. **Heaven & Hell** (Paseo de los Héroes 10501, ☎ 66/84–84–84) is less formal than most and extremely frenetic. **Baby Rock** (Calle Diego Rivera 1482, ☎ 66/84–94–38), an offshoot of a popular Acapulco disco, attracts a young, hip crowd. Tijuana's discos are elegant and sophisticated and usually have strict dress codes, with no T-shirts, jeans, or sandals allowed.

ROSARITO BEACH

Not long ago, Playas de Rosarito (Rosarito Beach) was a small seaside community with virtually no tourist trade. Part of the municipality of Tijuana, it was an overlooked suburb on the way to the port city of Ensenada. But as the roads improved, and particularly after Baja's Transpeninsular Highway was completed in 1973, Rosarito Beach began to flower. Vacation suites were added along the beach, and time-share and condo units were put up, although as recently as 1980, the Rosarito Beach Hotel was the only resort in the area. The '80s brought an amazing building boom to Rosarito. The main street, alternately known as the Old Ensenada Highway and Boulevard Benito Juárez, is now packed with restaurants, bars, and shops. Rosarito's population, nearly 100,000 in 1993, is growing steadily.

Still, it is a relaxing place to visit. Southern Californians have practically made Rosarito a weekend suburb. Surfers, swimmers, and sunbathers come here to enjoy the beach, one of the longest in northern Baja: It's an uninterrupted stretch of sand from the power plant at the far north end of town to below the Rosarito Beach Hotel, about 5 miles south. Horseback riding, jogging, and strolling are popular along this strand. Whales pass not far from shore on their winter migration; dolphins and sea lions sun on rocks jutting out from the sea.

One of the area's major draws is its seafood, especially lobster, shrimp, and abalone. Margaritas and beer are the favored thirst quenchers. People throw off their inhibitions here, at least to the degree permitted by the local constables. A typical Rosarito day may begin with a breakfast of eggs, refried beans, and tortillas, followed by a few hours of horseback riding on the beach. Lying in the sun or strolling through the shops takes care of midday. Siestas are imperative and are usually followed by more shopping, strolling, or sunbathing before dinner, dancing, and sleep.

Exploring

Rosarito Beach has few historic or cultural attractions, beaches and bars being the main draws. Sightseeing consists of strolling along the beach or down Boulevard Benito Juárez. Note: Street numbers and addresses are changing along Juárez. To reduce confusion, ask for landmarks when getting directions.

An immense PEMEX gasoline installation and electric plant anchor the northern end of Boulevard Juárez, which then runs along a collection of new shopping arcades, restaurants, and motels. The eight-story **La Quinta del Mar** hotel is the first major landmark, followed by the **Quinta Plaza** shopping center, which has a car wash, pharmacy, bakery, specialty shops, and restaurants, as well as the **tourism office** and the **Centro de Convenciones,** a 1,000-seat convention center. Across the street is the **Festival Plaza** hotel and shopping center, with a distinctive roller coaster–like facade.

TIME OUT   The long, glassed-in bar that sits on a little hill between the pool and the beach at the **Rosarito Beach Hotel** (☎ 661/2–01–44) is the best place for absorbing the hotel's ambience. The margaritas are a potent reminder that you're in Mexico, and the nachos are fairly good. Have Sunday brunch ($15) in the dining room overlooking the pool.

Off the Beaten Track

The most popular side trip from Rosarito Beach is **Puerto Nuevo** (Newport) at Km 44 on the old highway. A few years ago, the only way you could tell you'd reached this fishing community was by the huge painting of a 7-Up bottle on the side of a building. You'd drive down the rutted dirt road to a row of restaurants, where you were served the classic Newport meal: grilled lobster, refried beans, rice, homemade tortillas, butter, salsa, and lime. The meal became a legend, and now at least 30 restaurants have the identical menu. Try one of the family-run places, like Ponderosa (*see* Dining, *below*).

Shopping

The two major resort hotels have shopping arcades equipped with laundromats, taco stands, and some good crafts stores. The **Calimax** grocery store on Boulevard Juárez is a good place to stock up on necessities.

Rosarito is a great place to shop for pottery and wood furniture. Curio stands and open-air artisans' markets line Boulevard Juárez both north and south of town, with the best pottery stands on the highway to the south. Another cluster of stands appear at Puerto Nuevo, where diners sated on lobster and beer bargain for cotton blankets, seashell lamps, and piñatas. Within Rosarito proper, **Casa Torres** (Rosarito Beach Hotel Shopping Center, ☎ 661/2–10–08) carries a wide array of imported perfumes. **Margarita's** (Rosarito Beach Hotel Shopping Center, no ☎) has a great selection of Guatemalan textiles and clothing. **Oradia Imports** (Quinta Plaza Center, ☎ 661/2–16–37) focuses on imported perfumes and crystal. **Casa del Arte y La Madera** (Quinta del Mar Plaza, ☎ 661/2–13–00) always has an irresistible selection of Mexican folk art with a fish and sea theme, and creatively painted furnishings. The shelves of **Taxco Curious** (Quinta del Mar Plaza, ☎ 661/2–18–77) are filled with handblown glassware. **Casa la Carreta** (Km 29, Ensenada Hwy., ☎ 661/2–05–02), one of Rosarito's best furniture shops, is worth a visit just to see the woodcarvers create elaborate desks, dining tables, and armoires. **Rangel** (Blvd. Juárez 151-A, ☎ 661/2–14–26) specializes in rattan and wood furnishings. **La Hacienda** (Blvd. Juárez 97, ☎ 661/2–07–21) has a good selection of painted tiles. **Tony's Surf Shop** (Blvd. Juárez 312, ☎ 661/2–11–92) offers surfing gear for sale or rent.

Sports and Outdoor Activities

Fishing

There is a small fishing pier at Km 33 on the Old Ensenada Highway; surf casting is allowed on the beach. No place in Rosarito issues fishing licenses, but tourism officials say licenses are not necessary if you fish from shore. Unfortunately, the ocean tends to be polluted, especially in residential areas, so it is not a good idea to eat fish caught close to shore.

Golf

Two golf courses have opened in the Rosarito area, and more are in the planning stages. **Bajamar** (Km 77.5 Ensenada Hwy., ☎ 615/5–01–51 or 800/342–2644), a 1976 course revamped and reopened in late 1993, will be joined by a second resort course; the first nine holes are scheduled to open by the end of 1995. **Real del Mar** (☎ 661/3–34–01) has an 18-hole course in the center of a planned golf community; it's located at Km 19.2 on the toll highway Ensenada Cuota, 12 miles south of the border and 6 miles north of Rosarito. Golf packages are available at some Rosarito Beach hotels.

Horseback Riding

Horses can be rented at the north and south ends of Juárez and on the beach for $10 per hour. Check them carefully; some are pathetically thin. The number of horses on the beach is now restricted, and the horses are better cared for.

Surfing

The waves are particularly good at **Popotla** (Km 33), **Calafia** (Km 35.5), and **Costa Baja** (Km 36), on the Old Ensenada Highway.

Dining

Nearly all Rosarito's restaurants feature the same items—lobster, shrimp, fresh fish, and steak—at nearly the same prices: about $15–$18 for dinner. Some restaurants tack a 15% service charge on to your bill. Dress is casual and reservations are not required unless otherwise noted.

CATEGORY	COST*
$$$	$15–$20
$$	$8–$15
$	under $8

per person, excluding drinks and service

Rosarito Beach

$$$ Dragon del Mar. A miniature waterfall greets guests in the marble foyer of this elegant Chinese restaurant, which features a pianist. Carved wooden partitions in the expansive dining room help create an intimate dining experience. The food is well prepared and appealing to the eye as well as the palate. ✕ *Blvd. Juárez 283,* ☎ *661/2–06–04. MC, V.*

$$$ La Casa de la Langosta. You needn't drive to Puerto Nuevo for lobster; just visit this branch of one of that area's best restaurants. The traditional lobster dinner is the house specialty, of course, but you can also get grilled fish and shrimp. The second-story dining room and kitchen are impeccably clean, and the food dependable, though not overly exciting. ✕ *Quinta Plaza,* ☎ *661/2–09–24. MC, V.*

$$$ La Leña. You can see the ocean from the window tables of La Leña.
★ The dining room is spacious, with the tables spread far enough apart for privacy. Try any of the beef dishes, especially the tender grilled *carne asada* with tortillas and guacamole. ✕ *Quinta Plaza,* ☎ *661/2–08–26. MC, V.*

$$ El Nido. A dark, wood-paneled restaurant with leather booths and a large central fireplace, this is one of the oldest eateries in Rosarito. Diners unimpressed with the newer, fancier establishments come here for the good mesquite-grilled steaks. ✕ *Blvd. Juárez 67,* ☎ *661/2–14–30. MC, V.*

$$ Mariscos de Rosarito Vince's. This seafood restaurant and deli is popular with expatriate Americans, who swear that Vince's has the best lobster in town. Mariachis add to the nightly festivities. ✕ *Blvd. Juárez 77,* ☎ *661/2–12–53. No credit cards.*

$$ René's. One of the oldest restaurants in Rosarito (1924), René's features *chorizo* (Mexican sausage), quail, frogs' legs, and lobster. There's an ocean view from the dining room, a lively bar, and mariachi music. ✕ *Blvd. Juárez south of the Rosarito Beach Hotel,* ☎ *661/2–10–20. MC, V.*

$ Juice 'n Juice. Rosarito's Mexican/health-food restaurant is a no-frills lunch counter with lots of salads, juices, yogurt, and granola. Good cheese enchiladas and other meatless Mexican dishes give vegetarians a chance to sample the local fare. ✕ *Blvd. Juárez 98,* ☎ *661/2–03–38. No credit cards.*

$ La Flor de Michoacán. Carnitas Michoacán style, with homemade tor-
★ tillas, guacamole, and salsa, are the house specialty. The tacos *tortas* (marinated pork kebabs) and tostadas are great. The surroundings are simple but clean. Takeout is available. ✕ *Blvd. Juárez 291,* ☎ *661/2–18–58. No credit cards. Closed Wed.*

South of Rosarito Beach

$$$ Calafia. The owners of this restaurant and trailer park are in the process of transforming their establishment into a cultural center, with a museum devoted to historical artifacts from the region. Still, most visitors are drawn to Calafia's restaurant, where tables are scattered on small terraces down the cliffside to the crashing sea. The food is standard Mexican fare, but it all tastes great when combined with the fresh salt air and sea breezes. Calafia has an outdoor dance floor at the base of the cliffs, where live bands sometimes perform. Trailers are available for rent on a nightly or weekly basis at the top of the cliffs. ✕ *Km 35.5, Old Ensenada Hwy.,* ☎ *661/2–15–81 or 800/225–2342. MC, V.*

$$$ La Fonda. This popular restaurant has an outdoor patio overlooking
★ the beach where you can sip potent margaritas served with greasy nachos. Fresh lobster, grilled steaks, prime rib, and traditional Mexican

dishes come with a delicious black-bean soup. The bar is usually crowded with boisterous patrons. ✕ *Km 59 on the Old Ensenada Hwy., no ☎. No credit cards.*

$$ **Puerto Nuevo.** Of the 25–30 restaurants in Newport that serve the same dishes—grilled or deep-fried lobster or shrimp, Spanish rice, refried beans, and homemade tortillas with melted butter, lime, and hot sauce—**Ortega's,** with four branches in Newport and two in Rosarito, is the most crowded; **Ponderosa** is smaller and quieter and is run by a gracious family; **Costa Brava** is newer and more elegant, with tablecloths and an ocean view; and **La Casa de la Langosta** serves grilled fish along with lobster and shrimp. Lobsters in most places are priced as small, medium, and large—medium is about $15. The lobster served at Newport comes from local waters during lobster season (October through March) and is imported from Australia the rest of the year. There is some concern that the waters close to shore have become polluted, but fishers say they catch the lobsters a mile or so offshore, where the waters are safe. ✕ *Km 44 on the Old Ensenada Hwy., no ☎s. Most places are open for lunch and dinner on a first-come, first-served basis. Some take credit cards.*

Lodging

The Rosarito area has nearly 2,000 hotel rooms—and more in the planning stages. You can usually get a room without advance reservations, except during holiday periods, when the town fills up completely. Several agencies in the United States book reservations at Rosarito hotels and at nearby condo and time-share resorts, which may cost less than hotel rooms if you're traveling with a group of four or more. For details, contact **Baja Information** (7860 Mission Center Ct., Suite 202, San Diego, CA 92108, ☎ 619/298–4105, 800/225–2786, or 800/522–1516 in CA), or **Baja California Tours** (6986 La Jolla Blvd., No. 204, La Jolla, CA 92037, ☎ 619/454–7166, ⅂Ⅎ 619/454–2703). Reservations are a must on holiday weekends. Many hotels require a minimum two-night stay for a confirmed reservation, and inexpensive rooms are hard to find.

CATEGORY	COST*
$$$$	over $90
$$$	$60–$90
$$	$25–$60
$	under $25

All prices are for a standard double room, excluding service charge and sales tax (10%).

Rosarito Beach

$$$ **Brisas del Mar.** Built in 1992, this motel is especially good for families, since the large pastel rooms comfortably accommodate four persons. A few of the rooms on the second story have views of the ocean; all have air-conditioning and TV. 🖭 *Blvd. Juárez, at the south end of town, 22170, ☎ and fax 661/2–25–47 or 800/697–5223. 66 rooms. Bar, coffee shop, hot tub. MC, V.*

$$$ **Rosarito Beach Hotel.** Dating from the Prohibition era, this venerable
★ hotel continues to be Rosarito's centerpiece. Several buildings have been added over the years, and there always seems to be some sort of renovation going on to preserve the hotel's character while modernizing its services. It's still a charmer, with huge ballrooms, tiled public rest rooms, and a glassed-in pool deck overlooking a long beach. Rooms and suites in the low-rise buildings and tower that face the beach are modern, though somewhat sterile; more characterful accommodations

in the original building surrounding the swimming pool have been over-hauled. Midweek reduced rates are often available; ocean-view rooms are in the very expensive ($$$$) category. A 1930s mansion next door to the hotel has been refurbished as the Casa Playa Spa, a full-service European facility with a restaurant. ⊡ *Blvd. Juárez, at the south end of town,* ☎ *661/2–01–44 or 800/343–8582,* FAX *661/2–11–76; reservations: Box 430145, San Diego, CA 92143. 275 rooms and suites. 2 restaurants, bar, 2 pools, spa, 2 tennis courts, health club, beach, convention center. MC, V.*

$$ **Los Pelicanos Hotel.** Completed in 1990, this hotel—one of the few situated directly on the beach—has prices that vary depending on the location of the rooms and the presence or absence of a balcony with an ocean view. The second-story restaurant and bar are popular sunset-watching spots. ⊡ *Calle Cedros 115,* ☎ *661/2–04–45,* FAX *661/2–17–57. U.S. mailing address: Box 3871, San Ysidro, CA 92073. 39 rooms. Restaurant, bar. MC, V.*

$ **Cupalas del Mar.** Opened in 1991, this small hotel between Boulevard Juárez and the beach is quieter than most, with sunny, clean rooms and satellite TV. ⊡ *Calle Guadalupe Victoria 9, 22710,* ☎ *661/2–24–90,* FAX *661/2–24–94. 39 rooms. Pool, hot tub. No credit cards.*

South of Rosarito Beach

$$$ **Grand Baja Resort.** A good value for families and groups, this resort—a block from the Puerto Nuevo lobster restaurants—offers beachfront condo rentals with daily and long-term rates; split the cost of a suite or studio between two couples and you'll be in the moderate ($$) range. The units come in a variety of sizes, from studios to two-bedroom ocean-front condos; most have kitchens. ⊡ *Km 44.5 Old Ensenada Hwy.,* ☎ *661/4–14–84,* FAX *661/4–11–42; reservations in the U.S.: 3549 Camino del Rio South, San Diego, CA 92108. 150 units. Pool, tennis courts. MC, V.*

$$$ **La Fonda.** A longtime favorite with beachgoers, La Fonda's well-worn
★ rooms are decorated with carved-wood furniture and folk art and have great views of the ocean. The restaurant and bar are immensely popular; if you plan on getting any sleep, ask for a room as far away from them as possible. Reservations can be made by mail only. Allow two weeks to receive your confirmation. ⊡ *Km 59 on the Old Ensenada Hwy., no* ☎; *reservations in the U.S.: Box 268, San Ysidro, CA 92073. 18 rooms. Restaurant, bar, beach. No credit cards.*

$$$ **Las Rocas.** Perched on a cliff above the ocean, this elegant hotel is ter-
★ raced up a hillside, giving all the rooms ocean views. The white building, with blue-and-purple trim, stands out vividly against the surroundings. Some suites have fireplaces, coffeemakers, and microwaves. ⊡ *Km 37 on the Old Ensenada Hwy.,* ☎ *661/2–21–40; reservations in the U.S.: Box 8851, Chula Vista, CA 91912,* ☎ *619/425–2682 or 800/733–6394 outside CA. 74 rooms and suites. Restaurants, bar, hot tubs, beach. AE, MC, V.*

$$ **Oasis Resort.** This full-scale resort on a long, perfect beach has become incredibly popular since it opened in 1992. The hotel section has one-bedroom, ocean-view suites with heat, air-conditioning, cable TVs, and minibars; RVs with full kitchens and maid service are also available. Though not especially peaceful, the Oasis is a fun spot where guests quickly become friends and end up booking return visits together. ⊡ *Km 40 on the Old Ensenada Hwy., 22710,* ☎ *661/3–32–55,* FAX *661/3–32–52; reservations in the U.S.:* ☎ *800/462–7472. 100 suites, 12 RVs, 55 RV spaces. Restaurant, bar, 2 pools, wading pool, hot tub, sauna, miniature golf, tennis courts, exercise room, recreation room. MC, V.*

Nightlife

The many restaurants in Rosarito Beach keep customers entertained with live music, piano bars, or *folklórico* (folk music and dance) shows; the bar scene is also active. Drinking and driving laws are stiff—the police will fine you no matter how little you've had. If you plan to drink, take a cab or assign a designated driver.

There's a lot going on at night at **Rosarito Beach Hotel** (Blvd. Juárez, ☎ 661/2−01−44): live music at the ocean-view Beachcomber Bar and Hugo's, a Mexican Fiesta on Friday nights, and a live band at the cavernous disco. The Festival Plaza (*see* Lodging, *above*) has become party central for Rosarito's youthful crowd and presents live concerts on the hotel's courtyard stage most weekends. Dedicated to the art of drinking tequila, **El Museo Sal y Limón** (Festival Plaza, ☎ 661/2−08−42) offers more than 130 brands of the fiery drink. **Rock & Roll Taco** (Festival Plaza, ☎ 661/2−08−42) is just what its name suggests—a taco stand and boisterous bar all in one. **Papas and Beer** (Blvd. Juárez near the Rosarito Beach Hotel, ☎ 661/2−03−43) draws a young, energetic crowd. **Rene's** (Blvd. Juárez south of town, ☎ 661/2−10−61) often has live bands or mariachis; crowds fill the bar to watch sports events on satellite TV. **Calafia** (Km 35 on the Ensenada Hwy., ☎ 661/2−15−81) is alternately rowdy and subdued, depending on what type of band is playing by the dance floor.

ENSENADA

Ensenada is a major port, 104 kilometers (65 miles) south of Tijuana on Bahía de Todos Santos. The paved highway (Route 1) between the two cities often cuts a path between low mountains and high oceanside cliffs; exits lead to rural roads, oceanfront campgrounds, and an ever-increasing number of resort communities. The small fishing communities of San Miguel and El Sauzal sit off the highway to the north of town, and the Coronado Islands can be clearly seen off the coast.

Juan Rodríguez Cabrillo first discovered Ensenada, in 1542. Sebastián Vizcaino named the region Ensenada-Bahía de Todos Santos (All Saints' Bay) in 1602. Since then, the town has drawn a steady stream of "discoverers" and developers, ranchers, gold miners, and, later, shippers. Now it is one of Mexico's largest seaports and has a thriving fishing fleet and fish-processing industry.

There are no beaches in Ensenada proper, but beaches north and south of town are satisfactory for swimming, sunning, surfing, and camping. On weekends and school breaks, Californians throng down here to play, but during most weeks Ensenada is just a normal, relatively calm port city, with a population nearing 300,000.

For decades most hotels and bars have catered to groups of young people intent on drinking and carousing. The beachside strip between San Miguel and Ensenada has long been a haven of moderately priced oceanfront motels and trailer parks. But now there is a concerted effort to attract conventioneers and business travelers. A group of civic boosters has renovated the Riviera del Pacifico, the grand old gambling hall turned civic center that is Ensenada's most stately edifice. The waterfront area has been razed and rebuilt, with taco stands replaced by shopping centers, hotels, and the massive Plaza Marina, which opened in 1992. Several strip malls have opened in town, and cruise ships regularly anchor offshore. Marina Coral, a pleasure-boat marina and large hotel complex is under construction north of town, with completion projected for late 1995. Plans are also under way to move the cruise ship pier to the waterfront across the street from Riviera del Pacifico.

Exploring

Numbers in the margin correspond to points of interest on the Ensenada map.

The city of Ensenada, the third largest in Baja, hugs the harbor of **Bahía de Todos Santos.** If you have access to a car, begin your tour of Ensenada by driving north up Calle 2 or east on the Mexico Highway 1 bypass around town into the **Chapultepec Hills** to **El Mirador** (The Lookout). From here, you can see the entire Bahía de Todos Santos, from the canneries of San Miguel south to the town of Punta Banda and La Bufadora.

To tour the waterfront and downtown, you'll be better off on foot. As Alternate Route 1 leads into town from the north, it becomes Boulevard Costero, running past shipyards filled with massive freighters. To the right, between the water and the street, the massive Plaza Marina is completed but far from filled with the expected restaurants and shops. At the northernmost point at the water's edge sits an indoor-outdoor **Fish Market,** where row after row of counters display piles of shrimp, as well as tuna, dorado, marlin, snapper, and dozens of other species of fish caught off Baja's coasts. Outside, stands sell grilled or smoked fish, seafood cocktails, and fish tacos (don't leave town without trying one). Browsers can pick up some standard souvenirs, eat well for very little money, and take some great photographs. The hot-pink Plaza de Mariscos, which blocks the view of the traditional fish market from the street, is a comfortable place in which to eat. **Boulevard Costero** runs along the waterfront from the market and the **Sportfishing Pier,** where fishing and whale-watching tours depart. A large branch of the **Caliente Foreign Book** chain sits next door, blocking much of the waterfront view. Caliente offers wagering on sports events and horse races shown on satellite TV. At the intersection of Boulevard Costero and Avenida Riveroll is the **Plaza Cívica,** with sculptures of Benito Juárez, Miguel Hidalgo, and Venustiano Carranza. Cruise ships dock offshore from here, and passengers are ferried to the pier, where they can walk to the **Centro Artesenal de Ensenada** shopping center.

Boulevard Costero becomes Boulevard Lázaro Cárdenas at Avenida Riviera, site of the **Riviera del Pacífico.** This rambling white adobe hacienda-style mansion was built in the 1920s with money raised on both sides of the border. An enormous gambling palace, hotel, restaurant and bar, the glamorous Riviera was frequented by wealthy U.S. citizens and Mexicans, particularly during Prohibition. In 1977, the Tourism and Convention Bureau began refurbishing the palace and its lavish gardens. During daylight visitors can tour the elegant ballrooms and halls, which host occasional art shows and civic events. Riviera del Pacífico is officially called the Centro Social, Civico y Cultural de Ensenada (Social, Civic and Cultural Center of Ensenada), and there are plans to include it in a major convention-center complex along the waterfront. *Blvd. Costero and Av. Riviera,* ☎ *617/6–43–10.* ☛ *Free.* ☼ *Daily 9–5.*

The **State Tourist Office** (*see* Important Addresses and Numbers, *below*) is located south of Riviera del Pacifico, a short walk from the tourist zone.

8 Ensenada's traditional tourist zone is centered one block east of the waterfront along **Avenida López Mateos.** High-rise hotels, souvenir shops, restaurants, and bars line the avenue from its beginning at the foot of the Chapultepec Hills for eight blocks south to the dry channel of the Arroyo de Ensenada. Locals shop for furniture, clothing, and other necessities on **Avenida Juárez** in Ensenada's downtown area. The city's **9** largest cathedral, **Our Lady of Guadalupe,** is at Avenida Floresta and the south end of Juárez.

Off the Beaten Track

About 30 minutes south of Ensenada by car, **La Bufadora** is an impressive blowhole in the coastal cliffs at Punta Banda. Water splashes up to 75 feet in the air with startling power, spraying sightseers standing nearby. The blowhole has a long been a natural attraction, but the area around it had become littered with trash and rundown building. State officials have begun a major restoration of the area, and a paved parking lot, permanent artisans' stands, rest rooms, and restaurants are under construction. To reach La Bufadora drive south on Highway 1 to Maneadero, then turn right on Highway 23, a narrow two-lane road down the point.

The hillsides and valleys outside Ensenada are known for their grapes and olives; many of the wineries have tours that can be arranged through hotels in Ensenada. Most of them are in the Guadalupe Valley, on Route 3, north toward Tecate; it's about a 30-minute drive from Ensenada on a paved highway that runs up into the hills past cattle ranches and orchards.

Shopping

Most of the tourist shops are on Avenida López Mateos alongside the hotels and restaurants. There are several two-story shopping arcades, many with empty shops. Dozens of curio shops line the street, all selling similar selections of pottery, woven blankets and serapes, embroidered dresses, and onyx chess sets.

Good crafts stores in town include **Artes de Quijote** (Av. López Mateos 503, ☎ 617/6–94–76), **Girasoles** (Av. López Mateos, no ☎), **Xuchitl** (Av. López Mateos at Alvarado, ☎ 617/4–09–76), **La Mina de Salomón** (Av. López Mateos 1000, ☎ 617/8–28–36), and **Los Castillo** (Av. López Mateos 815, ☎ 617/6–11–87) and **Artesanías Castillo** (Av. López Mateos 656, ☎ 617/6–11–87), which both have extensive displays of silver jewelry from Taxco.

Centro Artesenal de Ensenada, a shopping center on the waterfront, caters to cruise-ship visitors. The best shop by far is the **Galería de Pérez Meillón** (Blvd. Costera 1094-39, ☎ 617/4–03–94), which carries museum-quality pottery and folk art by the indigenous peoples of northern Mexico.

Sports and Outdoor Activities

Golf

The Baja Country Club (Hwy. 1 south of Ensenada at Maneadero, ☎ 617/3–03–03) has a secluded 18-hole course in a resort development. *See also* Sports and Outdoor Activities *in* Rosarito Beach, *above,* for details on Bajamar Golf Resort, some 32 kilometers (20 miles) north of Ensenada.

Sportfishing

Fishing boats leave the **Ensenada Sportfishing Pier** regularly. The best angling takes place from April through November, with bottom fishing good in the winter. Charter vessels and party boats are available from several outfitters along Avenida López Mateos, Boulevard Costero, and off the sportfishing pier. Trips on group boats cost about $50 per day. You can book sportfishing packages that include transportation, accommodations, and fishing through **Baja California Tours** (☎ 619/454–7166 in CA). Licenses are available at the tourist office or from charter companies, among them **Ensenada Clipper Fleet** (pier, ☎ 617/8–21–85) and **Gordo's Sportfishing** (pier, ☎ 617/8–21–90). Gordo's also operates whale-watching trips from December through February.

Tennis

Bajamar and the **Baja Club** (*see* Golf, *above*) have courts open to guests.

Beaches

Since the waterfront in Ensenada proper is taken up by fishing boats, the best swimming beaches are south of town. **Estero Beach** is long and clean, with mild waves. Surfers populate the beaches off Route 1 north and south of Ensenada, particularly **San Miguel, California, Tres Marías,** and La Joya; scuba divers prefer **Punta Banda,** near La Bufadora. Lifeguards are rare; swimmers should be cautious. The tourist office in Ensenada has a map that shows safe diving and surfing beaches.

Dining

Since Ensenada is a sportfishing town, fish is the prime dining choice. The lobster, shrimp, and abalone are great, and a variety of fresh fish is prepared in French, Italian, and Mexican sauces. During the winter hunting season, quail and pheasant are popular. Some restaurants add a 10%–15% service charge to your bill (replacing the tip) in addition to the 15% tax. Dress is casual, and no reservations are necessary unless otherwise indicated.

CATEGORY	COST*
$$$	$15–$20
$$	$8–$15
$	under $8

per person for a three-course meal, excluding drinks and service

$$$ **El Rey Sol.** ★ A family-owned French restaurant more than 40 years old, El Rey Sol has stained-glass windows, wrought-iron chandeliers, and heavy oak tables and chairs. Specialties include French and Mexican presentations of fresh fish, poultry, and vegetables grown at the owner's farm in the Santo Tomás Valley. The excellent pastries are baked on the premises. ✗ *Av. López Mateos 1000,* ☎ *617/8–17–33. Reservations advised. AE, MC, V.*

$$$ **La Embotelladora Vieja.** ★ The most exciting new restaurant Ensenada has seen in years is set in a converted wine-aging room at the Santo Tomás winery. The decor is classic country French, with wine bins stacked floor-to-ceiling under brick arches and crystal goblets glistening on candlelit tables. The so-called Baja French menu includes appetizers of smoked tuna and French pâté; among the most sublime entrées are the grilled lobster in cabernet sauvignon sauce and beef Montpellier with green peppercorns. Teetotalers, note: Nearly every dish is prepared with wine, though you can order some without alcohol-laden sauces. All of Baja's wineries are represented on the impressive wine list. The restaurant is so outstanding that southern Californians drive to Ensenada for long lunches here. ✗ *Av. Miramar 666,* ☎ *617/4–08–07. MC, V.*

$$ **Casamar.** ★ A long-standing, dependable restaurant, Casamar is known for its wide variety of excellent seafood. Lobster and shrimp are prepared in several ways but seem freshest when grilled *con mojo y ajo* (with butter and garlic). The upstairs bar has live jazz on weekend nights. *Blvd. Lázaro Cárdenas 987,* ☎ *617/4–04–17. MC, V.*

$$ **El Charro.** You can get rotisserie chicken, beans, rice, and tortillas far more cheaply at other places in downtown, but El Charro still attracts a steady stream of locals and tourists. Part of the draw is the location, not far from Hussong's and other watering holes, and the food is consistently good. Hungry patrons hover over platters of chilies rellenos, enchiladas, and fresh chips and guacamole at heavy wooden picnic tables under a ceiling of charred wooden beams. Plump chickens slowly circle over a wood fire by the front window, and the aroma of grilled beef and simmering beans fills the air. ✗ *Av. López Mateos 475,* ☎ *617/8–38–81. MC, V.*

$ **Plaza Mariscos.** Several taco stands fill this bright pink plaza in front of the fish market. Check out the bowls of condiments arrayed on picnic tables between the stands—if the salsa, onions, cilantro, and pickled vegetables look good, you're bound to like the tacos as well. Most stands serve seviche and fish tacos; a few also have beef tacos. Mariachis stroll among the tables—if you request a song, you're expected to give the musicians a tip. ✗ *Blvd. Costero, no* ☎. *No credit cards.*

$ **Plaza Mexico.** You can eat in or take out your meals at this brightly lit café, where mariachis add to the festive ambience on Friday and Saturday nights. Thick grilled steaks and marinated *carne asada* are the best dinner bets; the tacos are good for inexpensive meals or snacks. Margaritas and beer are available. ✕ *Av. López Mateos 2184,* ☎ *617/7–21–51. No credit cards.*

Lodging

Ensenada has a glut of hotel rooms at the moment, and package deals abound. Most rooms are least expensive during mid-week and in the winter, when Ensenada can be chilly and breezy. Several companies can book rooms in Ensenada and throughout Baja. For information contact: IMPA/Mexico Information (7860 Mission Center Ct., Suite 202, San Diego CA 92108, ☎ 619/298–4105 or 800/522–1516, ͞Fᴀ͞x 619/294–7366); Baja California Tours (6986 La Jolla Blvd. No. 204, La Jolla, CA 92037, ☎ 619/454–7166, ͞Fᴀ͞x 619/454–2703); and Mexico Resorts International (Box 120637 Chula Vista, CA 91912, ☎ 619/422–6900 or 800/336–5454, ͞Fᴀ͞x 619/422–6910). Unless otherwise indicated, the postal code for all Ensenada lodgings listed is 22800.

CATEGORY	COST*
$$$$	over $90
$$$	$60–$90
$$	$25–$60
$	under $25

*All prices are for a standard double room, excluding service charge and tax (10%).

$$$$ **Las Rosas.** This elegant pink palace just north of town is by far the ★ most modern hotel in the area; the atrium lobby features marble floors, mint-green-and-pink-upholstered couches facing the sea, and a green-glass ceiling that glows at night. All rooms face the ocean and pool, some have fireplaces and whirlpools, and even the least expensive accommodations are lovely. Make reservations far in advance. ☎ *Mexico Hwy. 1 north of town,* ☎ *617/4–43–20,* ͞Fᴀ͞x *617/4–45–95. 32 rooms and suites. Restaurant, bar, pool, hot tub. AE, MC, V.*

$$$ **Villa Marina.** At 12 stories, the blue-and-white Villa Marina is the tallest hotel in town, though not necessarily the most luxurious. Rooms face either the waterfront or downtown and have small balconies, blue carpeting and walls, bathtubs with showers, and sinks outside the bathroom. The nightclub on top of the hotel has a spectacular view of the region, but noise from live bands on weekends makes rooms on the floor below less desirable. A small shopping plaza fronts the hotel on the main shopping and dining street. ☎ *Av. López Mateos at Balancarte,* ☎ *617/8–33–21,* ͞Fᴀ͞x *617/8–33–51; reservations in the U.S.: Box 727, Bonita, CA 91908. Restaurant, bar, pool, nightclub. MC, V.*

$$$ **Punta Morro.** For seclusion and the sound of crashing surf, you can't beat this all-suites hotel beside the university campus. The three-story tan building faces the north end of the bay; the restaurant sits on rock pilings above the waves. All accommodations have terraces facing the ocean, kitchenettes, and seating areas; some also feature fireplaces. ☎ *Mexico Hwy. 1, 2 mi north of town, Box 2891,* ☎ *617/8–35–07 or 800/726–6426;* ͞Fᴀ͞x *616/4–44–90; reservations in the U.S.: Box 43-4263, San Ysidro, CA 92143. 30 suites. Restaurant, bar, pool, hot tub, beach. MC, V.*

$$ **Quintas Papagayo.** A bungalow and low-rise seaside establishment that opened in 1947, Quintas Papagayo is a place where couples honeymoon and then return for their anniversaries. The accommodations are rustic, but you feel as if you've discovered a special hideaway where everyone remembers your name. Fireplaces, kitchens, patios, and decks

are available. ✆ *Mexico Hwy. 1 north of town,* ☎ *617/4–41–55 or 617/4–45–75; reservations: Box 150, Ensenada, BC, or* ☎ *619/491–0682 in the U.S. 50 rooms. Restaurant, bar, pool, tennis courts, beach. MC, V.*

$$ Villa Fontana. An architectural oddity in a town full of Spanish tiled roofs, this peak gabled hotel has a New England look. The rooms are decorated in pastels; choose one at the back, away from street noise. There is enclosed parking—a major plus in downtown Ensenada. ✆ *Av. López Mateos 1050,* ☎ *and* FAX *617/8–34–34; reservations in the U.S.: 800/329–7466. 60 rooms. Pool, hot tub. MC, V.*

$ Joker Hotel. A bizarre, brightly colored mishmash of styles makes it hard to miss this hotel, conveniently located for those traveling south of Ensenada. Spacious rooms have private balconies, satellite TV, and phones. ✆ *Mexico Hwy. 1, km 12.5,* ☎ *and* FAX *617/6–72–01; reservations in the U.S.: 800/22–JOKER. 40 rooms. Pool, hot tub. MC, V.*

Nightlife

Ensenada is a party town for college students, surfers, and other young tourists. **Hussong's Cantina** (Av. Ruíz 113, ☎ 617/8–32–10) has been an Ensenada landmark since 1892 and has changed little since then. A security guard stands by the front door to handle the often-rowdy crowd, a mix of locals and tourists of all ages over 18. The noise is usually deafening, pierced by mariachi and ranchera musicians and whoops and hollers from the inebriated. **Papas and Beer** (Av. Ruíz at López Mateos, ☎ 617/8–42–31) is oriented toward the college set, who hang out the second-story windows shouting at their friends.

Hotel Villa Marina (Av. López Mateos at Balancarte, ☎ 617/8–33–21) opened a night club on the 11th floor in late 1994. The views from the tallest building downtown are staggering, as is the noise of recorded disco music. Live dance bands play Thursday through Saturday nights.

TIJUANA, ROSARITO BEACH, AND ENSENADA ESSENTIALS

Getting There

Tijuana can be reached from San Diego by bus, trolley, or car; from there, you have the option of continuing south by bus or car. The 67-mile trek from Tijuana to Ensenada takes about 2½ hours by car.

By Bus

Greyhound (☎ 619/239–1288 or 800/231–2222) serves Tijuana from San Diego several times a day; the Greyhound terminal in Tijuana is on Avenida Mexico at Madero (☎ 66/86–06–95). **Mexicoach** (☎ 619/232–5049) has bus service from the trolley depot on the U.S. side of the border to Avenida Revolución in Tijuana. For listings of bus lines connecting San Diego, Rosarito Beach, and Ensenada, *see* Guided Tours, *below*.

Within Baja, **Autotransportes de Baja California** (☎ 66/85–84–72) has first-class buses to Tijuana and other points in Baja. **Autotransportes del Pacífico** (☎ 66/86–90–45) and **Tres Estrellas de Oro** (☎ 66/86–91–86) offer second-class service throughout Baja. The Tijuana central bus station is at Calz. Lázaro Cárdenas and Bd. Arroyo Alamar (☎ 66/80–90–60). In Rosarito Beach, the bus station is on Avenida Juárez across from the Rosarito Beach Hotel (no ☎). Ensenada's bus station is at Avenida Riveroll between Calles 10 and 11 (☏ 617/8–67–70).

By Car

U.S. 5 and I–805 end at the border crossing in San Ysidro. If you are visiting **Tijuana** for the day, consider parking in one of the lots on the U.S. side and walking across the border. If you do drive in, be sure to purchase Mexican auto insurance, available at many stands before the last exit of the border crossing. Many car-rental companies do not allow their cars to be driven into Mexico. If you do, you must inform the company of your destination and purchase Mexican auto insurance at the same time you are renting the car.

Mexico Route 1, called Ensenada Cuota (toll road), runs from the border at the Tijuana crossing to Rosarito and Ensenada along the coast; follow the ROSARITO, ENSENADA signs. Each toll is about U.S. $2.50, and there are three toll booths between Tijuana and Ensenada. The road is in good condition, but parts of it are often under construction, so drive with care.

Although the toll road is the quickest route from Tijuana to Ensenada, you'll bypass seeing Baja's charming coastal communities close up. To get a better look, leave the toll road at the Rosarito exit and travel Old Ensenada Highway (Ensenada Libre, the free road), a bit rough in spots but perfectly serviceable.

Beaches, restaurants, and other locations along the coast are often designated by the number of kilometers they are located from the beginning of the peninsular highway. A restaurant with an address of Km 55, therefore, would be 21 miles down the road; look for roadside markers to indicate these locations (to convert kilometers to miles, multiply by .621: km × .621 = mi).

Rosarito Beach is 18 miles south of Tijuana on the coast. You can tour Rosarito Beach proper on foot, which is a good idea on weekends, when Boulevard Juárez has bumper-to-bumper traffic. To reach Puerto Nuevo and other points south, continue on Boulevard Juárez, also called Ensenada Libre, through town and south.

Ensenada is an easy city to navigate; most streets are marked. If you want to get to the waterfront area, stay with Alternate Highway 1 as it travels along the fishing pier and becomes Boulevard Costero, also known as Lázaro Cárdenas and Carretera Transpeninsular.

By Boat

Starlite Cruises (☏ 800/488–7827) offers one-day cruises from San Diego to Ensenada, with gambling on board.

By Trolley

The bright red **San Diego Trolley** (☏ 619/233–3004) runs to within 100 feet of the border from the Santa Fe Depot, at Kettner Boulevard and Broadway, every 15 minutes from 5 am to midnight, and is the most convenient transportation for a day trip from San Diego to Tijuana. The 45-minute trip costs $1.75.

By Taxi

Taxis (called *rutas*) will drive you from downtown Tijuana, at Calle Madero and Calle 3, to Rosarito. The drivers usually won't leave until they have four passengers. The fare should be under $10 per person. In Ensenada, the central taxi stand (*sitio*) is located on López Mateos by the Bahia Hotel (☎ 617/8–34–75). Be sure to negotiate the price before the taxi starts moving. Destinations within the city should cost $10 or less.

Official Requirements

Passports and Tourist Cards

U.S. citizens entering Mexico by road are required to have proof of citizenship: The only acceptable proof of citizenship is either a valid passport or an original birth certificate plus a photo ID. Tourist cards are not needed unless you are traveling south of Ensenada or are planning to stay longer than 72 hours. Otherwise, tourist cards can be obtained from the information booth just inside the border. Passports are required of non-U.S. citizens for reentry at the San Ysidro or Otay Mesa border crossings.

Customs

U.S. residents may bring home duty-free up to $400 worth of foreign goods, as long as they have been out of the country for at least 48 hours. Each member of the family is entitled to the same exemption, regardless of age, and exemptions may be pooled. Included in the allowances for travelers 21 or older are one liter of alcohol, 100 cigars (non-Cuban), and 200 cigarettes. Only one bottle of perfume trademarked in the United States may be imported. There is no duty on antiques or works of art more than 100 years old. Anything exceeding these limits will be taxed at the port of entry and may be taxed in the traveler's home state.

Since Mexico is considered a "developing" country, many arts and handicrafts may be brought back into the United States duty-free. You will need to declare the items and state their value and use, but they won't count against your $400 limit.

Guided Tours

From the U.S.

Baja California Tours (6986 La Jolla Blvd. No. 204, La Jolla, CA 92037, ☎ 619/454–7166, FAX 619/454–2703) offers comfortable, informative bus trips throughout Baja. Vans depart daily from San Diego to Ensenada; midweek transportation-and-hotel packages are a real bargain. The company also offers customized Tijuana tours, including visits to private homes and tours of art galleries and artists' studios.

Gray Line Tours (1775 Hancock St., San Diego, CA 92110, ☎ 619/491–0011 or 800/331–5077) arranges shopping and sightseeing tours on air-conditioned buses. Tours including one night's accommodation are also available. Make reservations two weeks in advance.

San Diego Mini Tours (1726 Wilson Ave., National City, CA 91950, ☎ 619/477–8687, FAX 619/477–0705) has frequent departures throughout the day from San Diego hotels to Avenida Revolución in Tijuana and back and connections with a Mexican-operated trolley tour of Tijuana.

In Mexico

Gordo's Sportsfishing (Sportsfishing Pier, Ensenada, ☎ 617/8–21–90) operates whale-watching trips from December through February. The half-day trip, which goes to La Bufadora and Isla Todos Santos, costs $35 per person.

Servicios Turísticos (Av. Septiembre 213-B, ☎ 66/86–17–25; Viajes Harold, Av. Revolución 608, ☎ 66/88–11–11) offers assistance with tours of Tijuana and beyond.

In Ensenada, half-day bus tours of Ensenada and the surrounding countryside are available for $20 from **Viajes Guaycura** (López Mateos 1089, ☎ 617/8–37–18).

Important Addresses and Numbers

Emergencies
A three-digit emergency dialing system is in effect throughout Baja Norte—for **police,** dial 134; **Red Cross,** 132; **fire department,** 135.

Visitor Information
Getting information or arranging reservations is infinitely easier for most people in the United States than in Mexico. Whenever possible, make inquiries and/or reservations before you enter Mexico, through travel agents or other tourist information centers.

To call Baja Norte from the United States, dial 011–52, the area code, and the number. The area code for Tijuana has been changed from 668 to 66; the following number should have six digits. The area code for Rosarito Beach is 661, and for Ensenada, 617.

Baja Information (7860 Mission Center Ct., No. 202, San Diego, CA 92108, ☎ 619/299–8518 or 800/522–1516 in CA, AZ, and NV; FAX 619/294–7366) handles reservations and provides valuable information about the area.

Tijuana
A **tourism office** (☎ 66/83–13–10), at Avenida Revolución and Calle 1a, has maps, newspapers, and English-speaking clerks; it's open daily 9–5. Tourist-information booths are just inside the border and at the airport. **The Attorney General for the Protection of Tourists Hotline** (☎ 66/88–05–55) takes calls weekdays to help with tourist complaints and problems.

The **Tijuana Chamber of Commerce** (Av. Revolución and Calle 1, ☎ 66/85–84–72), open daily 9–7, is the best source of tourist information.

Main telephone office (Calle Pio Pico, between Calles 10 and 11).

Main post office and telegraph office (Corner of Av. Negrete and Calle 11, ☎ 66/85–26–82).

U.S. Consulate (Tapachula 96, Colonia Hipódromo, just behind the Tijuana Country Club, ☎ 66/86–38–86).

Rosarito
There is a **tourist information** office just south of La Quinta (Blvd. Juárez, 2nd floor of Quinta Plaza shopping center, ☎ 661/2–03–96 or 661/2–30–78).

Ensenada
Convention and Visitors Bureau (Av. López Mateos and Av. Espinoza, ☎ 617/8–24–11).

Police (Ortíz Rubio and Libertad, ☎ 134).

Hospital of the Americas (Av. Arenas 151, ☎ 617/6–03–01).

Post Office (Av. Juárez 1347).

Red Cross (☎ 617/8–12–12).

State Tourism Office (Blvd. Costera 1477, ☎ 617/2–30–22, FAX 617/2–30–81) is open weekdays 9–7, Saturday 10–3, Sunday 10–2; there's always an English-speaking clerk on hand to assist travelers.

12 Portraits of San Diego

IDYLLING IN SAN DIEGO

I'VE NEVER BEEN TO Sea World; performing fish give me the willies. And during the two years I lived within striking distance of Balboa Park, I had to take visiting friends to the zoo so many times I began having nightmares about koalas. But if I came to dislike various theme-park aspects of the city, I nevertheless loved San Diego. At first sight.

A typical easterner, I went out to San Diego in the late 1970s expecting to find a smaller version of Los Angeles. The freeways were there, along with a fair share of traffic congestion, but so was an oceanscape of surprisingly pristine beauty. The first drive I took from the University of California, where I was doing graduate research, knocked me for a loop: I rounded a curve on La Jolla Shores Drive to confront a coastline that could match any on the French Riviera.

I was also taken by the distinctiveness of the many shoreline communities. For one thing, the beaches tend to get funkier as you head south from the old-money enclave of La Jolla: Pacific Beach, with its Crystal Pier, is an aging Victorian resort taken over by teenagers, while transients and surfers share the turf at Ocean Beach. To the north, Del Mar has a strip of shops that rival those of Rodeo Drive, while Carlsbad and Oceanside show the democratizing influence of nearby Camp Pendleton.

Unlike Los Angeles, San Diego is still strongly defined by its relationship to the ocean—to some degree by default. During the latter half of the 19th century, the town was banking on a rail link to the east. A building boom in the 1880s was largely based on the assumption that San Diego would become the western terminus of the Santa Fe Railroad line; the city hoped in this way to compete with Los Angeles, which was already connected by rail to San Francisco and thus to the national railroad network. The link was completed in 1885, but it proved unsuccessful for a variety of reasons, including the placement of the line through Temecula Canyon, where 30 miles of track were washed out repeatedly in winter rainstorms. The Santa Fe soon moved its West Coast offices to San Bernardino and Los Angeles, and to this day there is no direct rail service from San Diego to the eastern part of the United States.

Instead, San Diego's future was sealed in 1908, when President Theodore Roosevelt's Great White Fleet stopped here on a world tour to demonstrate U.S. naval strength. The navy, impressed during that visit by the city's excellent harbor and temperate climate, decided to build a destroyer base on San Diego Bay in the 1920s; the newly developing aircraft industry soon followed (Charles Lindbergh's plane *Spirit of St. Louis* was built here). Over the years San Diego's economy became largely dependent on the military and its attendant enterprises, which provided jobs as well as a demand for local goods and services by those stationed here.

San Diego's character—conservative where Los Angeles's is cutting edge—was formed in large part by the presence of its military installations, which now occupy more than 165,000 acres of land in the area. And the city conducts most of its financial business in a single neighborhood, the district fronting San Diego Bay, in this way resembling New York more than its economic rival up the coast. San Diego has set some of its most prestigious scientific facilities on the water—Scripps Institute of Oceanography, naturally, but also Salk Institute. Jonas Salk didn't need the Pacific marine environment for his research, but his regular morning runs along Torrey Pines Beach no doubt cleared his head.

San Diego also has the ocean to thank for its near-perfect weather. A high-pressure system from the north Pacific is responsible for the city's sunshine and dry air; moderating breezes off the sea (caused by the water warming and cooling more slowly than the land) keep the summers relatively cool and the winters warm and help clear the air of pollution. In the late spring and early summer the difference between the earth and water temperatures generates coastal fogs. This phenomenon was another of San Diego's delightful surprises: I never tired of watching the mist roll in at night, wonderfully romantic, as thick as any I'd ever seen in London and easier to enjoy in the balmy air.

If I loved San Diego from the start, I had a hard time believing in its existence. It was difficult to imagine that a functioning American city could be so attractive, that people lived and worked in such a place every day. Although I'd never considered myself a Puritan, I quickly came to realize that I'd always assumed work and leisure environments had to be separate, that one was supposed to toil in unpleasant surroundings in order to earn the time spent in idyllic settings.

I found that I could get used to working on sunny days, but that it was impossible to remain unaffected by the city's physical presence. Rampant nature conspires in a variety of ways to force you to let your guard down here. In northern East Coast cities, plants are generally orderly and prim: shrubs trimmed, roses demurely draped around railings, tulips set in proper rows. Even the famed cherry blossoms of Washington, D.C., are profuse in neat columns. In San Diego, the flora, whimsical at best, sometimes border on obscenity. The ubiquitous palms come in comedic pairs: Short, squat trees that look like overgrown pineapples play Mutt to the Jeff of the tall, skinny variety. The aptly named bottle-brush bushes vie for attention with bright red flame trees, beaky orange birds of paradise, and rich purple bougainvillea spilling out over lush green lawns. Only in Hawaii had I previously encountered anthurium, a waxy red plant with a protruding white center that seems to be sticking its tongue out at you. "We're still on the mainland," I felt like telling them all on some days: "Behave yourselves."

Ironically, it was the Victorians who were largely responsible for this indecorous natural profusion. Difficult as it is to imagine now, it's the sparse brown vegetation of San Diego's undeveloped mesas that accurately reflects the climate of the region, technically a semiarid steppe. When Spanish explorer Juan Rodríguez Cabrillo sailed into San Diego Bay in 1542, looking for a shortcut to China, he and his crew encountered a barren, desolate landscape that did not inspire them to settle here, or even stop for very long.

It wasn't until the late 19th century, when the Mediterranean in general and Italy in particular were all the rage among wealthy residents, that the vegetation now considered characteristic of southern California was introduced to San Diego. In 1889, money raised by the Ladies Annex to the Chamber of Commerce was used to plant trees in Balboa Park, and between 1892 and 1903 a wide variety of exotic foliage was brought into the city: eucalyptus, cork oak, and rubber trees, to name a few. As homeowners in the area can attest, most of the landscaped local vegetation couldn't survive if it were not watered regularly.

NO DOUBT BOTH the natural setting and the relentlessly fine weather help contribute to the clash of cultures that exists here. The conservative traditionalism of the military presence in town is posed against the liberal hedonism of visiting sunseekers, as well as a large local student population. Nude bathing is popular at Black's Beach in La Jolla, a spot that's reasonably private because it's fairly inaccessible: You have to hike down steep cliffs in order to get to the water. Rumor has it that every year a few navy men are killed when they lose their footing on the cliffs, so intent are they at peering through their binoculars.

But I suspect it's the rare person of any political persuasion who can confront the southern California attitude toward nudity with equanimity. I hadn't wanted to believe all the stereotypes, but the first time I went to a dinner party in town, the host asked the group if we wanted to adjourn to the hot tub after we ate. I hadn't brought my bathing suit, so I declined.

The next day, I consulted a local expert in matters of whirlpool etiquette. "What does one do?" I asked. "Undress in front of a group of relative strangers and jump into the water with them? Does one rip off one's clothes with abandon? Fold them carefully afterward? Or go into another room and come out in the raw?" "All that's up to the individual," she answered. "Do whatever you feel comfortable with." "None of it," I asserted. "Where I come from, when people of different genders take their clothes off together, they tend to have sex." "That's optional, too," she said.

Nods to certain So-Cal conventions notwithstanding, San Diego has never come close to approaching the much-touted libertinism of Los Angeles. It has the porno theaters and sleazy clubs you'd expect in a liberty port, but little entertainment of a more sophisticated nature. Celebrities who came down from Hollywood in the 1920s and '30s sought out suites at the La Valencia Hotel and other chic La Jolla locales for the privacy, not the nightlife; the gambling they did at Del Mar racetrack to the north was of the tony, genteel sort. Those who sought thrills—and booze during Prohibition—headed farther south, to Mexico. Raymond Chandler, who spent most of his last 13 years in La Jolla and died there in 1959, wrote a friend that the town was "a nice place . . . for old people and their parents."

FOR ALL ITS conservatism, the one thing San Diego didn't conserve was its past—in some cases because there was little to save. When Father Junipero Serra arrived in 1769 to establish the first of the California missions, he did not find the complex dwellings that characterized so many of the Native American settlements he had encountered in Mexico. Nor did his fellow Spaniards improve much upon the site during their stay; the town that the Mexicans took over in 1822 was rudimentary, consisting mostly of rough adobe huts. The mission church had been moved to a new site in 1774, and the original Spanish presidio, abandoned in the 1830s, was in ruins by the next decade; some grass-covered mounds and a giant cross built in 1913 on Presidio Hill, incorporating the tiles of the original structure, are all that's left of it.

Though a romanticized version of the city during the Mexican period (1822–49), today's Old Town district gives a rough idea of San Diego's layout at that time, when somewhat more impressive structures, such as Casa Estudillo and the Bandini House, were built. San Diego didn't really begin to flourish, however, until 1850, the year that California became a state. At that point the dominant architectural influence came from the East Coast; their enthusiasm for becoming American caused San Diegans to reject their Spanish and Mexican roots as inappropriately "foreign." Thus the first brick structure in the state, the Whaley House (1856), was built in typical New England nautical style. Most of the original Old Town was destroyed by fire in 1872, and a good deal of what was left fell victim to the construction of I–5.

During the Victorian era (1880–1905), the site of the city's development moved south; entrepreneur Alonzo Horton may have miscalculated the success of the rail link to the East Coast, but when he bought up a huge lot of land in 1867 for his "Addition," he knew the city's future lay on the harbor. It was in this area, now the city's financial district, that many of the neo-Gothic structures characteristic of the period were built. Perhaps it's perversely fitting that a number of the Victorian relics in downtown San Diego were removed in conjunction with the 15-block Horton Redevelopment Project, of which the huge Horton Plaza shopping complex is the center.

San Diego finally began to reject the East Coast architectural style at the turn of the century, and at the Panama–California Exposition of 1915 the city celebrated its Spanish roots—as well as a Moroccan and Italian past it never had—with a vengeance. The beautiful Spanish-style structures built for the occasion fit right into the Mediterranean landscape that had been cultivated in Balboa Park during the Victorian era; today these buildings house most of the city's museums. San Diego became even more thoroughly Hispanicized during the 1920s and '30s as Spanish colonial–style homes became popular in new suburbs, such as Mission Hills and Kensington, as well as in the beach communities that were developing. Downtown buildings began looking like Italian palaces and Moorish towers.

SAN DIEGO'S LAND-
SCAPE of ravines and hills is partly responsible for the city's sprawling development in the 20th century, and the popularization of the automobile in the 1930s helped ensure its continuing growth in an outward direction. The physical barriers have been overcome by an ever-expanding highway system—though not by a viable public transportation network—but the discrete, individual neighborhoods created by them remain, if their populations sometimes shift. For example, Kearny Mesa, formerly a middle-class suburban neighborhood, is now one of the many Southeast Asian communities in the city.

In some ways, as residents and visitors alike have long feared, San Diego is coming to look more like Los Angeles. Faceless developments are cropping up all over once-deserted canyons and mesas, and the huge, castlelike Mormon temple built along I–5 north of La Jolla wouldn't look out of place in Disneyland. But in the years since I lived there, San Diego has also become more like a city—that is, what easterners know to be the city in its divinely ordained form.

As recently as the early 1980s, virtually no one went downtown unless required to. It was a desolate place after dark, and people who worked there during the day never stayed around in the evening to play. Gentrification of sorts began in the mid-1970s, as the low rents attracted artists and real-estate speculators. At about the same time the city designated the formerly rough Stingaree neighborhood as the Gaslamp Quarter, but revitalization, in the form of street-level shops and art galleries, didn't really take until Horton Plaza was completed in 1985. For many years the newly installed gaslights illuminated only the homeless.

The poor and disenfranchised are still here—indeed, many lost their homes to various redevelopment projects—but now the staff at the recently renovated historic U.S. Grant Hotel offers to accompany its guests across the street to Horton Plaza at night so they won't be bothered by vagrants. For the first time there's a concentration of good restaurants, and a serious art and theater scene is developing in the district, too.

The area is also a terminus for the San Diego Trolley. This inexpensive transportation link to Mexico has, among other things, allowed Mexican artists to bring their works to a wider market and fostered a cultural as well as a touristic exchange with Tijuana, which has cleaned up its own act considerably in recent years.

I like the infusion of life into downtown San Diego, and I even like Horton Plaza, which, with its odd angles and colorful banners, looks like it was designed by Alice in Wonderland's Red Queen. But maybe I miss that spot of unadulterated blight that once helped me to believe in San Diego's reality.

Reality seems to be setting in on a large scale these days. San Diego's bad neighborhoods still don't look like slums as I know them, but gang-related crime is on the increase in the southeast part of the city. In recent years, sewage spills have closed a number of southern beaches, and the problem is likely to grow, since neither San Diego nor Tijuana has enacted any large-scale programs for effective waste disposal. Friends tell me that even the weather is changing for the worse, a fact they attribute to global warming.

Would I move back to San Diego? In a minute. Like many temporary residents, I left the city vowing to return; unlike many, I've never managed to do more than visit. I used to think that if I had the chance I'd live in Hillcrest, a close-knit inland community with lots of ethnic restaurants and theaters that show foreign films, but I've come to realize that would only be transplanting my East Coast life into the sun. Now I think I'll wait until I'm rich and can afford to move to La Jolla; no doubt I'll be old enough by then to fit in, so I'll fully enjoy that suite in the La Valencia Hotel overlooking the cove

.— Edie Jarolim

MORE PORTRAITS

There is no better way to establish the mood for your visit to Old Town San Diego than by reading Helen Hunt Jackson's 105-year-old romantic novel, *Ramona,* a best-seller for more than 50 years and still readily available. The Casa de Estudillo in Old Town has been known for many years as Ramona's Marriage Place because of its close resemblance to the house described in the novel. Richard Henry Dana, Jr's *Two Years Before the Mast* (1869), based on the author's experiences as a merchant sailor, provides a masculine perspective on early San Diego history.

Other novels with a San Diego setting include Raymond Chandler's mystery about the waterfront, *Playback;* Wade Miller's mystery, *On Easy Street;* Eric Higgs's gothic thriller, *A Happy Man;* Tom Wolfe's satire of the La Jolla surfing scene, *The Pump House Gang;* and David Zielinski's modern-day story, *A Genuine Monster.*

INDEX

NOTES

Your guide to a picture-perfect vacation

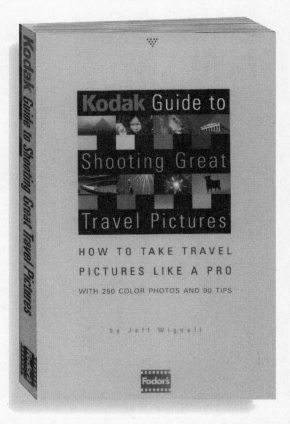

Kodak and Fodor's join together to create the guide that travelers everywhere have been asking for—one that covers the terms and techniques, the equipment and etiquette for taking first-rate travel photographs.

The most authoritative and up-to-date book of its kind, **The Kodak Guide to Shooting Great Travel Pictures** includes over 200 color photographs and spreads on 100 points of photography important to travelers, such as landscape basics, under sea shots, wildlife, city street, close-ups, photographing in museums and more.

$16.50   ($22.95 Canada)

At bookstores everywhere, or call 1-800-533-6478.

Fodor's Travel Publications

Available at bookstores everywhere, or call 1–800–533–6478, 24 hours a day.

Gold Guides

U.S.

Alaska	Florida	New Orleans	Santa Fe, Taos, Albuquerque
Arizona	Hawaii	New York City	
Boston	Las Vegas, Reno, Tahoe	Pacific North Coast	Seattle & Vancouver
California		Philadelphia & the Pennsylvania Dutch Country	The South
Cape Cod, Martha's Vineyard, Nantucket	Los Angeles		U.S. & British Virgin Islands
	Maine, Vermont, New Hampshire		
The Carolinas & the Georgia Coast		The Rockies	USA
Chicago	Maui	San Diego	Virginia & Maryland
Colorado	Miami & the Keys	San Francisco	Waikiki
	New England		Washington, D.C.

Foreign

Australia & New Zealand	Egypt	London	Provence & the Riviera
Austria	Europe	Madrid & Barcelona	Scandinavia
The Bahamas	Florence, Tuscany & Umbria	Mexico	Scotland
Bermuda	France	Montréal & Québec City	Singapore
Budapest	Germany	Moscow, St. Petersburg, Kiev	South America
Canada	Great Britain		South Pacific
Cancún, Cozumel, Yucatán Peninsula	Greece	The Netherlands, Belgium & Luxembourg	Southeast Asia
Caribbean	Hong Kong		Spain
China	India	New Zealand	Sweden
Costa Rica, Belize, Guatemala	Ireland	Norway	Switzerland
Cuba	Israel	Nova Scotia, New Brunswick, Prince Edward Island	Thailand
The Czech Republic & Slovakia	Italy		Tokyo
	Japan	Paris	Toronto
Eastern Europe	Kenya & Tanzania	Portugal	Turkey
	Korea		Vienna & the Danube

Fodor's Special-Interest Guides

Branson	Fodor's London Companion	Kodak Guide to Shooting Great Travel Pictures	Walt Disney World for Adults
Caribbean Ports of Call	France by Train		Where Should We Take the Kids? California
The Complete Guide to America's National Parks	Halliday's New England Food Explorer	Shadow Traffic's New York Shortcuts and Traffic Tips	
		Sunday in New York	Where Should We Take the Kids? Northeast
Condé Nast Traveler Caribbean Resort and Cruise Ship Finder	Healthy Escapes	Sunday in San Francisco	
	Italy by Train		
Cruises and Ports of Call		Walt Disney World, Universal Studios and Orlando	

Special Series

Affordables
Caribbean
Europe
Florida
France
Germany
Great Britain
Italy
London
Paris

Fodor's Bed & Breakfasts and Country Inns
America's Best B&Bs
California's Best B&Bs
Canada's Great Country Inns
Cottages, B&Bs and Country Inns of England and Wales
The Mid-Atlantic's Best B&Bs
New England's Best B&Bs
The Pacific Northwest's Best B&Bs
The South's Best B&Bs
The Southwest's Best B&Bs
The Upper Great Lakes' Best B&Bs

The Berkeley Guides
California
Central America
Eastern Europe
Europe
France
Germany & Austria
Great Britain & Ireland
Italy
London
Mexico

Pacific Northwest & Alaska
Paris
San Francisco

Compass American Guides
Arizona
Chicago
Colorado
Hawaii
Hollywood
Las Vegas
Maine
Manhattan
Montana
New Mexico
New Orleans
Oregon
San Francisco
Santa Fe
South Carolina
South Dakota
Southwest
Texas
Utah
Virginia
Washington
Wine Country
Wisconsin
Wyoming

Fodor's Español
California
Caribe Occidental
Caribe Oriental
Gran Bretaña
Londres
Mexico
Nueva York
Paris

Fodor's Exploring Guides
Australia
Boston & New England
Britain
California
Caribbean
China
Egypt
Florence & Tuscany
Florida
France
Germany
Ireland
Israel
Italy
Japan
London
Mexico
Moscow & St. Petersburg
New York City
Paris
Prague
Provence
Rome
San Francisco
Scotland
Singapore & Malaysia
Spain
Thailand
Turkey
Venice

Fodor's Flashmaps
Boston
New York
San Francisco
Washington, D.C.

Fodor's Pocket Guides
Acapulco
Atlanta
Barbados

Jamaica
London
New York City
Paris
Prague
Puerto Rico
Rome
San Francisco
Washington, D.C.

Rivages Guides
Bed and Breakfasts of Character and Charm in France
Hotels and Country Inns of Character and Charm in France
Hotels and Country Inns of Character and Charm in Italy

Short Escapes
Country Getaways in Britain
Country Getaways in France
Country Getaways Near New York City

Fodor's Sports
Golf Digest's Best Places to Play
Skiing USA
USA Today The Complete Four Sport Stadium Guide

Fodor's Vacation Planners
Great American Learning Vacations
Great American Sports & Adventure Vacations
Great American Vacations
National Parks and Seashores of the East
National Parks of the West

Before Catching Your Flight,
Catch Up With Your World.

Fueled by the global resources of CNN and available in major airports across America, CNN Airport Network provides a live source of current domestic and international news,

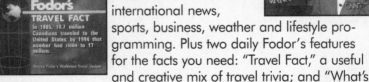

sports, business, weather and lifestyle programming. Plus two daily Fodor's features for the facts you need: "Travel Fact," a useful and creative mix of travel trivia; and "What's Happening," a comprehensive round-up of upcoming events in major cities around the world.

With CNN Airport Network, you'll never be out of the loop.

HERE'S YOUR OWN PERSONAL VIEW OF THE WORLD.

Here's the easiest way to get up-to-the-minute, objective, personalized information about what's going on in the city you'll be visiting—before you leave on your trip! Unique information you could get only if you knew someone personally in each of 160 destinations around the world. Everything from special places to dine to local events only a local would know about.

It's all yours—in your Travel Update from Worldview, the leading provider of time-sensitive destination information.

Review the following order form and fill it out by indicating your destination(s)

and travel dates and by checking off up to eight interest categories. Then mail or fax your order form to us, or call your order in. (We're here to help you 24 hours a day.)

Within 48 hours of receiving your order, we'll mail your convenient, pocket-sized custom guide to you, packed with information to make your travel more fun and interesting. And if you're in a hurry, we can even fax it.

Have a great trip with your Fodor's Worldview Travel Update!

Fodor's WORLDVIEW
TRAVEL UPDATE

Customized to your interests and dates of travel

Time-sensitive

Insider perspective

DESTINATIONS

Worldview covers more than 160 destinations worldwide. Choose the destination(s) that match your itinerary from the list below:

Europe
Amsterdam
Athens
Barcelona
Berlin
Brussels
Budapest
Copenhagen
Dublin
Edinburgh
Florence
Frankfurt
French Riviera
Geneva
Glasgow
Lausanne
Lisbon
London
Madrid
Milan
Moscow
Munich
Oslo
Paris
Prague
Provence
Rome
Salzburg
Seville
St. Petersburg
Stockholm
Venice
Vienna
Zurich

United States (Mainland)
Albuquerque
Atlanta
Atlantic City
Baltimore
Boston
Branson, MO
Charleston, SC
Chicago
Cincinnati
Cleveland
Dallas/Ft. Worth
Denver
Detroit
Houston
Indianapolis
Kansas City
Las Vegas
Los Angeles
Memphis
Miami
Milwaukee
Minneapolis/St. Paul
Nashville
New Orleans
New York City
Orlando
Palm Springs
Philadelphia
Phoenix
Pittsburgh
Portland
Reno/Lake Tahoe
St. Louis
Salt Lake City
San Antonio
San Diego
San Francisco
Santa Fe
Seattle
Tampa
Washington, DC

Alaska
Alaskan Destinations

Hawaii
Honolulu
Island of Hawaii
Kauai
Maui

Canada
Quebec City
Montreal
Ottawa
Toronto
Vancouver

Bahamas
Abaco
Eleuthera/
 Harbour Island
Exuma
Freeport
Nassau &
 Paradise Island

Bermuda
Bermuda Countryside
Hamilton

British Leeward Islands
Anguilla
Antigua & Barbuda
St. Kitts & Nevis

British Virgin Islands
Tortola & Virgin
Gorda

British Windward Islands
Barbados
Dominica
Grenada
St. Lucia
St. Vincent
Trinidad & Tobago

Cayman Islands
The Caymans

Dominican Republic
Santo Domingo

Dutch Leeward Islands
Aruba
Bonaire
Curacao

Dutch Windward Island
St. Maarten/St. Martin

French West Indies
Guadeloupe
Martinique
St. Barthelemy

Jamaica
Kingston
Montego Bay
Negril
Ocho Rios

Puerto Rico
Ponce
San Juan

Turks & Caicos
Grand Turk/
 Providenciales

U.S. Virgin Islands
St. Croix
St. John
St. Thomas

Mexico
Acapulco
Cancun & Isla Mujeres
Cozumel
Guadalajara
Ixtapa & Zihuatanejo
Los Cabos
Mazatlan
Mexico City
Monterrey
Oaxaca
Puerto Vallarta

South/Central America
Buenos Aires
Caracas
Rio de Janeiro
San Jose, Costa Rica
Sao Paulo

Middle East
Istanbul
Jerusalem

Australia & New Zealand
Auckland
Melbourne
South Island
Sydney

China
Beijing
Guangzhou
Shanghai

Japan
Kyoto
Nagoya
Osaka
Tokyo
Yokohama

Pacific Rim/Other
Bali
Bangkok
Hong Kong & Macau
Manila
Seoul
Singapore
Taipei

INTERESTS

For your personalized Travel Update, choose the eight (8) categories you're most interested in from the following list:

1.	**Business Services**	Fax & Overnight Mail, Computer Rentals, Protocol, Secretarial, Messenger, Translation Services

Dining

2.	**All-Day Dining**	Breakfast & Brunch, Cafes & Tea Rooms, Late-Night Dining
3.	**Local Cuisine**	Every Price Range — from Budget Restaurants to the Special Splurge
4.	**European Cuisine**	Continental, French, Italian
5.	**Asian Cuisine**	Chinese, Far Eastern, Japanese, Other
6.	**Americas Cuisine**	American, Mexican & Latin
7.	**Nightlife**	Bars, Dance Clubs, Casinos, Comedy Clubs, Ethnic, Pubs & Beer Halls
8.	**Entertainment**	Theater — Comedy, Drama, Musicals, Dance, Ticket Agencies
9.	**Music**	Classical, Opera, Traditional & Ethnic, Jazz & Blues, Pop, Rock
10.	**Children's Activites**	Events, Attractions
11.	**Tours**	Local Tours, Day Trips, Overnight Excursions
12.	**Exhibitions, Festivals & Shows**	Antiques & Flower, History & Cultural, Art Exhibitions, Fairs & Craft Shows, Music & Art Festivals
13.	**Shopping**	Districts & Malls, Markets, Regional Specialties
14.	**Fitness**	Bicycling, Health Clubs, Hiking, Jogging
15.	**Recreational Sports**	Boating/Sailing, Fishing, Golf, Skiing, Snorkeling/Scuba, Tennis/Racket
16.	**Spectator Sports**	Auto Racing, Baseball, Basketball, Golf, Football, Horse Racing, Ice Hockey, Soccer
17.	**Event Highlights**	The best of what's happening during the dates of your trip.
18.	**Sightseeing**	Sights, Buildings, Monuments
19.	**Museums**	Art, Cultural
20.	**Transportation**	Taxis, Car Rentals, Airports, Public Transportation
21.	**General Info**	Overview, Holidays, Currency, Tourist Info

Please note that content will vary by season, destination, and length of stay.

Name

Address

City   **State**   **Country**   **ZIP**

Tel # (   )   -   **Fax # (   )   -**

Title of this Fodor's guide:

Store and location where guide was purchased:

INDICATE YOUR DESTINATIONS/DATES: You can order up to three (3) destinations from the previous page. Fill in your arrival and departure dates for each destination. <u>**Your Travel Update itinerary (all destinations selected) cannot exceed 30 days from beginning to end.**</u>

		Month	Day	Month	Day
(Sample) **LONDON**	From:	**6** / **21**	To:	**6** / **30**
1	From:	/	To:	/
2	From:	/	To:	/
3	From:	/	To:	/

CHOOSE YOUR INTERESTS: Select up to eight (8) categories from the list of interest categories shown on the previous page and circle the numbers below:

1 2 3 4 5 6 7 8 9 10 11 12 13 14 15 16 17 18 19 20 21

CHOOSE WHEN YOU WANT YOUR TRAVEL UPDATE DELIVERED (Check one):
❏ Please send my Travel Update immediately.
❏ Please hold my order until a few weeks before my trip to include the most up-to-date information.
Completed orders will be sent within 48 hours. Allow 7–10 days for U.S. mail delivery.

ADD UP YOUR ORDER HERE. SPECIAL OFFER FOR FODOR'S PURCHASERS ONLY!

	Suggested Retail Price	Your Price	This Order
First destination ordered	$ 9.95	$ 7.95	$ 7.95
Second destination (if applicable)	$ 6.95	$ 4.95	+
Third destination (if applicable)	$ 6.95	$ 4.95	+

DELIVERY CHARGE (Check one and enter amount below)

	Within U.S. & Canada	Outside U.S. & Canada
First Class Mail	❏ $2.50	❏ $5.00
FAX	❏ $5.00	❏ $10.00
Priority Delivery	❏ $15.00	❏ $27.00

ENTER DELIVERY CHARGE FROM ABOVE: + [   ]

TOTAL: $ [   ]

METHOD OF PAYMENT IN U.S. FUNDS ONLY (Check one):
❏ AmEx ❏ MC ❏ Visa ❏ Discover ❏ Personal Check (U. S. & Canada only)
❏ Money Order/International Money Order

Make check or money order payable to: Fodor's Worldview Travel Update

Credit Card __/__/__/__/__/__/__/__/__/__/__/__/__/__/__/__/ **Expiration Date:** __/__

Authorized Signature

SEND THIS COMPLETED FORM WITH PAYMENT TO:
Fodor's Worldview Travel Update, 114 Sansome Street, Suite 700,
San Francisco, CA 94104

OR CALL OR FAX US 24-HOURS A DAY
Telephone **1-800-799-9609** • Fax **1-800-799-9619** (From within the U.S. & Canada)
(Outside the U.S. & Canada: Telephone 415-616-9988 • Fax 415-616-9989)

(Please have this guide in front of you when you call so we can verify purchase.)
Code: FTG   Offer valid until 12/31/97